Africa and the Blues

Africa and the Blues

Gerhard Kubik

University Press of Mississippi
Jackson

http://www.upress.state.ms.us

07   06   05   04   03   02   01   00   99   4   3   2   1

∞

Library of Congress Cataloging-in-Publication Data

Kubik, Gerhard, 1933–
    Africa and the blues / Gerhard Kubik.
        p. cm.
        Includes bibliographical references and index.
        ISBN 1-57806-145-8 (cloth : alk. paper).—ISBN 1-57806-146-6
    (paper : alk. Paper)
        1. Blues (Music)—African influences.   2. Blacks—Africa—Music—
    History and criticism.   3. Music—Africa—History and criticism.
    I. Title
    ML3521.K83 1999
    781.643'096—dc21 99-24343
    CIP

British Library Cataloging-in-Publication Data available

Contents

Contents

List of Examples

List of Figures

List of Photographs

Preface

As I am writing about the blues after a thirty-seven-year interval—the last time I had specifically touched the subject was in 1961—this book is unfolding before my eyes as if I were in a state of trance. Obviously, I haven't been sitting in idleness during the last three decades. Besides covering much of sub-Saharan Africa in field research and writing, I have also written much about the extensions of regional African cultures in the New World, notably in Brazil, and (in return) on the impact of jazz and other forms of African-American music in southern Africa. Since 1974 I have been a performer on clarinet and guitar in Donald Kachamba's Kwela Band from Malaŵi, playing a kind of music that is, at least in part, a jazz offspring.

In 1977 I visited American blues researcher David Evans in California and spent several days listening to historical blues recordings and material from his recent fieldwork in Mississippi and providing commentary from an Africanist perspective. In 1981 I paid him a second visit in Memphis, where he had settled; and together we visited a number of blues performers there and in northern Mississippi. Another trip followed in 1990, and in 1993 I revisited Mississippi as part of a remarkable research team that included the oral literature researcher Moya Aliya Malamusi from Malaŵi, Evans's wife Marice, music researcher Richard Graham, and myself. We recorded and videotaped storytelling by John Milton Alexander at Victoria about the trickster Rabbit, and we also visited Glen Faulkner near Senatobia, who played for us his "one-stringed guitar," both his older acoustic model and his more recent model with electric amplification. Other journeys within the United States in recent years, for lectures, research, and visits, have brought me to the Center for Popular Music at Middle Tennessee State University, Murfreesboro; the Archives of Traditional Music at Indiana University, Bloomington; Northwestern University in Evanston, Illinois; the Center for Black Music Research at Columbia College, Chicago; the Department of Musical Instruments of the Metropolitan Museum of Art in New York, where Moya and I held Andrew W. Mellon Senior Research Fellowships; an International Conference on Black Ethnicity at the North-South Center of the University of Miami (Florida); and lectures at ten other universities. During these trips the Chicago–Bloomington–Nashville–Memphis highways seem to have become a kind of north-south axis for my "rambling" spirit—occasionally meeting old friends on the Greyhound bus, such as the ghost of Robert Johnson, who in one of his songs said that after his death his body should be buried by the side of the highway so that his spirit could catch a Greyhound and keep traveling on.

Thus, while African-American studies have been an important focus of my work, at least since the mid-1970s, I did not anticipate that I would write again specifically about jazz or blues. I had developed an enormous respect for the learned and detailed literature that had accumulated since the 1960s, and thought it would be better left to other specialists with more African-American historical background knowledge. Until 1996 I didn't think that anything in the world could have the magical power to prompt me to write again extensively on jazz or blues. However, that magical nudge came when David Evans proposed that I contribute to an anthology he was editing an article on the blues' "round trip," i.e., their roots in Africa, their rise and development in the southern United States by the 1890s, and their "return" to selected areas of Africa during the second half of the twentieth century, where they have been picked up and reinterpreted by a variety of African musicians.

At the particular juncture when I received this request, I was about to prepare a lecture trip to Salvador, capital city of the state of Bahia, Brazil, for August and September 1996. I was also booked at Andrew Tracey's Fourteenth Symposium on Ethnomusicology at Rhodes University, Grahamstown, South Africa, for late September. Therefore, I registered the proposal with only one eye while continuing to read with the other eye Stephen J. Gould's thoughts on the fortuitous nature of the evolution of life. . . . Eventually, after completing the South African obligations, I flew to Malaŵi, retreating to family life in my home surroundings at Moya's Oral Literature Research Programme in Chileka, staying up to the end of the year. The daily perspiration at over 100 Fahrenheit during

October and November—the hottest months in southeast Africa—did not prevent me, however, from beginning work on the blues article. On December 31, 1996, I flew with an outline of the manuscript to my other desk in Vienna.

During the next six months I would commute between Vienna and Mainz, Germany, fulfilling my obligations as Professor of Cultural Anthropology and Ethnomusicology at those two universities. It was during that period that I began reading through the fascinating and ever-expanding universe of writings on the blues, and listening to some of the recorded gems on LPs and CDs. The sheer size and intellectual weight of all this material seemed unmanageable, particularly in view of the many other deadlines I had for publications, plus the teaching load of six courses at both universities with the attention needed by a hundred students writing homework, dissertations, and so on. But I became obsessed by the idea of the blues article, and I often worked in a dreamlike state, as if the blues' ancestral spirits, among them one of my favorites, Skip James, were actually dictating the text to me. James's "Devil Got My Woman," Jessie Mae Hemphill's "She-Wolf," and Robert "Wolfman" Belfour's wonderful "Catfish Blues" and "Poor Boy Long Way from Home" enhanced my flow state. Robert Johnson appeared to me again and proposed a simple solution to my problem: I had better sign up with the devil and I would finish the work successfully!

By June 1997, I had a preliminary typed manuscript in my hand. David Evans happened to be on a concert tour as a solo blues guitarist in Germany, and he came to see me in Mainz. He read my manuscript through the midnight hours, making comments and writing suggestions in the margins. He said he was unable to make any quick decision but pointed out to me the obvious—that the manuscript was far too long for an article. It was too early, however, to say whether it might best be split into two articles, or shortened, or published in a series of extracts. Just a week earlier, Robert Farris Thompson, professor of Art History at Yale University, had also come to see me in Mainz in connection with his new book on Kikongo conceptualizations about music and dance. He reacted to my blues manuscript with enthusiasm and encouraged me to pursue the subject and get it into a finished form.

Eventually, on July 9, Moya, his children Monika and Yohana, and I traveled to Chicago on a two-month joint Rockefeller Foundation Residence Fellowship at the invitation of the Center for Black Music Research of Columbia College.

Although not directly connected with my blues article manuscript, this new commitment turned out to tip the scales. As stated in our research proposal, we would have a fresh look at a variety of contemporary and historical African-American musical traditions in the United States, the Caribbean, and South America, against the background of our field experience in a broad variety of African cultures, with the objective of delineating their historical links with *specific* African culture areas. My field data, accumulated from research since 1959 and covering no less than eighteen countries of Africa (altogether 159 societies) had passed the 26,000-item mark. Together with Moya's own coverage of south central Africa since 1979, this was a unique database against which we could examine selected African-American traditions, paying particular attention to the ever fluent processes of change, innovation, and intra-American migration the Africa-derived traditions have undergone during their histories in the Americas. Included in this project was a brief fieldwork period in selected areas of the southern United States.

When I discussed the details of my various plans with the Center's director, Dr. Samuel A. Floyd Jr., he had very encouraging words, stating his desire to get Africanist researchers involved in African-American studies. We then focused on some of my ideas about the so-called "blue notes" and the blues tonal system and its origins, a subject that is also dealt with in this book. At the Center I had not only the facilities of a substantial library with many badly needed references, and especially hard-to-obtain dissertations on the shelves, but also a quiet and pleasant office in which to do the final writing for what had now quite clearly grown to a book-length manuscript.

During the two-week fieldwork period, Moya, the children, and I were able to revisit the South, first working for a week with Bruce Nemerov at the Center for Popular Music at Middle Tennessee State University, Murfreesboro, recording blues harmonica player William Howse Jr., and other blues and country musicians, then for another week with David Evans in Memphis. David and I concentrated on editing parts of the blues manuscript, screening his library and record collection. We made visits to the home of bluesman Robert "Wolfman" Belfour in Memphis and the Tenth Annual Sunflower River Blues and Gospel Festival in Clarksdale, Mississippi, where we heard more blues as well as the fife and drum music of Othar Turner.

Back at the Center for Black Music Research in Chicago on August 3, I had just one more full month to complete the manuscript. With the Center's staff actively helping me with my requests for references, I accomplished what seemed to be a marathon. By the end of August I had completed most of the main text of this book. Further correspondence with David Evans, and a brief visit to Chicago and Memphis in April 1998, enabled me to refine certain elements of content and expression in the manuscript as well as to experience more live blues by Memphis artists "Big Lucky" Carter and Mose Vinson.

There are so many friends and colleagues who have been helpful in this endeavor that I hardly know where to start and in which order I should express my thanks. Let me then thank everybody in alphabetical order for their interest, help, wonderful discussions, and friendly reception.

Gerard Béhague (Department of Music, University of Texas at Austin)

Robert Belfour (bluesman, Memphis)

Wolfgang Bender (African Music Archive, University of Mainz)

Paul Berliner (The School of Music, Northwestern University, Evanston, Illinois)

Johann Buis (Center for Black Music Research, Columbia College, Chicago)

Dena Epstein (Music historian and ethnomusicologist, Chicago)

David Evans and Marice Evans (Department of Music, The University of Memphis)

Glen Faulkner (bluesman, Senatobia, Mississippi)

Thelma Fitzgerald and daughter (Music educator, Chicago)

Suzanne Flandreau (Librarian and Archivist, Center for Black Music Research, Columbia College, Chicago)

Samuel A. Floyd Jr., and staff (Center for Black Music Research, Columbia College, Chicago)

Richard Graham (Music historian, Memphis)

Donald and Ernestine Hopkins (Guinea Worm Eradication Scheme, Chicago)

Kazadi wa Mukuna (School of Music, Kent State University, Kent, Ohio)

Carol Lems-Dworkin (Northwestern University, Evanston, Illinois)

Laurence Libin (Department of Musical Instruments, The Metropolitan Museum of Art, New York)

Alan Lomax (The Association for Cultural Equity, Hunter College, New York)

Moya Aliya Malamusi (Oral Literature Research Programme, Chileka, Malaŵi)

John Minton (Indiana University-Purdue University, Fort Wayne)

Ken Moore (Department of Musical Instruments, The Metropolitan Museum of Art, New York)

Bruce Nemerov, Mayo Nemerov and children (Center for Popular Music, Middle Tennessee State University, Murfreesboro)

Sylvester Oliver (Rust College, Holly Springs, Mississippi)

Hans Panofsky (Curator of Africana Emeritus, Northwestern University Library, Evanston, Illinois)

Cynthia Schmidt (University of Washington, Seattle)

Ruth Stone and Verlon Stone (Archives for Traditional Music, Indiana University, Bloomington)

Robert Farris Thompson (Timothy Dwight College, Yale University, New Haven, Connecticut)

Andrew Tracey (International Library of African Music, Grahamstown, South Africa)

Paul Wells (Center for Popular Music, Middle Tennessee State University, Murfreesboro)

Africa and the Blues

Part I

Out of Africa

Introduction

Historically oriented research on the blues embraces several disparate areas of inquiry:

1. The study of the musical, literary, and social factors leading in the late nineteenth century to the gradual development of a new, distinct genre of accompanied solo song in rural areas of the South—a genre that would later be labeled "blues."

2. The study of the remote history of this previously unnamed genre's musico-structural and literary characteristics with regard to their origins in African and other cultures.

3. The study of the developments and changes that took place in the blues after the first publication of sheet music versions in 1912 and commercial gramophone records beginning in 1920.

4. The study of the influences exerted by the blues and its contemporary rural and urban derivatives upon other types of American music and upon other musical cultures of the world from the 1920s to the present.

Within these areas of inquiry, the third has been the best covered. Besides written sources, pictorial documents, and oral tradition, commercial recordings have been our most important twentieth-century source for the history of the blues. These are augmented by the immense field recording work done by researchers since the 1930s.

In respect to its earlier history, most authors agree that the blues is a tradition that developed in the Deep South at the end of the nineteenth century under specific circumstances, molding together traits whose remote origins can be traced to distinctive African regions with other traits from Euro-American traditions, such as the use of ending rhymes in most of the lyrics, reference to

3

I–IV–V degrees, strophic form, and certain Western musical instruments. The search for the blues' "African roots" has been a persistent concern in African-American studies.

History can be conceptualized as an uninterrupted continuum in time and space. This framework also suits the study of the origins and rise of the blues. The blues as such did not begin in Africa, nor on the Middle Passage, nor at the moment the first African set foot on American soil; not even necessarily with the inception of plantation life in the southern United States. Like any other innovative development, the nineteenth- and twentieth-century genre to be called blues was the result of a chain of determinants linked by cause and effect that can be traced to various other times and places until the traces vanish in the anonymity of sourceless history. We proceed from the notion that there is no such thing as "roots" of the blues, but that the American blues were a logical development that resulted from specific processes of cultural interaction among eighteenth- to nineteenth-century African descendants in the United States, under certain economic and social conditions.

However, just as Brazilian samba developed out of older traditions transplanted to early nineteenth-century Brazil specifically from within the cultural radiation area of the ancient Lunda Empire in northeastern Angola (cf. Kubik 1979, 1986), so must the blues have come out of something. That it should have been invented out of "social needs" alone is an idea that only perpetuates the stereotype of a *tabula rasa* state among African captives. One of our questions then is: which African eighteenth- to nineteenth-century traditions preceded the blues, channeling experiences and energies into the formative processes of this music? And in which parts of Africa were these traditions established?

1 - Sources, Adaptation, and Innovation

Anyone studying the history of the early rural blues and its proclaimed "roots" will be aware of the complexity of such an undertaking. To recall a few basic data of the general history of the United States might therefore help us to avoid the most serious errors, such as suggesting a direct, unilinear descent of the blues from any specific eighteenth- to nineteenth-century ethnic African musical genre.

The first British settlement in North America was Jamestown, established in 1607. By the 1640s only a narrow strip along the Atlantic coast had been settled. In 1682 the French under La Salle penetrated the Mississippi River area from the south. Nouvelle Orleans was founded in 1718. Florida was under Spanish administration. Although some British pioneers did reach the Mississippi by the 1770s, the area called Louisiana—much larger than today's state—was firmly under Spanish or French control. During the seventeenth and eighteenth centuries the British slave trade brought ever increasing numbers of West Africans, first only from the Gambia/Senegal area, then from all along the Guinea coast, to Jamestown and other Atlantic coastal towns. Contemporaneous sources testify that during that period the African population was particularly concentrated in rural areas of Maryland, Virginia, North Carolina, South Carolina, and Georgia.

Dena Epstein (1973: 61) writes:

Among the most tantalizing questions about African music in the New World are those concerning its earliest period. What kind of music did the Africans bring with them when they first arrived on the North American mainland? How long did that music persist in its new environment, and how was it transformed into something we now call Afro-American?

FIGURE 1. The southern United States today. Outline of the broad geographical region under consideration in this book.

She deplores the lacunae in the seventeenth- and eighteenth-century literature:

Authentic answers to these questions are not at all easy to find, for the published literature on the thirteen colonies says really very little about the black population and still less about its music. Those contemporary documents which have been examined barely mention them. (1973: 61)

However, her meticulous work has uncovered a few significant sources. Concerning the mode of deportation of Africans to the New World, Epstein cites several eighteenth-century sources to testify that slave traders often encouraged dance and music among the captives on slave ships, to prevent their falling into depression and dying. Dances and songs were practiced on deck to "air" the captives from time to time (Epstein 1973: 66–67). Musical instruments of various provenance were used for that purpose, including African musical instruments purchased on the Guinea coast. Epstein quotes, among other sources, Bryan Edwards (1793: 116): "In the intervals between their meals they [the slaves] are encouraged to divert themselves with music and dancing; for which purpose such rude and uncouth instruments as are used in Africa, are collected before their departure" (quoted in Epstein 1973: 67). It is not surprising therefore that the knowledge of several African musical instruments reached North America, including one-stringed West African bowed lutes, two-stringed plucked lutes (cf. Kubik 1989a: 80–81, 86–87, 189; Charry 1996 for a historical overview and typology), flutes, and drums. Dena Epstein has even traced a Senegambian *"barrafoo"* and an eighteenth-century "African drum" from Virginia in the British Museum (Exhibit 1368 of the Sloane bequest of 1753; see Epstein 1977: 47–62). This type of goblet-shaped single-headed drum is only known from the Guinea Coast; it has a characteristic type of attachment of the single skin: the so-called cord-and-peg tension (cf. Wieschhoff 1933) prominent in southern Ghana, Togo, Dahomey, and southwestern Nigeria. It is of secondary importance here whether any of these West African instruments actually reached the New World in the hands of the captives or their captors, or whether they were constructed in the new environment from memory, using local materials. John Michael Vlach compares the eighteenth-century drum from Virginia to the Asante *apentemma*, and suggests that "the patina of red clay which cakes the surface of the drum indicates that it had been buried, hidden away" (1978: 21–22).

The presence of more West African instruments in the New World, especially ones from the savanna and Sahel zones of the so-called Western Sudan, is attested to by Sir Hans Sloane (1707) also from another then British territory: Jamaica. Sloane's famous illustration (reproduced in Epstein 1973: 74) shows two two-stringed West African lutes, the plant fibers that were used for the strings, and in the background an eight-stringed bridge-harp clearly manufactured after models common in the western Sudan, somewhat close in typology to those found among the Tem (northern Togo) and other ethnic groups in the area of speakers of I.A.3 (Voltaic) languages in Joseph Greenberg's 1966 classification of the African languages (cf. objects no. 317 and 318, late nineteenth century, in the Museum für Völkerkunde, Berlin; Wegner 1984: 175, 269–70).

What kind of songs and instruments could be found among Africans and their descendants in eighteenth-century Maryland, Virginia, North and South Carolina, and Georgia? We get some idea from the sources Epstein unearthed, although much has also to be extrapolated from accounts relating to the Bahamas and other Caribbean islands, which were much better covered by the sources. In the *Glossary of Archaic and Provincial Words* (1832) by the Reverend Jonathan Boucher, a philologist and missionary who spent many years in Maryland and Virginia until 1775, there is this testimony:

I well remember, that in Virginia and Maryland the favourite and almost only instrument in use among the slaves then was a *bandore*; or, as they pronounced the word, *banjer*. Its body was a large hollow gourd, with a long handle attached to it, strung with catgut and played on with the finger.

He then transcribes a "couplet" of one of the songs:

Negro Sambo play fine banjer,
Make his fingers go like handsaw. (cited in Epstein 1973: 76)

To anyone familiar with the cultures of the western and central geographical Sudan, the regional origins of the models for such long-necked plucked lutes as described in this eighteenth-century source are clear. They are spike-lutes found across the west-central Sudan, from Hausa minstrels and their neighbors in Cameroon and northern Nigeria to the Wolof and others in Senegambia with their *xalam* (Coolen 1982; Charry 1996). The tradition has survived into the late twentieth century, and I for one recorded such unfretted plucked lutes in northeastern Nigeria and northern Cameroon (cf. Kubik 1989a: 80–81, 86–87; recordings Phonogrammarchiv Vienna, B 8610, 8921, etc.). Boucher's Virginia performer was a virtuoso, if his fingers went "like handsaw." This compares to the spike-lute players I met two centuries later in Africa. Most were professionals, usually traders or minstrels who traveled long distances. Hausa traders in northeastern Nigeria used to call the instrument *garaya* (Kubik 1989a:80). Michael Theodore Coolen, who researched the *xalam* of the Wolof of Gambia in the 1970s, writes:

Until recent times, one of the common Senegambian ensembles consisted of a plucked-lute (the *xalam*), a bowed-lute (called *riti* by the Wolof and *nyanyaur* by the Fula), and a tapped calabash. There is a remarkable similarity between this ensemble and the fiddle, banjo, and tambourine ensembles so popular in the United States from the late seventeenth through the nineteenth centuries. (Coolen 1982: 74)

Indirectly, then, Boucher's testimony suggests the retention in the southern Atlantic coastal region of the United States of a performance tradition that came from a certain broad region of West Africa, and subsequently may have become vital to the rise of the blues in a quite different part of the United States. On a more individual basis, such professionalism in music is often connected with an itinerant lifestyle. Solo singing of "the improvisatori kind" (Boucher 1832), self-accompanied by a plucked stringed instrument of west-central African design, thus had formed a cultural bridgehead in the southeastern United States, and become a favorite pastime among the region's slaves.

A story by an African descendent, "Dick the Negro," quoted by John Davis (1803: 381), describes another aspect of life before the American War of Independence (1775–83): "I made my court to a wholesome girl, who had never bored her ears, and went constantly to meeting . . . by moonlight I used to play my *banger* under her window, and sing a *Guinea* love-song my mother had taught me" (quoted in Epstein 1973: 81). Many of the sources uncovered by Epstein coalesce to give us a picture of the kind of culture perpetuated by captives in South Carolina, Virginia, and elsewhere during the eighteenth century. These sources give us a lead to some likely regional African connections. Even the text of the so-called Slave Act of 1740 in South Carolina following the Stono insurrection is conclusive not only of the fact that dancing in public was common and accompanied by a variety of instruments, but that initially the slaves displayed passive resistance to various attempts at their Christianization. Efforts by the evangelical missionaries to stamp out all secular music were to a degree successful, so that by the mid-nineteenth century most dance gatherings by the African descendants seem to have disappeared in their original forms (Epstein 1973: 90, citing contemporaneous sources). Some were transformed into Protestant religious expression, such as the ring-shouts (Parrish 1942: 54–92; Floyd 1991, 1995: 37–38, 43).

For the earlier periods, however, the testimony of the Reverend Morgan Godwin (1680), who came to Virginia in 1665, is particularly revealing, since he mentions even dances to procure rain, and the fact that the converted slaves were loyal Christians apparently throughout the week *except* on Sundays (cf.

PHOTO 1. Performers of one-stringed bowed lutes from northern Ghana during a public festival in Accra, February 1970. (Photo: Author [Archive no. G 457])

PHOTO 2. A Hausa trader playing the *garaya*, two-stringed plucked lute. At Disol, near Genye/Sugu, south of Yola, northeastern Nigeria, November 1963. (Photo: Author [Recording No. 8610, Phonogrammarchiv Vienna])

FIGURE 2. Details of the *garaya* lute's construction: (compare to Photo 2)

Epstein 1973: 79–80). Sunday was, of course, their only full day off from work, except for holidays like Christmas. Epstein (1973: 80) also cites another source, a letter by the Reverend George Whitefield, who wrote in 1739–40 to the inhabitants of Maryland, Virginia, and North and South Carolina about "their" Negroes: "I have great reason to believe that most of you on Purpose, keep your Negroes ignorant of Christianity; or otherwise, why are they permitted thro' your Provinces, openly to prophane the Lord's Day, by their Dancing, Piping and such like?" There were also signs of acceptance by European-Americans of the music played by the African descendants, a pattern that would continue throughout history. Epstein (1973: 83) discovered a report from Virginia in the 1690s in the Accomac County Records, telling "of a Negro fiddler playing for the dancing of whites." We do not know what kind of fiddle this was. Probably it was a European fiddle, but in all likelihood it was also a conceptual extension of the west-central Sudanic *goje* or *goge* (one-stringed fiddle) as played by Hausa, Dagomba, and other minstrels. The expertise and specific style of this musician must have come from somewhere, after all, to make him attractive to "whites" as an entertainer. Many of them would certainly have played the current Euro-American popular tunes, to which their audience was accustomed, and not any African music, but with novel accentuations, techniques, and improvisations that would have struck such audiences as "virtuoso." Indirectly, therefore, this source also suggests that techniques inherited from the playing of one-stringed fiddles common in the west-central Sudanic belt (cf. DjeDje 1980, 1982, 1984; Minton 1996a) would ultimately be transferred to status-enhancing European instruments, notably the violin. Expertise on such instruments could make a performer of African descent a prodigy in the eyes of his startled audience. Eventually this would result in a revival of African musical professionalism, though now for a different public and with a different repertoire. (See also Southern 1971; Winans 1990; Jabbour 1993.)

After the American War of Independence, 1775–83, the situation of the slaves changed dramatically. Within two decades a process became effective that could be summarized as *secondary proliferation of African-derived styles*. Independence forged together thirteen states on the Atlantic coast, including Maryland, Virginia, North Carolina, South Carolina, and Georgia. After the invention of the cotton gin in 1793, increasingly profitable cotton plantations began to be established in these states and west of the Appalachian mountains. In 1803 a large territory called Louisiana, covering vast expanses of land on both sides of the Mississippi River, was purchased by the United States from the needy Napoleon Bonaparte for $15 million. That opened up the Mississippi region for settlement by English-speaking farmers. Following the removal over the next three decades of most of the Amerindian population, slave workers were transferred wholesale from southeastern Atlantic seaboard states to these new places, into a social environment of relatively scattered settlements, with social interaction often reduced to the radius of individual farming communities. That was the geographical and social turf upon which the blues later developed.

The westward migration of English-speaking farmers and their slaves to Alabama, western Tennessee, Mississippi, Arkansas, northern Louisiana, and eventually to east Texas, for a life on the regimented cotton plantations can also be followed up by numerous "dropped leaves" on the path. Some of these were documented recently by Richard Graham (1994) in the Appalachian and Ozark mountains, in European-American communities. Graham studied mouth-resonated bows, and he expanded his field data by archival work uncovering a number of nineteenth- to twentieth-century written sources. The remote ancestry of these musical bows in specific African bow traditions is perceptible to the naked eye by an Africanist who is familiar with musical bows on that continent, in spite of the considerable mutation in organology and playing technique they have undergone in the course of time. An example was recorded by Alan Lomax in 1959 in Arkansas (cf. Lomax 1962), and it has persisted to this day (Irwin 1979: 59–63). The convex side of the bow's stave (instead of the string) is turned toward the player's mouth. We have come to the conclusion that the remote genealogy of these bows points in the direction of mouthbows in central and southern Mozambique, such as the *nyakatangali* (cf. Malamusi 1996: 63) and the *chipendani* (Lutero and Pereira 1981: 82; Dias 1986: 155–56; Brenner 1997). Two different playing techniques are found with the *chipendani*: striking the string with

PHOTO 3. An old cotton gin still in operation at Lula in the Mississippi Delta, August 3, 1997. (Photo: Moya Aliya Malamusi)

a stick, as for example among the -Tsonga, or pulling it with thumb and index finger, as among the Shona-Karanga and -Zezuru (recordings AMA *The Sound of Africa Series*, by Hugh Tracey, TR-82, TR-173, and TR-174).

Mozambicans were certainly also deported to the United States. Graham (1994: 374) quoted one source from 1804, i.e., four years before the legal importation of African slaves to the United States came to an end, testifying to the arrival of 243 Mozambicans in Charleston, South Carolina. The startling extent of the Mozambique slave trade in the early nineteenth century was researched by António Carreira (1979).

People from southeastern Africa in the United States may have been few in number, but this would not necessarily inhibit their cultural influence. Here, as always, we have to bear in mind that culture is not necessarily transmitted in proportion to people's numbers. *One* charismatic personality will suffice to release a chain reaction. *One* virtuoso musician can end up being imitated by hundreds. This fact has often been neglected by researchers proceeding from a collectivistic perception of culture.

Characteristically, there seems to be no memory among the present-day cul-

Photo 4. *Chipendani* (mouth-resonated musical bow) played by a Mozambican labor migrant at a South African mine. The performer, using a stick for striking the string, probably came from the -Tsonga ethnic group. Near Krugersdorp, Transvaal, South Africa, 1969. (Photo: Author)

tural bearers of those bows now sold to tourists as authentic "hillbilly" artifacts (Graham 1994: 361) of a possible African background. Kinship tradition is usually cited, and occasionally even Amerindian origins are suggested, contrary to compelling evidence that native Americans in the southeastern United States did not use mouth bows. Graham's findings not only testify to the relative ease with which traditions can migrate from one ethnic group to another, but also to how quickly historical memory fades; no one among his informants suggested any African background to these bows.

How did the knowledge of those specific types of musical bows take root among the mountaineers? My guess is that slaves from Mozambique, and perhaps also from Angola, during the late eighteenth to early nineteenth century spread this knowledge to the newly established scattered European communities. It was toward the end of the eighteenth century that the Atlantic slave trade shifted increasingly to areas south of the equator—to Angola and (to a some-

PHOTO 5. Appalachian-Mountains-type mouth-bow played with the convex side of the stave directed to the lips and one end of the stave pressed against the left corner of the mouth. The performer is the famous Alex Stewart at the age of 86, who made his bow at his home on Panther Creek in Hancock County, Tennessee. (Photograph by John Rice Irwin, summer 1974. Reproduced from John Rice Irwin, *Musical Instruments of the Southern Appalachian Mountains* [1979:60]. Courtesy of the Museum of Appalachia, Norris, Tennessee)

what lesser extent) to Mozambique. Captives from those areas were beginning to be preferred to those from the Guinea Coast. Musical bow playing seen among Mozambicans and southwestern Angolans, where the technique of passing the back of the bow stave by the lips is prominent (cf. Kubik 1987: 109, 136), was perhaps first imitated by children among the European settlers. Children in many cultures are known to be in the vanguard of artistic innovation. When people of European descent migrated increasingly to the Appalachian mountains, and later the Ozark mountains in Arkansas, such critical experiences could have gained general acceptance, once contacts with Africans had become minimal. Tony Russell (1970: 10) and Richard Graham (1994: 367) have both suggested that such traditions could have been more easily assimilated in the

European-American communities once they were settled far away from African descendants, and could thereby perceive such cultural interaction as "less threatening" (Graham 1994: 367). This idea could be corroborated by the fact that the five-stringed *banjo*, an American derivative of western and central Sudanic plucked lutes (cf. Epstein 1975), is also especially concentrated in that relatively small area of European-American communities "no more than one hundred fifty miles in any direction from Knoxville in eastern Tennessee" (Graham 1994: 367) as well as in the Ozark Mountains extension of this region.

The Appalachian mountains also seem to foster the persistence of strange tonal and scalar concepts. Annabel Morris Buchanan drew attention to "the neutral 3ds and varying 7ths that constantly recur in our Anglo-American folk music, especially in the Appalachians" (Buchanan 1940: 81). This was suggested by Cecil J. Sharp's 1917 and 1918 fieldwork, as well as Buchanan's own, such as in a piece sung "by a primitive Baptist elder of eastern Tennessee, as learned in childhood from a very old preacher in North Carolina" (1940: 85). Buchanan writes: "Moreover, having recognized this same neutral mode in the tonal structure of American Indian, native African and American Negro folk melodies, I conclude that it exists, doubtless in other nationalities as well" (Buchanan 1940: 84). Important for us in this statement is that the Anglo-American settlers in the Appalachians and surrounding areas apparently shared that "neutral mode" with the African-American "folk."

In the Deep South, the knowledge of musical bows and other one-stringed instruments of African background has survived among African Americans to this day, especially among children and particularly in communities in Mississippi whose progenitors created the blues. David Evans has carried out pathbreaking research on these traditions; as early as 1970 he published a stunning account under the title "African-American One-Stringed Instruments," which was followed by the publication of many recordings, and cinematographic documentation. One type, sometimes called a "diddley bow," "bo diddley," "jitterbug," "unitar," or "one-stringed guitar," among other terms, is based on the remembrance and development of central and west-central African monochord zithers. This is obvious, although there are no nineteenth-century U. S. sources that would testify to its presence at that time. Like many other African traditions and culture traits, the idea of the monochord zither seems to have smoldered on through the nineteenth century in an underground existence, perpetuated especially by children, and in the rare cases in which the instrument was perhaps observed by outsiders, it was not considered even worthy of report. Only when systematic research of the southern cultures began, in the 1930s, does it become documented through photographs, and it was not recorded until the 1950s. It is first *recalled* from about 1910–1915 by Mississippi bluesman Big Joe Williams (cf. Evans and Welding 1995, CD notes).

In Africa too these instruments have been overlooked or not found worth reporting. For this reason we have notable gaps in our African distribution map. Monochord zithers are common in a relatively compact region of Africa including southeastern Nigeria, southern Cameroon, Gabon, Equatorial Guinea, the Republic of Congo, and the southwestern tip of the Central African Republic. This is a region where the raffia palm marks the ecology and is a basic material for the manufacture of furniture and various musical instruments such as lamellophones, the stick zither called *mvet*, *ngombi*, and so on. African monochord zithers, which serve as a children's pastime, are made of a length of raffia leaf stem, from which a thin strip of the hard epidermis is peeled off to form the string. They are played mostly by two (male) youngsters, one striking the string with two sticks, the other altering its pitch by stopping the string with a knife, bottle, or other object, often sliding along it. From the Gũ of the Dahomeyan coast it was reported that the monochord zither was used in games of hide-and-seek, the players directing the candidate toward the hidden object by using alternative, speech-tone based melodic phrases (Rouget 1982: 310–11). Significantly, musical associations with the game of hide-and-seek have also been reported from the southern United States, by the musical bow and quill player Eli Owens, not for a monochord zither but for the mouth-resonated musical bow Owens had used during his youth (Evans 1994: 347). No doubt, this represents an African survival, but as so often in New World cultures, the association *shifted*, in this case from one type of one-stringed instrument (the monochord zither) to another (the mouthbow).

The idea of the central African monochord zither, even in its original idiochord form, has survived in several places in South America (e.g., the *carángano* of Venezuela), the Caribbean, and the United States. From his fieldwork in Jamaica in 1997, Richard Graham recorded and obtained a specimen called *benta*, made from bamboo. In the United States the monochord zither transmuted into a soloist instrument. The string can be mounted either on the wall of a

Photo 6. Mono-idiochord zither made from a raffia stalk and performed in a typical arrangement by two Mpyɛmɔ̃ (= a Bantu language) speaking boys, Maurice Djenda and Moise Mbongo, one using two sticks for agitating the string, the other using a knife as a slider. At Bigene village, Nola District, Central African Republic, May 1966. (Photo: Author)

house (cf. recordings of Compton Jones, Jessie Mae Hemphill, and Napoleon Strickland on Evans 1978c, Evans 1998, and Evans and Welding 1995) or on a length of board (cf. recordings of Eddie "One-String" Jones and Glen Faulkner on Charters 1993 and Evans and Albold 1994, and video document no. 20, joint field trip D. Evans, R. Graham, G. Kubik, and M. A. Malamusi in 1993). In the United States these derivatives of the west-central African monochord zither became part of the blues scene. The knowledge of the slider technique, inherited

PHOTO 7. African American monochord zither ("jitterbug") with the string mounted on the wall of a house, played by Napoleon Strickland near Senatobia, Mississippi, March 1969. (Photo: David Evans)

from central Africa, can be traced in the southern United States at least to the early twentieth century. W. C. Handy, who was in large part responsible for popularizing the blues during the early decades of the twentieth century, reports in his autobiography how in around 1903 he came across a musician at Tutwiler, a Mississippi Delta town, who played a guitar using a knife to slide along the strings (Handy 1970: 78). Big Joe Williams (b. 1903), another important slide guitar player, has stated that one-stringed zithers built by children in his youth "on the wall with a strand of baling wire, two thread spools for bridges, and a half-pint whiskey bottle for a slider" were definitely the "source of the slide guitar style" (Evans and Welding 1995, CD notes by Evans).

The knowledge of the slider technique may have reached the Deep South from various sources. One possibility is that it reached the area with the bulk of African descendants who were transported there from the eastern seaboard states in the first four decades of the nineteenth century, after the Louisiana Purchase and the Amerindian removal. In any case, some of "the more archaic-sounding" African-American music has been recorded in the delta bottoms of Mississippi, the swamps of Louisiana, and the canebrakes of Texas, "all remote, rural areas settled late in the history of the South," to quote blues researcher Bob Eagle (1993: n.p.).

2 - The Rise of a Sung Literary Genre

Many proposals have been put forward as to the possible "African roots" of the music called blues. The blues as oral literature—though studied in great detail by various authors (cf. Dauer 1964–65, 1979, 1983a and b; Oliver 1990; Evans 1978b, 1982; Ferris 1973; etc.) for their social and historical commentary, their literary value, and their compositional structures—have remained somewhat neglected as concerns their African backgrounds in content, diction, and psychology. In part, this could be the result of a prevailing musicological tendency—also encountered in some studies of African music—to underrate literary aspects in favor of an abstract appreciation of the music, or, alternatively, to study each realm separately. For this reason I recommended in 1988 "an integrated approach towards west African music and oral literature," as demonstrated in my earlier fieldwork on Yoruba *chantefables* in Nigeria (Kubik 1988a: 129–82).

So far, the African background of the oral literature dimension of the blues has been studied mainly in one specific area—"magic" and "voodoo," including the permeating presence of the "devil." (On some of these subjects see Evans 1996; Ferris 1989; Finn 1986; Katz 1969; Kubik 1996; Oakley 1976; Oliver 1990: 117–37; Spencer 1993; LaVere 1990; and others.) A basic thesis of Finn and Spencer is that blues as "devil's music," as it was popularly called, demonstrates a process of reinterpretation of the Yoruba and Fõ religious concepts of *Èṣù* and *Legba* respectively. The bluesman is seen as a "voodoo" priest in disguise and also as a trickster (see also Floyd 1995: 72–78, for an assessment).

As fascinating as such conjectures may be, my own field experience in Togo and Dahomey among the Fõ, and in Nigeria among the Yoruba (cf. Kubik 1988a, 1989d: 110–43, 1994b) has taught me to exercise restraint when faced with the pleasures of freewheeling thought associations. Traditionally, Èṣù and Legba have no negativistic connotations such as "the devil." Legba mud sculptures found in the courtyards of many houses in Dahomey and Togo function to warn the inhabitants through dreams about any imminent danger of illness, even early death, caused by witchcraft. Legba is also intimately connected with the fa (in Fõ; ifa in Yoruba) oracle. A communal Legba called Tolegba is put up some two hundred meters from the village to protect against epidemic disease and arson, even harmful insects. Legba is a male being in love of truth. Nothing can be hidden before him, not even one's sexual organ. He himself is usually shown with a pronounced male sexual organ.

African-American studies seem often to pass through a stage in which the cognitive worlds of several distinctive African cultures are mixed up and grossly reinterpreted by the authors, with the Guinea Coast and particularly Nigeria providing the most easily accessible materials. What for a long time had been a dominant trend in the literature on Afro-Brazilian cultures (cf. criticism by Mourão 1980: 7; Kubik 1991: 147) is now being repeated in the United States: the Nigerianization of African-American studies, notably since Henry Louis Gates Jr.'s The Signifying Monkey (1988). It is true that the Yoruba òrìṣa (transcendental being) called Èṣù and the Fõ vodu equivalent called Legba, about whose connotations Danhin Amagbenyõ Kofi (in Kubik 1989a: 126–35) has informed us through firsthand observation, were variously targeted by Christians in Africa and in the New World and recategorized as "devils." Somewhat later, anthropologists labeled them "trickster Gods." But they have shared that fate with some other religious ideas in Africa. For example, in southeastern Angola Kavole, one of the masked characters appearing during the season of the mukanda initiation rites for boys, was reinterpreted by Christians as the "devil" (Kubik, field notes 1965/ Angola). In Venezuela certain masks used in carnival manifestations with (possibly) remote African components are called "devils' masks" (las máscaras de los diablos—cf. Pollak-Eltz 1977, 1979). In Malaŵi and Zambia, Seventh Day Adventists and other Protestant American churches have been in the vanguard up to the 1990s in calling the traditional masks of the Acheŵa and Amaŋanja people zausatana (things of Satan).

Probably no one will suggest that all those African religious traditions, variously stigmatized by Christians as "devil's things," must have survived in the back of the mind of blues singers. But why then also pick Èṣù and Legba, who incorporate religious ideas from just one delineated culture area of west Africa? Surely Yoruba and Fõ religious ideas have had notable extensions in the Caribbean and in Brazil, but little nineteenth-century presence in the United States. Even in Louisiana the concept of *vodu* imported with Haitians was soon reinterpreted and made into something quite different, now popularly called "hoodoo."

The "devil" is an ancient Mediterranean/Near East religious concept, prominent in Christianity and Islam. In his treatise on music in Mauritania, Senegal, and Niger, Tolia Nikiprowetsky (n.d.: 47) testifies to its presence among the Serer of the Kaolack region in Senegal. From Hausa culture in the Sudanic belt David Ames (1973: 141) reports: "The muslim scholar, macho and mosque head never plays an instrument or sings secular music or dance. They consider many kinds of Hausa music to be wicked, particularly *gogé* music which is called the music of the devil." In west Africa, *this* is the much more likely background to the idea of blues as "devil's music," not religious concepts associated with *Èṣù* or *Legba*. The "devil" as a concept has been used stereotypically by adherents, especially fundamentalists, to the Mediterranean/Near East religions for castigating nonconformist ideas and behavior. In fact, the entire United States was at one time labeled the "Great Satan" by the late Ayatollah Khomeini. Earlier, in the New World, the "black man" as such was regularly equated by Christians with the "devil." In Venezuela, characteristically, during the annual church theatrical festivals documented in Paul Henley's film *Cuyagua* (Granada Centre for Visual Anthropology, University of Manchester, 1977; for a review see Kubik 1988b: 255–57), the devil is always acted out by an Afro-Venezuelan person. Given this database, the lyrics and lifestyles of the blues singers must have been a thorn in the side of fundamentalist Christians.

Certainly, parallels to African thought styles can be detected in blues lyrics. They exist in the structure and patterning of symbolic ideas, in certain thematic preferences, and—contrary to what has been claimed in most of the literature—in the blues *non*-preoccupation with religion (cf. Garon 1975: 130–36; Prévos 1996). "Where I go when I die, can't nobody tell" is how Son House in 1930 expressed his rejection of the good people's hopes for an afterlife. He had given up preaching in about 1927 to become a blues singer, though he remained under some pressure from Christian beliefs.

Confidence in a nice afterlife is also a strange idea for most rural people in sub-Saharan Africa, as long as they are left alone by Christian missionaries. Nobody in any of the remote rural areas of southeastern Angola, where I conducted many months of fieldwork in 1965 and had to undergo my own initiation processes, ever "worshipped" something like "God." But there was an awareness of spiritual beings, *mahamba* (dissatisfied spirits) and *vakulu* (the "shadows" of persons who had died). Human beings had to cope with these dangerous entities. And there were *vulozi* (witchcraft) and *vandumba zyavantu* (the "lion-men"). The chance that any of these concepts would have survived and continued in the culture of the Deep South of the United States is just as high, if not higher, than for *Èsù* and *Legba*.

Robert Johnson (1911–1938) has been cited as a bluesman whose texts "alluded to or directly addressed themes of sorcery and/or the supernatural in about two-thirds of his recorded songs" (Evans 1996: 13). This was so because anxiety, feelings of guilt, and fear of others' revenge through witchcraft were psychological determinants of his short and "rambling" life. Popular beliefs began to spread that he had "made a pact with the devil." With the fashion of Hollywood "Zombies" (a word that derives from *Nzambi, Njambi*, etc., in various Congo/Angola languages, usually translated by Christians there as "God") fading, the movie industry recently picked up the rumors about Robert Johnson, using them in the 1986 movie *Crossroads*, directed by Walter Hill (cf. also Greenberg 1983, the published screenplay of Johnson's life). Sometimes, of course, it is in the musicians' interest to confirm such rumors. For example, William Bunch (1902–1941) called himself "Peetie Wheatstraw, The Devil's Son-in-Law" and "The High Sheriff From Hell" (Garon 1971).

While the "pact with the devil," preferably at a crossroads at midnight, is a well-known occult motif, traceable through European oral literature into Romanticism and beyond, it is characteristic of the African parallels that they evolve in a different setting and do not demonstrate extreme bipolar concepts such as the "Devil" versus "God." In Africa the idea that a musician makes a pact with a dangerous spiritual being in return for phenomenal musical powers is well documented. It is even thought generally that no one can develop extraordinary skills or attain fame without some "medicine" or secret liaison with the supernatural. The spectrum covers musicians, statesmen, and so on. Azande harpists in the Central African Republic can make a deal with the *mami wata* (mermaid, half woman-half fish) to obtain wonderful musical powers (cf. Kubik

1994a: 128–29). The Nigerian guitarist Sir Victor Uwaifo suggested the same thing by being photographed in a beach chair at the shores of the Atlantic Ocean for his 45 rpm disc *Dancing Time* (no. 8, 420034 PE, Philips West African Records), featuring his song "Guitar Boy and Mamywater." In the performance, the mermaid speaks to him with a tiny voice materializing in single-note high-pitched guitar patterns. Many more examples from Africa could be cited. *Mamiwata*, however, is not equated with the "Devil." In any case, musicians normally decide to confirm their audiences' belief in the spiritual implications of their lyrics. It is in that sense that Robert Johnson's choice of textual motifs can be understood as a continuation of African patterns of sociopsychological interaction. His mention of God and the Devil in his lyrics represents a coming to terms with Western dualistic religious thought.

One of the first recollections of blues is by William Christopher Handy, who heard them in St. Louis in 1892. From the content of the song it appears that the guitarist he heard on the streets "may well have been playing for tips" (cf. Evans 1973: 12). By 1902 the blues were already being commercialized. Ma Rainey in that year integrated blues into her stage shows. In 1903 Handy saw some more local bluesmen in the Mississippi Delta (Handy 1970: 147–48). One blues singer quoted by William Ferris (1971–72: 258) testified that blues existed in the Delta at least as early as 1890. It can be concluded, therefore, that blues or prototypes of the blues existed in Mississippi and other areas at least some years before Handy first heard them.

David Evans summarizes the pre-blues genres that arose in the nineteenth century as follows: "Throughout the South new musical forms emerged, among them worksongs for field work, corn shucking, tree cutting, rowing and riverboat work; social and dance songs, frequently accompanied by the fiddle and/or banjo and occasionally other instruments, and spiritual songs" (1994: 332).

Another summary, with reference to the most likely pre-Civil War antecedent vocal traditions in the Deep South, is given by Harriet Joseph Ottenheimer (1987), who states that the singing styles heard in work song leaders' parts probably drew from bardic traditions. Street cries of urban vendors of fruits, vegetables, and flowers, and the field hollers sung throughout the South, also could have retained elements of bardic traditions. Ottenheimer notes that such genres must have been rarely noted by European observers in the eighteenth and nineteenth centuries.

The street cries would have been considered such an ordinary, everyday, functional occurrence that they would not have been written about. Riverboatmen's cries on the Mississippi were noted by a few European travelers but were said to be impossible to describe. However, they also drew comments that indicate melodies of a melismatic bardic nature. Field hollers, also called *arhoolies*, were probably not heard at all by Europeans—except for the occasional white overseer, none of whom wrote any memoirs that have been discovered. (Ottenheimer 1987: 498–99)

Some of these melodic, textual, and stylistic ingredients were eventually absorbed by what would become the blues.

Blues is both a literary and a musical genre, and the two realms are inseparably linked by the very forces that also bind together music and text in most African cultures: semantic and grammatical tone, phonetic structure leading to offbeat phrasing of melodic accents (Waterman 1952; Kubik 1961a: 157–58, 1988a: 149–52), and the concept—widespread in African cultures—that the meaning of a song derives from its lyrics rather than from "melody," "rhythm," or chord sequences. Devoid of words, the sound patterns lose much of their original meaning. For this reason abstract melodies in African cultures often assume meaning only by the processes of *verbalization*, i.e., the projection of words or mere syllables into the pitch sequences and timbre patterns by musicians and audiences on the basis of analogy to speech rhythms and tones. *Mu chana cha Kapekula* ("In the river grasslands of Kapekula") is a famous southeastern Angolan mnemonic associated with a certain eight-pulse stick pattern (cf. Kubik 1972), while in Yoruba-speaking areas a certain melodic pattern might evoke the playful syllables *kɔŋ-kɔlɔ lakɔ kɔŋ-kɔla* symbolizing the way children act.

This way of looking at music can also be traced in African-American cultures. It is likely that in their early expressions the blues were somewhat more literary than abstract-musical, in the sense that we have before us essentially and originally a *song* genre, in which word, diction, content, and sound are intimately linked. That includes the kind of language used in the blues. While African-American vernacular English in its variations is certainly not a "Niger-Congo language" (see the 1996–97 media discussions on "ebonics," discussed in Gibbs 1997), it has incorporated tonal, phonetic, and also grammatical structural elements, even a few lexical items, notably from Benue-Congo (I.A.5), Kwa (I.A.4) and Voltaic (I.A.3) languages (cf. Greenberg's 1966 classification), projected by the original speakers upon English, thereby gradually modifying it. In an analogous manner this has happened to patois spoken in Louisiana (cf. Kubik 1993: 434).

Genealogically, blues can be considered an offspring of several African literary traditions incorporating music not usually associated with dance, most often performed either by a soloist accompanying himself or herself with a stringed or other instrument, or by a narrator supported by a participating audience. The music of itinerant musicians in the west African hinterland and elsewhere is one likely background, and so are some types of soloist work songs (grinding songs, etc.), and the practice of performing *chantefables*. By this term we embrace two relatively different African performance traditions: (a) sung narratives to the accompaniment of an instrument by a soloist; and (b) stories incorporating songs, told to small audiences of adults and children, especially in the evenings, with the audience participating as a responding chorus. All these traditions incorporate complex literary symbolism. It is in such individual or "small community" African settings that we have to look for the genealogical threads of the blues.

Alfons M. Dauer (1961: 51ff) pointed out that many blues texts might also be based on another well-known genre the slaves brought along from Africa: songs of mockery and denunciation by which unacceptable social behavior is castigated in a symbolic manner. Songs of denunciation and songs of praise are both part of a larger class of songs of social commentary. While we cannot deny certain retentions from those genres in the blues, they are more characteristic of calypso and other New World genres (van Dam 1954). There is, of course, plenty of mockery and denunciation in the blues, but it is much more "egocentric" than in calypso, i.e., the blues singer denounces the one who has mistreated him or her. Calypso and some African traditions tend to assume a *public knowledge* of the character to be denounced, either someone living nearby and therefore easily identified or known to the public from the mass media, e.g., a politician. The singer then acts as a public spokesman. Dauer's idea does not account for one striking difference between the lyrics of the blues and most African and New World songs of derision: that most blues are sung in the *first person*. Their messages are delivered from a first-person viewpoint and their emotional dimension is defined by performers as a "worried feeling caused by problems in life" (Evans 1982: 16–22). Thus their contents are derived from personal concerns and complaints, especially regarding man/woman relationships. The highly personal point of view in blues lyrics is, in fact, a significant lead in helping us to unlock their remote origins in comparable, especially first-person solo singing traditions in Africa, and in the lifestyle of itinerant musicians accompanying their songs with instruments such as lutes, fiddles, even lamellophones.

How was the psychological background in the southern United States conducive to the development of a genre that would incorporate many of the traits and performance characteristics of African itinerant music, *chantefables*, work songs, and so on? On an individual psychological basis, how could Leadbelly have imagined that he had grasshoppers in his pillow, crickets in his meal, and tacks in his shoes (Record Capitol A 40038, 27 October 1944)? Under what circumstances do dreamlike images of this sort occur to an individual?

A psychologist is entitled to ask such questions. Obviously, blues is not the product of a self-replenishing society with a community-oriented lifestyle. In most village-based agricultural African societies the community is the permanent background noise to an individual from an early age. Children are seen in a twelve-hour day-by-day interaction with their peers. A lonesome, introverted child is considered abnormal.

People growing up in societies thriving on intensive day-to-day community interaction often slide into depression when transplanted into an environment with a more individualistic lifestyle. Music may then assume the function of autotherapy and psychological compensation. Paul Oliver (1980: 813) stated that "a blues performer sings or plays to rid himself of 'the blues.'" The kind of society that evolved on the cotton plantations of the Mississippi Delta and elsewhere in the Deep South was in my opinion conducive to the rise of a genre like the blues, precisely for these reasons. The planters' unwritten policy was that the slaves should perhaps *work* in groups, but should not gather in large groups during leisure time. Much of the work was solitary (e.g., plowing fields), and many slaves in the frontier areas were isolated on small farms that had only one slave family or even a single slave. After Emancipation, many obtained small plots—perhaps forty acres—that they worked as single isolated families. Others began a life of wandering in search of better conditions or wage work. A lucid revelation of the psychology of an itinerant Delta bluesman (b. 1915) can be found in the autobiography of David "Honeyboy" Edwards (1997).

Such scenarios explain in part why even a hundred years later, in the mid-twentieth century, the sampling of African-American recordings we have from the Deep South displays a high number of work songs, disproportionately high as compared with our African samples. The rest of the Deep South sample consists of individual or small group performances, with the notable exception of some types of children's game songs and religious music which were often the only outlets for community spirit tolerated by the dominant Euro-American culture (cf. Evans 1987a; Lomax 1993).

While the concepts "blue," "blue devil," and so on had been current in the English language at least since the late eighteenth century, referring to specific states of mind, it is not known who first applied the term "blues" to the new genre and whether it was an insider or outsider appellation. Blues texts, with their complaints and intense imagery, occasionally read like quotations from the diary of a patient experiencing or recovering from clinical depression. For psychological reasons, therefore, they could not have emerged in the relaxed social atmosphere of New Orleans, nor probably in the eighteenth century before the development of intensive cotton plantation agriculture. Like rural Louisiana (cf. Minton 1996b: 484–85), New Orleans society was also highly stratified, but it was a multilayer stratification that eventually allowed for some social mobility, whereas the plantation society was essentially bipolar (cf. Cobb 1992).

Christopher Lornell suggested that "these dimensions include economic depression and the social disorientation caused by the movement from rural to urban areas" (1981: 117). Much earlier, however, the suppression of community-oriented forms of expression among the slaves on the plantations may also have played a significant role. The experience of social deprivation and individual loneliness under the circumstances of farm life were perhaps the dominant factors in determining the literary content of the blues. One could also note the response by African Americans in the late nineteenth century to the increasing individualism of American society as well as the disruption of communities after the Civil War (1861–65), which ended slavery.

All this stimulated a selective revival of exactly those African traditions (still lingering in the mind and reinforced by other behavioral patterns) that had responded most effectively to such situations in Africa, i.e., some of the itinerant, individual music, solitary work songs, and so on (cf. Kubik 1979, 1991 for theoretical discussion of processes of unconscious transmission of culture traits).

Why is it that the songs of the itinerant *bangwe* zither player Limited Mfundo from Malaŵi (cf. Double Album, Kubik and Malamusi 1989, items B6–B9) strike audiences as so blues-like? Is it because of the pentatonic tuning system or the melodic ductus of the sung pitch lines? The use of a stringed instrument to accompany himself? The slow tempo?

I believe Limited Mfundo's music and that of some other African minstrels transmits something that is psychologically comparable to the blues, and this becomes even more obvious if one reads their life histories. Limited Mfundo was an itinerant musician who sang songs of moral content, complaining about society's shortcomings and people's ruthlessness, and about his personal grief, his vain attempt to save the life of his mother, and so on (text example 1). In a sense, this compares to Blind Willie McTell's experience recorded in "Death Room Blues," from 1933 (text example 2). Limited Mfundo was almost an ascetic, living in a house devoid of any possessions except a sleeping mat. Much of his music radiates a mood that is virtually identical with that of many blues, if such a subjective judgment is permissible. The same applies to some of the songs of the late guitarist and composer Daniel Kachamba from the same region, who like bluesmen Blind Lemon Jefferson and Bukka White once composed a song about his own future funeral, characteristically in the first person (text examples 3, 4, and 5). It also applies to *chantefables* of the blind singer and *bangwe* player Chitenje Tambala, whose texts were studied by Moya A. Malamusi (1990)—also a minstrel from the same region. Moods can be transmitted non-verbally and perhaps even cross-culturally. Have the cultures of the central Mozambique/southern Malaŵi area perhaps also contributed something to the blues, besides their likely contribution to the mouthbow tradition in the Appalachian and Ozark mountains?

Minstrel traditions exist in many African societies, and they tend periodically to emerge and reemerge as distinct art forms, when circumstances in the changing social environment and individual experience are conducive. That is what must have happened on the cotton plantations of the Deep South during the nineteenth century. I propose that the social environment had a selective influence upon the bulk of African music and performance traditions, whose structural codes were still vaguely transmitted at that time, determining *which ones* would respond most suitably to the new situation. Once such a historical step had been accomplished, however, the emerging new literary forms changed again

EXAMPLE 1

Text of one of Limited Mfundo's songs, accompanied on his seven-stringed *bangwe* board zither. Recorded at Namila, T.A. Kasisi, Chikwawa District, 22 February 1984. Recording published on the double album *Opeka Nyimbo*–Musician-composers from southern Malaŵi, by Gerhard Kubik and Moya Aliya Malamusi, MC 15, Berlin: Museum für Völkerkunde. (Item B 9)

Text in Chimaŋanja:

Kwa chaGoma! Kwa chaGoma!

Kwadzala nsale

Kwadzala nsale, nsale, nsale wa chaGoma . . .

Amayi akudwala.

Ndipite kumankhwala

Ndikatenge mankhwala

Kuti amayi adzachile!

Pobwera ku mankhwala kuja

Kudzapeza amayi amwalira.

Anyamata bwerani!

Tingolira maliro!

Mankhwala tikataye.

Oo! Tatsala tokha ife,

Tatsala tokha ife

Tatsala tokha ife

Ga! Ga! Ga! Ga! Ga! Ga!

English Translation

There at [the healer] Mr. Goma's place!(2x)

Where they plant sweet millet stalks,

Where they plant the sweet millet stalks of Mr. Goma . . .

My mother is sick.

I should go to find medicine!

I should fetch medicine from there!

So that my mother gets cured!

Coming back from the place of the medicine,

I find that my mother has died.

Young men assemble!

We just cry for the funeral!

The medicine we throw it away.
Oh! We have remained alone!
We have remained alone!
We have remained alone!
Ga! Ga! Ga! Ga! Ga! Ga!

Note:
nsale (bot. *Saccharum officinarum L.*), also written *msale* (pl. *misale*), is a species of millet planted for the sweet stalks. The grain is not eaten.

PHOTO 8. The great Limited Mfundo, Chimaŋanja speaking minstrel, performing on his seven- stringed *bangwe* board zither at his home village Namira, near Chikwawa, southern Malaŵi, March 1984. (Photo: Author)

EXAMPLE 2

Text of "Death Room Blues," by Blind Willie McTell. Recorded in New York, 19 September 1933 (14048-2). Text reproduced from booklet notes written by David Evans and Bruce Bastin for *Atlanta Blues: 1933*, JEMF-106, 12″ LP, 1979.

1. Tombstones is my pillow, cold grounds is my bed.
   Tombstones is my pillow, cold grounds is my bed.
   Blue skies is my blanket, the moonlight is my spread.
2. Early one morning Death walked into my room.
   Early one morning Death walked into my room.
   Oh, it taken my dear mother early one morning soon.
3. She left me moaning and crying just like a turtle dove.
   She left me moaning and crying just like a turtle dove.
   Death walked in and taken my mother and came back and got the friend I love.
4. Eeeeeeh, eeeeeeh.
   Eeeeeeh, eeeeeeh.
   Hey, crying, Lord, have mercy. She came back and got the friend I love.
5. Every since my mother died and left me all alone,
   Every since my mother died and left me all alone,
   All my friends have forsaked me. People, I haven't even got no home.
6. Mmmmmmmm, feel like moaning and crying.
   Mmmmmmmm, feel just like moaning and crying.
   And death walked in and got my mother. That was the only friend of mine.

in content and meaning just as quickly as they had come into being, as soon as they were transferred to yet another environment. That would explain why the urbanized, commercialized forms of the blues that evolved in U.S. cities during the 1910s and later are of such a different matrix. Blues transformed into vaudeville stage entertainment and into boogie-woogie piano, it expanded the repertoire of swing orchestras, and it nourished rock 'n' roll.

The content of the blues in its literary message sometimes transmits images of almost paranoiac magnitude. There may be an obsession that will not go away. You try to run away from an unpleasant idea, an obstructive, ghastly image, but it constantly reemerges from your own unconscious, putting you under its spell.

Unconscious feelings of guilt can be the cause of the paranoiac mood—also a common syndrome in African societies, with their tense family relationships and frequent unconscious death wishes toward close relatives (brothers, sisters, uncles, etc.) triggering intense anticipations of revenge from the targeted per-

PHOTO 9A. Two shots of Daniel Kachamba performing at a dance party in his home village. To his left is his young brother, Donald, on the flute; on the right is eight-year-old Moya Aliya Malamusi on the tin rattle. Such dance parties lasted until late in the night. As in a blues performance, these two photographs seem to convey two moods on the same occasion. At Singano village near Chileka, 12 km from Blantyre, Malaŵi, September 1967. (Photos: Maurice Djenda)

sons. These are verbalized as anxiety about those relatives perhaps having witchcraft power (cf. the overview of the psychology and cognitive aspects of sorcery and antisorcery in sub-Saharan Africa in Multhaupt 1989: 10–11, 20–22, 53–54, etc.). Herein lies one of the deeper reasons why accusations of sorcery are so much a part of daily life in most African societies (G. Kubik, field research documentation on intrafamily relationships and sorcery, 1964 and 1966/Gabon; 1965/Angola; 1960 and 1962/Tanganyika; 1971, 1973, 1979, and 1987/Zambia).

Such fear can take possession of the individual and paralyze him or her. The

PHOTO 9B.

moment one wakes up, blues is around and seems to permeate everything. In such cases the blues almost become personified, as "Mr. Blues," or—on another level of perception—like little blue devils emerging from the most unexpected, innocent objects: from the pillow upon which one sleeps, from a kitchen shelf. And just when one thinks it's over and all gone, there it is again and the ghastly thought is now tagged to the most unlikely place or object. In Africa, Daniel Kachamba has expressed this paranoiac pattern in his description of *misece* (back-biting, slander). Slander was following him like a demon wherever he went to escape, even to the graveyard (cf. Kubik 1974: 48–50; see also text example 3). He was hardly forty years old when he slid more and more into depression, and after other ailments had accumulated, he died of virtual self-starvation. In America, Blind Lemon Jefferson was one of those who expressed how one feels if caught and pursued by an obsessional idea, in his "Long Lonesome Blues" (Paramount 12354, rec. 1926):

> I got up this mornin', these blues all around my bed.
> I got up this mornin', these blues all around my bed.
> Couldn't eat my breakfast, and there's blues all in my bread.

EXAMPLE 3

Daniel Kachamba's song about his own funeral (cf. Kubik 1974: 48–49). Recorded at Mr. Rice's Bar, Chirimba, Blantyre District, Malaŵi, 16 January 1972 by G. Kubik; publ. LP record *The Kachamba Brothers' Band*. A.E.L. Series Phonographica No. 1, ed. E. Stiglmayr, Wien-Föhrenau: E. Stiglmayr Verlag.

Text (in Cinyanja/Chicheŵa):
Ndinke ku Lilongwe, mayo! Ndabwera ine
KuMulanje mayo! Ndabwera ine
Maliro aKachamba mayo! Mudzabwere ine (2x)
Mudzabwere, mudzalire, mudzantaye kumanda (2x)
Ndatopa ine, mavuto aculuka ine (2x)
Cisoni mayo, kulila ine (2x)
Ndatopa ine, ndikapume ine (2x)
. . .
Anthu ali pano, mayo! misece awa (2x)
Ndinke kumadzi, mayo! ali nane, kunkhuni, mayo! ali nane
Ndatopa ine, ndikapume ine (2x)
. . .
Osinja nasinja, ophika naphika, oimba naimba, olila nalila
Cisoni mayo, ndadabwa ine (2x)
Ndatopa ine, ndikapume ine (2x)

Translation:
If I run away to Lilongwe, dear me! I am back,
To Mulanje, dear me! I am back,
The funeral of Kachamba. Dear me! You should come! (2x)
You should come, you should cry, you should throw me into the grave! (2x)
I am tired, troubles grow upon me. (2x)

Oh, the pity of it! I am crying! (2x)
I am so tired, I ought to rest! (2x)

. . .

These people here, dear me! with their delight in scandal.
If I run to the river, dear! they are still with me; to the firewood, dear, they are
with me!
I am so tired, I ought to rest! (2x)

. . .

Those who pound (corn) they are pounding; those who cook (food) are
cooking; those who sing are singing; those who cry are crying.
Oh, the pity of it, I am shocked.
I am so tired, I ought to rest! (2x)

PHOTO 10. Blind Lemon
Jefferson. Paramount
Records publicity photo,
late 1920s. (Photo is
courtesy of Texas
African American
Photography Archive)

The Rise of a Sung Literary Genre

Example 4

Text of "See That My Grave Is Kept Clean," by Blind Lemon Jefferson (vocal and guitar). Recorded in Chicago, ca. February 1928. Paramount 12608; reissued on Document DOCD-5019, *Blind Lemon Jefferson, Vol. 3.*

1. Well, it's one kind favor I ask of you.
   Well, it's one kind favor I ask of you.
   Lord, it's one kind favor I'll ask of you.
   See that my grave is kept clean.
2. It's a long old lane ain't got no end.
   It's a long lane that's got no end.
   It's a long lane ain't got no end.
   And it's a bad wind that never change.
3. Lord, it's two white horses in a line.
   Well, it's two white horses in a line.
   Well, it's two white horses in a line.
   Gonna take me to my burying ground.
4. My heart stopped beating, and my hands got cold.
   My heart stopped beating, and my hands got cold.
   Well, my heart stopped beating, Lord, my hands got cold.
   It wasn't long 'fore service by the cypress grove.
5. Have you ever heard a coffin sound?
   Have you ever heard a coffin sound?
   Have you ever heard a coffin sound?
   Then you know that the poor boy is in the ground.
6. Oh, dig my grave with a silver spade.
   Just dig my grave with a silver spade.
   Well, dig my grave with a silver spade.
   You may lead me down with a golden chain.
7. Have you ever heard a church bell tone?
   Have you ever heard a church bell tone?
   Have you ever heard a church bell tone?
   Then you know that the poor boy is dead and gone.

But there is also a more aggressive, extrovert position in some of the blues. Epithets such as "Howlin' Wolf" (Chester Burnett), "She-Wolf" (Jessie Mae Hemphill), "Wolfman" (Robert Belfour), and so on are in a sense psychograms, because they are indicators of demonic forces of the soul, a ferocious part of the psyche with which the singer purports to identify. These tags serve as a warning to the community about the extraordinary powers of this or that blues singer. In a sense, Sigmund Freud's famous "rat man" also belongs to this psychological realm.

EXAMPLE 5

Bukka White, "Fixin' to Die Blues," Vocalion 05588. Booker T. Washington White, vocal and guitar; Washboard Sam (Robert Brown), washboard. Recorded in Chicago, 8 March 1940. Reissued on *The Complete Bukka White*, Columbia/Legacy CK 52782, track 11 (1994).

1. I'm looking funny in my eyes, 'n I b'lieve I'm fixin' to die, b'lieve I'm fixin' to die.
   I'm looking funny in my eyes, 'n I b'lieve I'm fixin' to die.
   I know I was born to die, but I hate to leave my children crying.

2. Just as sure as we live today, sure we's born to die, sure we's born to die.
   Just as sure as we live, sure we's born to die.
   I know I was born to die, but I hate to leave my children crying.

3. Your mother treated me, children, like I was her baby child, was her baby child.
   You mother treated me like I was her baby child.
   That's why I tried so hard to come back home to die.

4. So many nights at the fireside, how my children's mother would cry, how my
      children's mother would cry.
   So many nights at the fireside, how my children's mother would cry.
   'Cause I ain't told their mother I had to say good-bye.

5. Look over yonder on the burying ground, on the burying ground.
   Look over yonder on the burying ground.
   Yonder stand ten thousand, standing to see 'em let me down.

PHOTO 11. Bukka White playing guitar in the slide style, Memphis, Tennessee, January 28, 1969. (Photo: F. Jack Hurley)

Instrumental Chorus

6. Mother, take my children back, please, 'fore they let me down, please, 'fore they let
   me down
   Mother, take my children back 'fore they let me down.
   Ain't no need of them screaming and crying on the graveyard ground.

It is often the fate of artists to function in a society as psychological seismo-graphs. In many cultures there is a high incidence of mood disorders in artists, including cyclothymic or hypomanic tendencies, and major depression. This was confirmed for living blues musicians in a study of artists and writers by Hagop S. and Kareen Akiskal of the University of California, San Diego, in collaboration with David Evans (cf. Jamison 1955: 49). While they do not repre-sent a category apart, but confirm the general picture, blues musicians express these tendencies in their poetry in a particular, culture-specific manner.

David Evans (1978b: 425) has distinguished between texts that are *thematic* "in the sense that from listening to the text it is possible for one to reconstruct a coherent story or visualize a scene clearly," and those that are *non-thematic*, "in the sense that a single theme is not maintained throughout and the listener cannot reconstruct a coherent story or visualize a single scene clearly." He has given several very instructive text examples. He also found that rural blues in its early forms were usually non-thematic and "relied mainly on traditional verses that the singers would recombine in a number of different ways in the processes of learning and composing their songs" (cf. also Titon 1977; Evans 1982). This corresponds strikingly with widespread African practice. An apparently non-thematic structure can also come about through the extensive use of symbolism, whereby deeper connections may be obscured. On one blues recorded from John Henry "Bubba" Brown, "Canned Heat Blues" (text example 6), the basic idea, according to my evaluation, is persistent frustration, deprivation, and dis-appointment, leading to suicidal tendencies. While many lines, such as the one about drinking "canned heat" (a paraffin-based cooking fuel containing alcohol that was used as an intoxicant during Prohibition), can be understood directly, the lines containing the image of a dog that fails to catch a rabbit seem obscure. The contextual nature of these lines only becomes clear if one realizes that the idea "dog" symbolizes an alter ego, the deprived animal in the singer's soul, his basic needs seeking satisfaction but finding barriers and frustrations in real life.

EXAMPLE 6
The text of "Canned Heat Blues," by John Henry "Bubba" Brown (reproduced from Evans 1978b: 440–42).
1. Oh well, I drink so much canned heat 'til I walked all in my sleep.
   Says, I drink so much canned heat, I walked all in my sleep.
   Says, I had to drink that canned heat. Lord, I didn't have nothing else to eat.
2. Says, my dog, he jumped a rabbit, and he run him a solid mile.
   Says, my dog jumped a rabbit, and he run the rabbit a solid mile.
   Well, he seen he couldn't catch the rabbit; he sit down and cried just like a child.
3. Says, I'm going to Memphis, from there to Baltimore.
   Says, I'm going back to Memphis, boys, from Memphis back to Baltimore.
   'Cause when I was around your place, you drove me 'way from your door.
4. Says, now I done drinked so much canned heat until that canned heat's a'killing me.
   Well, I done drinked so much canned heat, babe, 'til canned heat's a'killing me.
   I'm gonna get me a train; I'm going back to Memphis, Tennessee.
5. Says, and my dog, he jumped a wild fox, and he run him 'round in front of my door.
   And my dog, he jumped a wild fox; he brought him right in front of my door.
   I says, "Just looky here, dog, don't run no chicken-eater up here no more."

The blues *form* is normally strophic, in contrast to many African literary forms that are either cyclic, following the cyclic structure of the instrumental accompaniment, or short themes that are developed by variation and extension. Many blues begin with a (textual) *statement* (A), followed by the reinforcing *repetition of the statement* (A), and then by a *concluding text-line* (B), all performed within twelve bars (measures). The B line has often been erroneously called "response" in the literature. But although the more or less universal African call-and-response scheme is an integral part of the blues, it is not the last text line that functions as a response. *Each* four-bar sequence is bisected so that the second half can carry a response of equal length, as a rule performed instrumentally, for example on a guitar (fig. 3) (cf. Kubik 1961a: 159). The vocal statement extends into the first beat unit of the instrumental response, creating a brief overlap.

FIGURE 3. Structuring of a three-line (twelve-bar) strophic blues form:

Vocal statement (A)	Instrumental response
Repeated vocal statement (A)	Instrumental response
Concluding text-line (B)	Instrumental response

Besides the standard twelve-bar form, there are also eight- and sixteen-bar blues, as well as irregular numbers of bars (Evans 1973: 13). Alfons M. Dauer (1979) has surveyed the great number of textual patterns of blues strophic structures. These demonstrate entrenchment of the blues in literary form rather than metricized music. Although we lack the evidence of sound-recordings of late nineteenth-century blues, it can be taken for granted that the "standard" chord scheme for accompanying blues with tonic, subdominant, and dominant Western chords (I I I I / IV IV I I / V IV I I) was present in at least one strand of the blues from its earliest beginnings as a distinct musical genre. It was promoted by those blues musicians and their clients who had come to perceive the use of these chords as status-enhancing. But there was also another strand. Big Bill Broonzy (1893–1958; see his autobiography, Broonzy 1964) expressed his reservations this way:

It's all just a racket. First I got to pay a guy to take down what I'm playin on guitar. He fool around three or four hours on a piano and make himself maybe ten or twenty dollars. See, *he* say I don't play correctly chords, and he has to change um. Then I got to call in another racketeer to make parts for the different instruments in the combo. Then comes rehearsal. I got to pay for that, too. . . .

And I got to change my stuff to suit *them*. If I get really in the blues, they can't play with me and it ain't no band in the world *can*. . . . (Cited after Lomax 1993: 455)

Is the 12-bar AAB form of the blues an African-American invention, or can it be found (minus the Western chords) in some African tradition? No systematic survey of African music regarding this question has been undertaken. But the presence of an AAB form in west Africa is testified, if only (so far) by a single case I came across by chance in 1960 in Nigeria, studying a little-known song tradition among the Ọ̀yọ̀ Yoruba, free of both Arabic/Islamic influences that had been absorbed in the nineteenth century from Hausa music, and European influences. This genre, called àló, includes storytelling with intermediate songs by a story's protagonists. It is performed in the intimate environment of family gatherings near the fireplace in the impluvial houses of old Yoruba towns, or at nearby farms, usually in the evenings (cf. Kubik 1988a). In 1960 and 1963 I took note of some 171 such chantefables, and in only one I came across a strophic form that could be compared in structure to a twelve-bar blues (for transcription, see example 7). I first published my findings in an article in the

German magazine *Jazz Podium* (Kubik 1961a) including a transcription of this song, "Baba ol'odo". It is reproduced below in a modernized notational system that we now variously use in the transcription of African music (cf. Kubik 1988a; 1994a).

In this notational system, the elementary pulsation (i.e., the smallest units for rhythmic orientation) is visualized by vertical lines through the staff. Beat unit 1, the inception point of a metrical entity, is shown by reinforcing the appropriate vertical line. Duration of the notes on the staff is expressed indirectly. A tone is to be held until the black dot of another note or the stop sign (/). The encircled number at the beginning of the staff indicates the number of elementary pulse-units contained in a cycle, or—in the present case—in one text-line. Notation is *relative*, i.e., related to the "keynote" C, irrespective of the actual pitch level of the singer's voice.

The story is to warn young girls who allow adult men to follow them home. The text of the song is sung by the protagonist in the story. At every stage of the event the girl, identified as the daughter of Ládèjo Àwèlé Oniterena, addresses the man who will seduce her.

The structural parallels in form between this song and the twelve-bar blues cover several dimensions. There is even quite clearly a bipartite division of the vocal statements, with a caesura between them. And there is the characteristic ending of the vocal statements at the midpoint of each line, as in most blues. In this chantefable tradition the response to each line is *sung*; in the song transcribed it is a phrase, "Tere natere," with no verbal meaning, but obviously derived from Oniterena, the name of the girl's father in the story. The response remains unchanged throughout the AAB stanza form.

One notable difference between this story song and most of the blues is that the text does not stand in the first person. Another is that, if the *àló* piece were actually written in twelve bars, each bar would contain six pulses, which is something not found in the blues. But in west Africa the superposition of two different, related pulse schemes is common and is like a grid in the mind. Thus, one could experimentally superimpose the six-pulse scheme on a simultaneous eight-pulse scheme. Strangely, if accompanied with cluster chords and even a flatted fifth chord in one place, on a piano—the *d* of the first line reinterpreted as part of C^9—"Baba ol'odo" can be comfortably restated as a twelve-bar modern jazz theme, for example by someone like Modern Jazz Quartet leader John

Example 7

"Baba ol'ódò" (Father of the river)—Yoruba story song showing three-line strophic form structurally comparable to the 12-bar blues (transcription and text reproduced from G. Kubik, "Àló—Yoruba chantefables," 1988a: 178–80)

Elementary pulsation: 250 M.M.

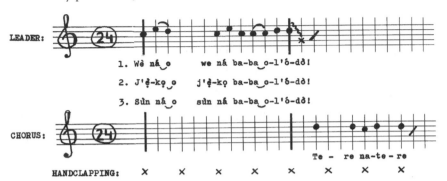

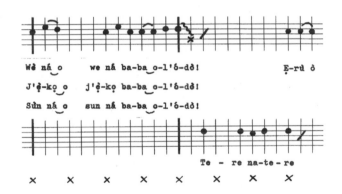

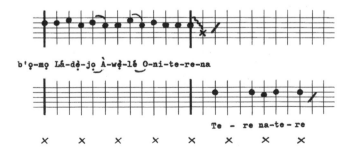

Yoruba text:	Translation:
LEADER: *Wẹ ná o, wẹ ná baba ol'ódò!*	Wash now, wash now, Father of the River!
CHORUS: *Tere natere.*	*Tere natere.*
L.: *Wẹ ná o, wẹ ná baba ol'ódò!*	Wash now, wash now, Father of the River!
CH.: *Tere natere.*	*Tere natere.*
L.: *Erù ò b'ọmọ Ládèjọ Àwẹ́lé Oniterena.*	Fear does not worry the daughter of Ládèjọ Àwẹ́lé Oniterena.
CH.: *Tere natere.*	*Tere natere.*
L.: *J'ẹkọ o, j'ẹkọ baba ol'ódò!*	Eat ẹko, eat ẹko, Father of the River!
CH.: *Tere natere.*	*Tere natere.*
L.: *J'ẹkọ o, j'ẹkọ baba ol'ódò!*	Eat ẹko, eat ẹko, Father of the River!
CH.: *Tere natere.*	*Tere natere.*
L.: *Erù ò b'ọmọ Ládèjọ Àwẹ́lé Oniterena.*	Fear does not worry the daughter of Ládèjọ Àwẹ́lé Oniterena.
CH.: *Tere natere.*	*Tere natere.*
L.: *Sùn ná o, sùn ná baba ol'ódò!*	Sleep now, sleep now, Father of the River!
CH.: *Tere natere.*	*Tere natere.*
L.: *Sùn ná o, sùn ná baba ol'ódò!*	Sleep now, sleep now, Father of the River!
CH.: *Tere natere.*	*Tere natere.*
L.: *Erù ò b'ọmọ Ládèjọ Àwẹ́lé Oniterena.*	Fear does not worry the daughter of Ládèjọ Àwẹ́lé Oniterena.
CH.: *Tere natere.*	*Tere natere.*

Lewis on a piano, or at least as a piece that could have been arranged in the Count Basie band.

There are other *àlọ́* chantefable songs with some traits vaguely reminiscent of the blues; for example, "Ma d'enia," the story song about a monkey who wants to become a human being (transcription in Kubik 1988a: 181–82), has a four-line stanza form with two statement lines followed by two different conclusion lines. While the theme of "Baba ol'odo" does not suggest any of the *tune families* isolated by Titon (1977), the four-line "Ma d'enia" is comparable to the blues in its descending melodic ductus. It is also sung in the first person.

I do not suggest that blues is a derivative of Yoruba chantefables; but such literary genres with minimal accompaniment, performed within small communities, should have had a greater chance for survival in oppressive contexts than any music dependent on drums and large participating crowds. While I only have this *one* testimony in my collection, I would not be surprised if more songs in a comparable three-line AAB strophic form were discovered, for example in

Nupe, to the north of the Ọ̀yọ̀ Yoruba, or in other places off the west African coast, in rural traditions of hinterland people who had been primary targets of slave raids. Actually, Michael Theodore Coolen suggested that the *fodet* in Senegambia, defined as "a recurring musical structure . . . of a fixed number of beats (from six to twenty-four) with specific melodic, rhythmic, and even harmonic characteristics" and being "the main structural principle of Wolof *xalam* music," also "displays remarkable similarities to blues structure" (1982: 77, 82). He even claimed to have detected an AAB song text format in one common song called "Alfa Yaya" (Coolen 1982: 84 n. 19). Unfortunately, his transcriptions do not support that statement.

In any case, the answer to our initial question is yes, the AAB form in a comparable structural layout *is* found in west Africa. For the songs cited, "Baba ol'odo" and "Ma d'enia," any kind of recent American or European influence can be excluded. *Àló* was a culturally reclusive genre that had preserved an older stratum of pentatonic west African pitch patterns, unaffected by Hausa and Arabic/Islamic influences such as are obvious in *ṣakara, apala, fuji,* and other Yoruba traditions.

Intrafamily song traditions from west Africa, such as story songs, and those carried by professional, itinerant artists, such as by the *jali* ("griots") in Mali or the *xalamkat* (player of the *xalam* plucked lute) in Senegambia, are two likely candidates for early models that were still remembered by African Americans in the late eighteenth and early nineteenth century, eventually becoming a factor in the development of the blues. The question is, of course, how such a "memory" could have survived until the *end* of the nineteenth century. Here, my theory of "unconscious transmission of culture traits" (cf. Kubik 1979: 49–51, 1991: 188–91) might give an answer, but its empirical basis lies in data gathered by so-called *cultural comprehension tests* with the carriers of such an unconscious awareness. In contrast to Brazil, where I was able to carry out such tests with startling results (cf. Kubik 1979), we are at least eighty years too late for reconstructing proto-blues forms. On the other hand, the absence of written sources testifying to such memory does not present a puzzle. Just as the monochord zither remained unreported in the nineteenth century, so would observers have neglected other African-American traditions and reported them only if they came to the surface in imitations by "whites." For us today, such reports constitute compelling indirect evidence. For example, the analogies drawn by Coolen (1982: 74) between Senegambian ensembles involving a plucked lute, a bowed lute, and a tapped calabash and popular African-American fiddle, banjo, and tambourine ensembles from the "late seventeenth through the nineteenth centuries" are not substantiated by any American sources before the 1840s. But then all of a sudden this combination of instruments is found among *European*-American professional minstrels.

Late reinforcements of the "memory" from Africa could also have played a role. Legal importation of slaves to the United States was officially banned in 1808. But some illegal importation persisted up to the Civil War (1861–1865). According to George Howe (1890), the last slave ship arrived in the United States in 1859. We do not know, of course, how many African, Caribbean, Mexican, and other slaves were brought in by professional "touts," "blind" customs inspectors, or through the Republic of Texas, which existed between 1836 and 1845, and other channels, but Randolph B. Campbell in an article on slavery in the *New Handbook of Texas* writes that the Peculiar Institution's

rate of growth accelerated rapidly during the 1840s and 1850s. The rich soil of Texas held much of the future of slavery. . . . The census of 1850 reported 58,161 slaves. 27.4 percent of the 212,592 people in Texas, and the census of 1860 enumerated 182,566 bondsmen, 30.2 percent of the total population. Slaves were increasing more rapidly than the population as a whole. —The great majority of slaves in Texas came with their owners from the older slave states. Sizable numbers, however, came through the domestic slave trade. New Orleans was the center of this trade in the Deep South, but there were slave dealers in Galveston and Houston, too. A few slaves, perhaps as many as 2,000 between 1835 and 1865, came through the illegal African trade. (Campbell 1996: 1081–82)

Cultural reinforcement of any of these song traditions by newcomers cannot therefore be excluded, until at least the mid-nineteenth century. These latest cultural imports may have come from odd places in Africa. Alternatively, a lingering memory of such traditions could have survived from the time of the eighteenth-century slave concentrations on the south Atlantic seaboard, and resurged or been reinstalled under the circumstances of the later Deep South cotton plantations.

Recently, Harriet Joseph Ottenheimer has come up with what she calls "a radical proposal." She argues that "we have been looking in the wrong places to explain the origins of the blues as a unique musical form" (Ottenheimer 1992:

34). She recommends that we look not at west Africa, but at east Africa, reminding us that "a formal structure as unique as the three-line AAB blues verse must have emerged from some pre-existing musical 'grammar'" (1992: 34). She then argues "that the answer can be found in the East African bardic style."

Thirty-eight years ago, I briefly cited blues-like harmony from east Africa in a little-known report to the *Jazz Podium* (Kubik 1960). Some of this music, especially by Alur singers and harpists such as Lazaro Albinga Olamoto, can actually be heard on an LP record I published in Nairobi (cf. *The Blind Musicians of Salama*, GKA 02, A.I.T. Records). In 1962, during a recording trip to western Kenya, and again in 1976 (cf. Kubik 1982: 106–7) I was amazed at how Abaluhya musicians played and sang to their eight-stringed lyres (*litungu, lunkhani,* etc.) tuned to a hexatonic "gapped scale." Motional organization of this music was characterized by a strongly audible reference beat objectified by the musician's stamping with the right foot, to which a small bell was attached. On top of this reference beat the lyre player developed highly interruptive melodic phrases with prominent off-beat accentuation. The vocal line followed the lyre patterns mostly in unisons or octave parallels. In between, the lyre assumed a commenting function, often reacting abruptly to vocal statements. Sometimes abrupt silence occurred for a fraction of a second. This was an extreme tension-producing device, especially if such an acoustic blackout was followed by a sharp sound attack, while the beat was continuing unperturbed (cf. recordings B 7425-9, 7438-9, 7453-6, 7467-70, Phonogrammarchiv Vienna, 1962/Kubik). In 1962, the music of the *litungu* lyre players was for me quite a culture shock. It reminded me intensely of the blues, especially some patterns by the lyre player Chioso, 40, with his parallel octaves, but I had no explanation for it.

Ottenheimer remains somewhat uncommitted as to what precisely constitutes "*the* East African bardic style." Would it embrace the music of minstrels such as Lazaro Albinga Olamoto (Uganda), the Abaluhya lyre players (Kenya), or Limited Mfundo (Malaŵi)? Or, as I suspect, does she limit its application to the coastal music of Tanzania and Kenya (particularly in *taarab* style) and that on the islands off the east African coast showing a pronounced impact of Omani Arab and other Near East Islamic cultural elements? She cites John Storm Roberts's *Songs the Swahili Sing* (OMA 103) and the verses in several of Roberts's examples. Eventually she explains her central idea, citing a song in a (14-bar) AAB form with lute accompaniment she collected during fieldwork in the Comoro Islands (cf. Ottenheimer and Ottenheimer 1982: I.1). Obviously, this song with a text in ShiNzwani, in her transcription and translation, shows the presence of a three-line AAB poetic form, but hardly anything else that could be safely related to the blues. In addition, the east African ancestry of the various African descendants on the Comoros is not clear-cut. Harriet and Martin Ottenheimer (1982: 2) point to the likelihood that most came from southeast Africa. But apparently there were also some people brought in from *west Africa* by the French planters.

In another section of her paper Ottenheimer explains that a common Shi-Nzwani phrase, *huana ngoma*, could be "smoothly" translated into English as "To have the blues" (Ottenheimer 1992: 35). Connoisseurs of Bantu languages will not easily subscribe to that. The semantic field of the word *ngoma* in the various forms of Kiswahili is admittedly wider than in other Bantu languages; it not only refers to drum(s), but by implication also to community events in which drums and/or other instruments play a role. (This is also confirmed for the Comoros in the Ottenheimers' earlier statement, 1982: 2.) But stretching the semantics of that word to include "an emotional state" analogous to what in the United States is called "to have the blues" (Ottenheimer 1992: 35) is not supported by linguistic analysis.

Ottenheimer is correct when she challenges Melville J. Herskovits's earlier thesis "that the predominant cultural styles in any New World area were set by the earliest arrivals in that area" (Ottenheimer 1992: 32). Brazil is a formidable example to the contrary, demonstrating the complexities of cultural superpositions in time and their mutual adaptations in space (cf. Kubik 1979, 1991). But her "simplified scenario," which "would have Bantu-speaking East Africans or Comorians (particularly musicians) arriving in the United States in the mid-eighteen hundreds" (1992: 36), bringing "the proto-blues form" with them as part of their intellectual baggage, is less "radical" than it is far-fetched.

Monophyletic schemes such as "the possibility that the Comoros were indeed the African birthplace of the blues" (Ottenheimer 1992: 35) neglect—like any other African "birthplace" hypothesis—the complex interplay of retention, reinterpretation, adaptation, modification, and innovation of single traits, operating diachronically in cultural transplants and culture contact. I am afraid the "birthplace" of the blues is in the United States, and the "birthdate" in the 1890s. While it is important and worthwhile to collect and report any genres from

The Rise of a Sung Literary Genre

outside the United States showing *traits* that could have contributed to the formation of the new genre, we have to be aware that instances of an AAB verse form collected in Africa or anywhere else in the world can only be conclusive in a scheme for diffusion if they are part of a trait *cluster* that links both traditions to be compared. "Modes," "three-line" poetry, twelve bars, "neutral thirds," or some strange "voice quality" yield insufficient evidence if the underlying systems cannot be decoded and compared cross-culturally. For this reason, my *àló* find presents, so far, the most solid analogy to the blues form from a tradition outside the United States. As an isolated find, however, it does not discredit the view that the twelve-bar AAB blues form must be considered primarily an African-*American* development that crystallized at the beginning of the twentieth century from a variety of expressions: field hollers, chanted prayers and preaching, some folk ballads, especially in AB-plus-refrain forms, African concepts of call-and-response, the "riff" (frequently in the instrumental response), and even possibly iambic pentameter poetry perhaps learned in school (cf. Evans 1982: 46), besides the continuity of various African storytelling and "bardic" traditions.

3 - A Strange Absence

For those of us with training in the percussive rhythms of Guinea Coast music (cf. Richard A. Waterman 1952, discussion in Merriam 1953), much of our Guinea Coast experience is inapplicable to the blues. This is so not just because of the absence of drums and complex polyrhythms in early blues; there is, in addition, the very specific absence of *asymmetric time-line patterns* in virtually all early twentieth-century U.S. African-American music, except in cases where these patterns were borrowed from Puerto Rico or Cuba. Only in some New Orleans genres does a hint at simple time-line patterns occasionally appear in the form of transient so-called "stomp" patterns or a stop-time chorus (cf. Brothers 1994: 492 for an example). These do not function in the same way as African time-line patterns. New Orleans is, after all, a rather different culture. The nineteenth-century so-called Creole dances, such as "counjaille," "bamboula," "chacta," and "juba," had an influence on early jazz (Borneman 1969: 103). Jelly Roll Morton's "New Orleans Blues," based on a Creole song, is the most famous example. There are also other tunes in Morton's work exemplifying the fact that New Orleans is culturally also part of the Caribbean. In Ernest Borneman's opinion, what preceded New Orleans jazz before 1890 was "Afro-Latin music similar to that of Martinique, Guadeloupe, Trinidad and San Domingo" (1969: 104). Surely, this music must have incorporated some notion of time-line patterns, while other popular music in late nineteenth-century New Orleans, based on European dance forms such as the mazurka, polka, waltz, schottische, and quadrille, and the standard European instrumentation and even line-up perpetuated in early New Orleans Jazz ensembles (cf. zur Heide 1994) obviously did not incorporate them. (On New Orleans dance music of the 1890s

PHOTO 12. Fife and drum music played at a picnic near Senatobia, Mississippi, September 1970. Napoleon Strickland, fife; R. L. Boyce, snare drum; Jimmie Buford, bass drum; Othar Turner, dancing. (Photo: David Evans)

see also Gushee 1994, where its transformation to jazz is dated rather specifically to ca. 1893–95).

Borneman (1969: 100) eventually postulated that it was precisely during the years when New Orleans jazzmen migrated to Chicago to be recorded for the first time that jazz lost its "Spanish tinge" and was reduced to straight 2/4 and 4/4 time. However, in other more European-derived and only slightly African-ized traditions of the South, time-line patterns were absent from the start—for example, in post-Civil War fife-and-drum music, in spite of its various verbal-ized rhythms such as "Granny, will your dog bite? No, child, no" (Evans 1972a). A performance by the last surviving exponent of this tradition, eighty-nine-year-old Othar Turner, videorecorded by us at Clarksdale, Mississippi, on August 2, 1997, vividly demonstrates how *additive* metrical patterns—no doubt African in concept—persist in the rolling drum rhythms within his various cycles; but there are no asymmetric time-line patterns. The absence of Guinea Coast time-line patterns in U.S. African-American music, therefore, does not constitute a later-state "loss."

What are time-line patterns? Under this term, coined by J. H. Kwabena Nketia in the 1950s (cf. Nketia 1961: 78), we understand mostly single-pitch structures struck on an object of penetrating timbre, such as a bell, the body of a drum, concussion sticks, and so forth, to serve as time-keeping devices, orienting musicians and dancers. It was A. M. Jones who first uncovered their structure, transcribing such patterns among the Babemba of Zambia (Jones 1954: 59) and later among the Ewe (Jones 1959: 210) with a transcription machine of his own invention.

These patterns are characterized by an irregular, asymmetric structure within a regular cycle, and they range from ubiquitous eight-pulse cycles to the most complex asymmetries filled into a 24-pulse frame. A unique structure, whose invention could have coincided with the early stages of formation of the Kwa (I.A.4) and Benue-Congo (I.A.5) families of African languages on the Guinea Coast and in the Nigeria/Cameroon grassland areas, is a well-known twelve-pulse pattern that has been called the "standard pattern," a term coined by A. M. Jones during lectures in the 1950s and introduced into the literature by Anthony King (1960). With the slave trade this pattern was exported to various places in the Caribbean, notably Cuba, and to Brazil, where it survives in the Candomblé religious ceremonies. An early transcription of this pattern in a Ketu cult performance for the "Orixa" transcendental being called "Exu" in Brazil can be found in an article by Richard A. Waterman (1948: 28).

The African time-line patterns are determined mathematically by (a) their *cycle number*, the number of constituent elementary pulse units contained in the repeating cycle, usually 8, 12, 16, or 24; (b) the *number of strokes* distributed across the cycle, e.g., 5, 6, 7, or 9 strokes; and (c) the *asymmetric nature of their distribution* generating two adjunct subpatterns such as 3 + 5, 5 + 7, 7 + 9, or 11 + 13 pulses.

Each asymmetric time-line pattern has a manifest and a latent appearance. The auditively perceptible part is supplemented by a silent inaudible pattern. Like patrix and matrix, the two parts together form the total motional structure (fig. 4; cf. Kubik 1972: 173). In this notation x represents a struck/sounded pulse, while a dot represents a silent pulse. Both symbols have the *same* time value, and are therefore printed equidistantly.

FIGURE 4. Patrix and matrix of the 12-pulse asymmetric time-line pattern:

7-stroke version ⑫ [X . X . X X . X . X . X]

5-stroke version ⑫ [. X . X . . X . X . X .]

One of the two phenotypes is usually dominant within a culture, while the other is implied or may sometimes be silently tapped with a finger, as I observed with the great Fõ itinerant singer Sosu Njakɔ, at village Sada Gbonjɛnji, east Mono river area, Togo, in January 1970 (cf. Kubik 1972: 171–72). In some other cultures, the two complementary shapes are actually struck together, the seven-stroke version with a right-hand stick, the five-stroke version with a left-hand stick, for example on the body of a drum (videorecording of a *makishi* masked dance performance in northwestern Zambia, Kubik/September 1987, copy deposited in the Center for Black Music Research, Columbia College, Chicago).

At the broadest level, the African asymmetrical time-line patterns are all interrelated, and can be arranged visually according to progressing cycle numbers in the form of a pyramid base, with each new step downward on both sides of the pyramid defined arithmetically by the addition of two pulses (fig. 5).

The trapezoidal shape shows the mathematical interrelationship of the most

FIGURE 5. The mathematics of West and Central African asymmetric time-line patterns; their structural relationships shown as a pyramid stump (illustration after Kubik 1983:336).

Cycle number	Pattern Structure	Notation
⑧	3 + 5	[x x . x . | x x .]
⑫	5 + 7	[x . x x . x . | x . x x .]
⑯	7 + 9	[x . x . x x . x . | x . x . x x .]
⑳	9 + 11	[x . x . x . x x . x . | x . x . x . x x .]
㉔	11 + 13	[x . x . x . x . x x . x . | x . x . x . x . x x .]

common African time-line patterns. Each new pattern down the slopes is defined at each side by an extension: one stroke covering two elementary pulses. Note in the figure that there is one series of double strokes in the mid-left area of the pyramid base forming a *vertical column*, and another, at the figure's right side, forming a *staircase pattern*. This visual representation of the various time-line patterns demonstrates their underlying asymmetry.

The mathematical content of the African time-line patterns exists independently of their cognitional dimension. The latter, of course, is always best studied culture by culture through the mnemonics used for teaching. These vary a great deal from language to language.

Here we discovered (cf. Kubik 1969, 1972) that sound and timbre values of the mnemonics (which can be mere syllables without any specific verbal meaning, or verbal patterns) represent, by their phonetics, the strokes to be executed. Plosive sounds such as [k], [p], and [t] usually symbolize a hard, firm timbre of the stroke to be carried out, while liquid sounds and velar fricatives like [l] and [γ] symbolize strokes requiring less physical effort, with a soft, weak timbre. [tʃ] usually indicates the reference beat; if it refers to the sounds of a rattle played on-beat, it is often conceptualized as *cha-cha-cha-cha*.

Mnemonic patterns transmit to the learner something about the structure and timbre sequences of the musical patterns to be played. For example, the syllables used in Yoruba-speaking areas of west Africa to transmit the essence of the seven-stroke 12-pulse "standard" pattern are highly indicative of this

Figure 6. The Yoruba 12-pulse pattern: how it is conceptualized.
↓ This is the actual starting point of the pattern and its mnemonics as conceptualized by musicians.
* This is the "weakest" timbre-value and one of the pattern's two unobtrusive points.

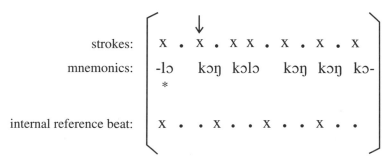

pattern's structure. Thus they can serve as a tool for analyzing how the pattern is conceptualized.

The Yoruba mnemonic syllables confirm that the pattern has two subsections: a shorter one covering 5 pulses (to the syllables kɔŋ kɔlɔ) and a longer one covering 7 pulses (syllables kɔŋ kɔŋ kɔlɔ). They also reveal that the pattern is hooked to the inner reference beat of musicians and dancers, objectified by the dance steps, in such a manner that a "weak" timbre-value (= the least physically enforced stroke), symbolized by b, coincides with the starting point of the underlying cycle and metrical scheme.

This lengthy excursion into the mathematics and cognitional aspects of the time-line patterns might perhaps appear to be irrelevant in a book on blues. However, in order to understand the implications of their "strange absence" in the blues we have to know precisely what they are.

The most important fact about the asymmetric time-line patterns is that their mathematical structures are *cultural invariables*, i.e., their mathematics cannot be changed by cultural determinants. They are immune to all social, cultural, or environmental influences. One can change a time-line pattern's instrumentation, accentuation, speed, starting point, and the mnemonic syllables used to teach it, but not its mathematical structure. Any attempt to change that dissolves the pattern. For this reason time-line patterns are formidable diagnostic markers for detecting historical connections between certain New World African diaspora musical styles and those of distinctive language zones on the African continent, as I have demonstrated elsewhere (Kubik 1979).

In cultural transplants time-line patterns are either transmitted or not transmitted. Their absence in U.S. music expresses a major characteristic that sets the rhythmic structure of blues, jazz, and most U.S. popular music apart from much of the music heard in the Caribbean and in South America. Referring to the 16-pulse Cuban clave pattern (in my notation: (16) [x . . x . . x . | . . x . x . . .]), Joseph H. Howard (1967) observed a notable culture gap between African-American styles in the Caribbean and in the United States:

In areas of the Americas where the clave pattern is not traditional—for example, the United States—local musicians have difficulty in accurately playing the clave pattern. Similarly many Cuban drummers have migrated to the United States and begun to play jazz only to find that in fast tempo they revert to clave patterns; and their solos are nearly always within the clave framework. Like a first language, clave becomes part of the subconscious: musicians brought up in the clave tradition hear music in "clave" and express themselves musically in reference to clave. (Howard 1967: 239)

Jazz, blues, and other U.S. African-American traditions share with most Caribbean and South American traditions of people of African descent the first three levels of subjective timing inherited from African music (cf. Kubik 1994a: 42–46):

> 1. The *elementary pulsation*, which is a kind of basic grid engraved in the mind. It incorporates the smallest units of orientation in time, and it has no beginning and no end.
>
> 2. The *reference beat*. It combines a regular number of elementary pulses, usually three or four, into larger units that steer the dancers' steps, and constitute beat awareness, for example, in jazz musicians. In some African culture areas there is, in addition, the phenomenon of an interlocking, relative reference beat (cf. Kubik 1994a: 17–11), for example, in southern Uganda and northern Mozambique xylophone music. This is rare in New World musical cultures, but seems to have been retained in some Afro-Venezuelan drumming traditions. In contrast to Western music, the reference beat in African and African-American music does not embody the notion of pre-accentuation, i.e., "strong" and "weak" parts of the meter. *Beat 1* of a metrical scheme can be so unobtrusive acoustically that it functions like a black hole (with a powerful gravity, but virtual invisibility). Not pre-accented, accents can then be set on-beat or off-beat according to the melodic-rhythmic structures to be developed.
>
> 3. The *cycle*. It combines a regular number of elementary pulses (8, 9, 12, 16, 18, 24, 32, 36, 48, etc.) to form yet larger entities that are to be repeated. In African-American music short repeating melodic-rhythmic cycles are often called "riffs." In several forms of African music, such as *mukanda* circumcision songs in Angola (cf. the double album *Mukanda na Makisi*, MC 11, Kubik 1981), there are also strophic forms. The 32-bar chorus form in many jazz pieces combines African form ideas with popular European-derived song forms.

Asymmetric time-line patterns constitute a fourth level of subjective timing operating in some African musical cultures and their African-American extensions across the Caribbean (Cuba, Haiti, Dominican Republic, Puerto Rico, Trinidad, etc.) and in Brazil. In view of this, what is the likely explanation for their absence in North America? Is it possible to reconstruct exactly what happened to the various traditions that were brought to Virginia and other British colonies from 1619 on, and to the United States between 1783 and 1859? What exactly was played on the famous "bones" accompanying stringed instruments in late eighteenth-century Virginia? "Bones" are concussion rather than percussion sticks, and it is unlikely that they were used to mark the beat. In conformity with African small-group traditions, almost certainly patterns were played on the "bones" in America, probably one of the ubiquitous eight-pulse time-lines, as it also survives in the hand-clapping of some ring-shouts.

Did Africans deported from west, central, and southeast Africa originally bring along the same variety of traditions (with drums, time-line pattern, etc.) to the southeastern and southern United States as they brought to Cuba and Brazil, and could their subsequent absence be explained as merely a forced disappearance due to Anglo-Saxon oppression and religious Protestantism that stopped people from drumming? Or, seen from a cultural-materialist viewpoint, could the absence be explained by social specifics arising from the differences in the slave economy, the cotton and tobacco plantations in the southern United States as compared to sugar-cane plantations in Brazil and Cuba (Harris 1968: 22)? These two explanations (Protestant intolerance and economic differences) are the ones usually given by scholars, although Janheinz Jahn (1959) adds an interesting twist—that extreme monotheistic Protestantism in the southern United States wiped out the alleged "polytheistic basis" of African polyrhythm (cf. also my review and criticism of Jahn's book *Muntu*, Kubik 1961b).

Various viewpoints and assumptions exist in the literature. Earlier researchers often tended to assume a certain uniformity in the cultural commodities imported by African captives to all parts of the New World, and a subsequent regional differentiation due to different processes of acculturation. Richard A. Waterman (1948: 29–30) outlined in great detail the social and religious circumstances of a "white" North American society, with its own "folk music," that would have made it difficult for African descendants to retain African polyrhythms. This theory implies that the *initial cultural position* of the deportees to different New World places was everywhere more or less the same, and that the panorama of different African-American musical cultures we see in the twentieth century across the hemisphere resulted principally from the interaction of the slaves with different "master-cultures," such as Portuguese, Spanish, French, English, and Dutch. Waterman summarizes this position:

The situation of the African slaves in the United States, then, was obviously not one that afforded them much opportunity to retain their African musical style. In the main, African percussion instruments disappeared, and with them the multiple-metred poly-rhythms so characteristic of African music. The off-beat phrasing, which requires merely a dependable percussion beat as a point of departure, became attached to simple rhyth-mic patterns represented by European time-signatures. (1948: 29)

Less committed to generalizations, Dena Epstein has formulated this posi-tion in another way.

The cultural heritage brought from Africa, common to the slaves both on the mainland and in the islands, met with less overt opposition in the islands and so was able to maintain itself freely and for a longer time. The conditions in the islands conducive to the preservation of African cultural patterns included absentee landowning with an accompanying lack of interest in the leisure activities of the slaves, frequent influxes of new arrivals from Africa, and a very high proportion of blacks to whites ranging from 9 to 1. The blacks on the mainland on the other hand were relatively fewer in number and dispersed among a much larger white population. Moreover, not all of them came directly from Africa; slaves already "seasoned" in the West Indies were considered more desirable since they could already understand some English or French and had become accustomed to plantation labor. (1973: 63)

A slight modification of Waterman's perspective may then be advisable, replac-ing the panoramic and uniform vision of Africa that characterized many works written during the 1940s. We know that there is no "African musical style." Even generalizing schemes such as Lomax's (1968) song style areas do not under-write the thesis of a pan-African culture world, as Christopher Ehret observed: "Polyrhythmic music and dance . . . is often thought of as quintessentially African. In fact it appears to be a feature of culture particularly associated with Niger-Congo peoples. . . . Outside the Niger-Congo speaking regions in Africa other styles, frequently based on stringed instruments, tend to prevail, along with quite different styles of dance" (1981: 28).

We know that percussion instruments are not everywhere so important as they are on the Guinea Coast, from whence a major portion of the sample collected by Melville J. Herskovits (1938a and b, 1941) and his disciples came; and we also know that there are sharp stylistic delineations across Africa, for example between the Guinea Coast and the west-central Sudanic Belt, or the music of speakers of Nilotic languages in East Africa and that of the Bantu. Across Africa, the music of pastoral peoples, who tend to have very few or even no musical instruments at all, contrasts sharply with that of their settled neighbors.

Asymmetric time-line patterns are not universally distributed in sub-Saharan Africa. Actually, they are a distinctive Kwa (I.A.4) and Benue-Congo (I.A.5) phenomenon, and even there they are not known among all speakers of this language family. Some of the more complex time-lines, such as the twelve-pulse standard pattern, are confined to well demarcated African regions: the Guinea Coast with its speakers of Akan, Ewe, Fõ, Yoruba, and so on; west-central Africa from eastern Nigeria to Gabon, Congo, Angola; southern Congo-Zaire, into Zambia; and to southeast Africa in a broad belt, covering the Zambezi and Ruvuma cultures. Characteristically, asymmetric time-line patterns are unknown in most of East Africa, in South Africa, and elsewhere. The few exceptions to this rule can all be accounted for historically. Speakers of Afro-Asiatic languages in northeast Africa and into the Sahara do not normally use them, nor do speakers of Nilo-Saharan languages, except in a few linguistic border areas of Uganda and Congo-Zaire, such as the Alur and Logo (Field documentation 1960/Kubik in the Phonogrammarchiv Vienna).

In many areas of Africa time-line patterns were not used prior to the impact of Congolese and West African popular music through the mass media. Speakers of languages outside the Kwa (I.A.4) and Benue-Congo (I.A.5) families of African languages did not use time-line patterns in their music, unless these patterns had been adopted in recent times through close contacts with the former. This is the case with the Azande, Gbaya, and others in the Central African Republic, or the Alur in northwestern Uganda.

Social and economic factors alone cannot explain the presence or absence of time-line patterns in New World musical cultures. Nor can they account for the specific geographical distribution picture in Africa itself (1) for all time-line patterns together, or (2) for each of them separately (cf. Kubik 1998a and b). Neither the hypothesis of extreme cultural repression during plantation life in North America, nor that of a general amnesia in the deportees from Africa due to the sufferings of the Middle Passage can explain their absence in U.S. music. There is, of course, ample evidence from the contemporaneous literature that drums were soon forbidden in some New World cultures, for fear that coded

FIGURE 7. Linguistic regions of Africa and major slave-recruiting areas ca. 1800.

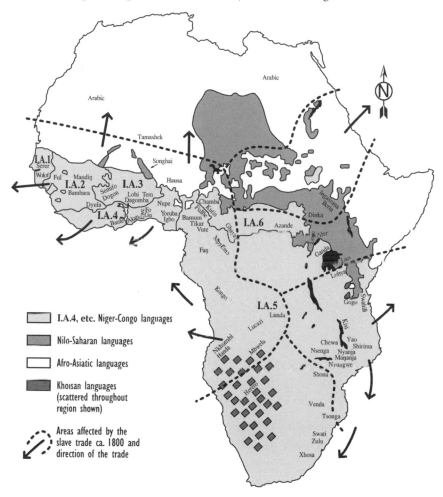

messages might be sent to incite rebellion. But drums are not floppy discs with time-line patterns electronically inscribed. One can prevent people from making drums, or from gathering in large groups, or from playing loud music, if that was what the authorities found so threatening; but time-line patterns can be tapped silently on any object—they are permanently engraved in the brain once they have been implanted through enculturation. Rhythmic structures can also transcend the auditory and motional realms and be encoded by analogy in visual forms of expression, as is demonstrated in cross-relations between African music and abstract African designs, and in some of the fabulous African-American appliqué quilts exhibited in the Cleveland Museum of Art (cf. Vlach 1978). Cultural transmission works through codes, and the individual can switch between channels, from the auditory to the motional to the visual. As long as the codes are transmitted intact, the individual's unconscious can reassemble the missing patterns. The outcome depends on stimuli and constraints exerted by the social environment variable in place and time.

4 - The West Central Sudanic Belt

The explanation for the absence of time-line patterns in the blues, and from the North American scenario in general—with the exception of their shadowy appearance in Louisiana early in the twentieth century, and in more recent times, for example in Bo Diddley's music (cf. Kubik 1993: 443–44; see also his recent biography based on interviews, White 1995)—must therefore be something other than repression or amnesia. Paul Oliver, on the basis of fieldwork in northern Ghana (Oliver 1970, 1972, 1973), suggested that if there was any affinity at all in musical structure between the blues and certain African musical traditions, it should be sought in the broad savanna hinterland of west Africa, from Senegal and Gambia, across Mali, northern Ghana, and Burkina Faso, to northern Nigeria, rather than along the Guinea Coast where previous researchers had sought it.

Stylistically, the music played in the west African savanna hinterland, such as, for example, on certain stringed instruments, especially the long-necked lutes (*xalam, garaya,* etc.) and one-stringed fiddles (*gogé, gojé, riti,* etc.), is characterized by the predominance of pentatonic tuning patterns, the absence of the concept of asymmetric time-line patterns, a relatively simple motional structure lacking complex polyrhythm but using subtle off-beat accents, and a declamatory vocal style with wavy intonation, melisma, raspy voices, heterophony, and so on. Some of these characteristics are, of course, shared with the broader realm of Islamic music and reflect longstanding historical contact between the west African savanna and sahel zone through the Sahara with North Africa and even the Near East in view of regular pilgrimages to Mecca. One of the most celebrated journeys remembered in heroic songs is that of King Mansa Musa of the Mali Empire (fourteenth century). The west central Sudanic belt is the style world that presents the closest stylistic parallel from any part of Africa to what can be heard in the blues.

In addition, there is also the rather unsavory and sometimes demonic reputation of musicians in the blues (cf. Oliver 1970: 49, 98–101). That could be matched with the social status of many of the so-called "griots" in west Africa (*jali* in Mandiŋ) and that of other itinerant African instrumentalists. Coolen (1982: 75) points out that parallels can "be drawn between the lifestyles of professional *xalamkats* and the songsters and bluesmen of Texas and the Mississippi Delta." In other New World areas, for example Brazil, Mandiŋ slaves regularly ended up as social outcasts. They were believed to have a demonic character and to practice evil magic. Brazilians coined the term "mandingueiros" for practitioners of sorcery (Kubik 1991: 19). The Mandiŋ have a similar reputation in Venezuela (Martínez Suárez 1994: 53–54).

In his book *Savannah Syncopators—African Retentions in the Blues*, Paul Oliver (1970) laid out his conclusions, which then revolutionized the search for historical connections between African-American music in the United States and that of west Africa. He criticized those authors who had up to then looked for the "roots" of jazz on the Guinea Coast, and pointed out—proceeding from his fresh field research in northern Ghana—that in North America many more traits, particularly in the realm of blues, lived on that had obviously originated in the western Sudan. He stressed the pronounced differences in the type of instruments and in musical style between the west African savanna hinterland and the musical cultures close to the coast. Oliver's work was the first attempt to paint an interconnected profile for the west central Sudanic region, pointing among other things to the importance of chordophones (lutes, fiddles, etc.) in this region, in contrast to the dominant role of idiophones (bells, rattles, etc.) and membranophones (drums) in the cultures of the Guinea coast. He also drew attention to the much simpler rhythmic framework in the music of the "savanna" peoples, without complex Guinea-Coast-style polyrhythm in the accompaniment, and to specific melismatic vocal techniques.

Oliver postulated that essential elements of the North American blues could only have come from the west African savanna hinterland. Rural U.S. bands composed of fiddle, banjo, and sometimes other string or percussion instruments, as they are mentioned in nineteenth-century sources, would have perpetuated western Sudanic instrumental traditions under the changed circumstances.

These changes obviously included ensemble formation. It is rare in the west central Sudanic belt for fiddle and plucked lute to play *together*. In the United States the combination of fiddle and banjo is reported beginning in 1843 in so-called "blackface" minstrelsy. Before that they were normally played separately, either solo or with added percussion. Paul Oliver cited the bowed-lute music of two of his northern Ghanaian musician friends, Sosira and Kunaal, who—in his view—combined vocal, rhythmic, and instrumental characteristics that suggested analogies with the blues. He also discovered in this music something that could be compared to "swing," an important kinetic element in African-American music of the United States, though one that is objectively difficult to define. In another section of his book, Oliver pointed to the presence in northern Ghana of a declamatory song style, widespread in the savanna culture area,

PHOTO 13. The persistence of the banjo and fiddle combination into the blues era. Left to right: unknown player, violin; Conlie Willis, banjo; Vollie Wiggins, banjo, Johnson City, Tennessee, ca. 1932-33. The banjos are 8-string and 6-string varieties, normally tuned and played respectively like a mandolin and a guitar. Thus, this group is a variant of the standard violin-mandolin-guitar string trio of the late nineteenth and early twentieth centuries, but with the musical timbre of the older banjo-fiddle combination. (Photo from the Lester Willis collection, courtesy of David Evans)

which in his assessment could have given rise to the historical forms of "field hollers" in the southern United States and some vocal techniques in the blues (Oliver 1970: 66). A most interesting issue has been raised in this context by David Evans:

I think the field holler tradition may spring largely from a cattle herding song tradition, thus adapted to another type of largely *solitary* rural activity. The U.S. South was mostly devoted to crop agriculture, although there was some dairy and beef cattle activity and much more in Louisiana/Texas where there were many black cowboys. I have heard cattle herding songs from Colombia (recorded by George List on an LP, List 1973) that sound very much like field hollers. Of course the west African savannah is an area of much cattle herding. (Evans, personal communication, June 25, 1997)

The west African savanna and sahel zone was also the playground for one of the relatively rare long-distance migrations in that region: the migration of the Fulɓe cattle herders, some of whom, in the nineteenth century, eventually settled under the strong centralized rule of their *lamido* (as in places like Toungo, northeastern Nigeria, and Kontcha, Cameroon—cf. Kubik 1989a: 82–85), while another branch, usually referred to as the Bororo in the literature, continued a pastoral lifestyle. That some of the vocal styles of cattle pastoralists even in other parts of Africa show traits reminiscent of field hollers and blues has struck me for some time; most recently during our work in Namibia among the Herero (cf. videorecording no. 6, Kubik/Malamusi, Namibia 1991, archival copy at the Center for Black Music Research, Columbia College Chicago). The "east African cattle complex" has had repercussions in southwest Africa due to a wave of migrations of cattle people passing from east Africa through the tsetse-free corridor between Lake Tanganyika and Lake Malaŵi in a southwest direction during the first millennium A.D. The Herero and Himba in Namibia continue their pastoral lifestyle to this day, while in Huila Province, southwestern Angola, millet agriculturalists mixed with pastoralists, giving rise to ethnic groups such as the Ovankhumbi, Ovahanda, Ovacipungu, and others. Southwestern Angola was, incidentally, one of the primary targets of the slave trade conducted by the Ovimbundu in Angola to the Port of Benguela in the eighteenth century (information obtained from oral tradition, Angola 1965/Kubik).

Although the presentation of his thesis drew some criticism with regard to methodology and the very small African sample upon which he based his conclusions (see my review, Kubik 1970a; Summers 1971, interview with Richard A. Waterman; Oliver 1972; Evans 1972b; Oliver 1973), Oliver's intuition did hit the mark, and his ideas have become generally accepted and have been followed up (cf. Samuel Charters 1982; various African tracks placed for comparison on record sets edited by Samuel Charters and John Storm Roberts; Oliver's own Fra-Fra track from northern Ghana on an LP set that accompanied another book of his, *The Story of the Blues*, Oliver 1975). Bob Eagle (1993: n.p.) has even suggested that the area for the "roots" of the blues should be extended beyond the savanna belt into the sahel zone, if not even into the Sahara, and that it should include, for example, the "negroid members of the Tuareg tribes in Mali and Niger," those who "prefer to call themselves Tamashek." On the other hand, Michael Theodore Coolen (1982: 76ff.) suggested a possible influence of the melodic and tuning tradition called *fodet* among the Wolof of Gambia, associated with the *xalam* (plucked lute), upon the genesis of the blues. In analogy to the retention of structural, tonal, and other characteristics of African languages in Black American vernacular English, Coolen finds it unlikely that such "calques" (fr: tracings, blueprints) should exist only at the linguistic level; "why not also at the musical level?" (Coolen 1982: 76). He writes: "It is possible to posit that *fodet* could have been introduced into the United States as a kind of musical calque, thereby influencing the development of the Afro-American blues, much as African languages, via linguistic calques, have influenced the emergence of Black-American English" (1982: 82).

Similarly, one might also investigate Mauritanian music (cf. Nikiprowetzky n.d.), including its modal theory. An echo of blues-like patterns can even be traced in the music of descendants of slaves in Morocco and southern Algeria (Kubik, field notes 1977/ during a joint lecture and concert tour with Donald Kachamba to these countries).

While the choices made by the various scholars for similarities between blues and African musical traditions can always be contested, the exercise is not worthless. Oliver's own savanna hinterland from northern Ghana into Burkina Faso and neighboring areas falls linguistically into Joseph Greenberg's I.A.3 (Voltaic) language family. Besides culture, linguistic affiliation links these populations, the Tem, Lobi, Kurumba, Senufo, Dogon, and others. However, Oliver's fieldwork region can also be expanded horizontally on the map (as he himself suggested) to include with justification the whole of the so-called western and central Sudanic belt. A considerable number of people from all these areas—often from defenseless small ethnic groups in the mountains—were forcibly taken away into slavery. Some of these are classed in the ethnographic literature as "Ancient Nigritic Cultures," ever since Bernhard Ankermann (1905) introduced and Hermann Baumann (1940) defined the term (see also Hirschberg 1988: 21), pointing to the likelihood that these people were descendants of millet agriculturalists settled in the same areas for several thousand years. In northeastern Nigeria, even in 1963 when I researched the area between Yola and Toungo, there were people such as the little-known Zanganyi still hiding in inaccessible mountain areas, in fear of slave raids. (Kubik, field notes 1964/Toungo). In contrast to what has been claimed over and over, the slave trade did not extend just 100 miles inland from the African coast; it cast its nets far into the interior regions of Africa, especially during the late eighteenth and early nineteenth centuries. This was marvelously demonstrated by Sigismund W. Koelle in his early nineteenth-century survey of the languages spoken by liberated slaves in Freetown, Sierra Leone (cf. Koelle 1854; Curtin 1969: 291–98; Kubik 1991: 27–28). In the first systematic survey of African languages, Koelle (1854) listed names such as Jupa, Dibo, Gbari, Kakanda, Basange, Ebe, Igbira-Panda, and Igbira-Hima, which sometimes do not even appear on modern linguistic maps. He also mentioned that Ọyọ Yoruba from far off the coast were numerous among ex-slaves in his times.

The ex-slaves whose languages he examined in Freetown, Sierra Leone, had been taken there on British ships raiding slave ships of other nations found north of the equator. Most of these ships were arrested off the Guinea Coast. However, at Africa's westernmost extension there was a French-controlled outlet near Dakar (Senegal), of great strategic importance for the trans-Atlantic slave trade: the Ile de Gorée. St. Louis, north of Dakar, was founded in 1638, and from the eighteenth century the Island of Gorée, about 3 km off the mainland near Dakar, became involved in the slave trade. It often changed owners, though, until in 1817 it finally fell under French authority. Much of its past is preserved in the Musée Historique situated in the Rue Malavois. Not far from there, on this island totally devoid of motor traffic, is the "slave house" (*maison d'esclaves*), where the cells can still be seen in which slaves were kept for weeks before embarkation to New World destinations. A painting dated February 20,

PHOTO 14. The notorious slave house on the Ile de Gorée (Goree Island) near Dakar, Senegal, 1981. (Photo: Author)

1839, by Adolphe d'Hastre (copy in the collections of the "Maison d'Esclaves," Gorée) shows the brisk life in front of this building.

No doubt, many people from Mali, Senegal, Guinea, and other places who were transported to North America via New Orleans (legally up to 1808 and clandestinely for many years thereafter) must have passed through this "monument of human misery," the "slave house" on the Ile de Gorée. The geographical position of the island near Dakar suggests that it was an important outlet for the population drainage in the western Sudan. Even today, Dakar is a springboard to the New World. The city is an important hub for air travel to Recife, New York, and Paris, with Dakar–Recife the shortest route from Africa to South America.

In spite of the logic of some of these arguments, and of Samuel Charters's emphasis on Senegambia as an area relevant for the "roots" of the blues, I tend to give a stronger weight to the more central Sudanic region as one core area of provenance of some of the rural blues' most characteristic traits: the region from Mali across northern Ghana and northern Nigeria into northern and central

Cameroon, rather than the westernmost geographical Sudan (Senegal, The Gambia). Other possible core areas include northern Guinea and the Sahel zone from Mali into Mauritania, where Nikiprowetzky (n.d.) has described a conjunction of culture traits including some "modes" that seem to match blues traits, at least at face value.

There are three major reasons for this delineation:

(1) The profiles I obtained from my own field recordings in northern Nigeria and northern and central Cameroon show a particularly dense accumulation of blues traits in certain genres found in that area. The pentatonic scales prevalent in the more interior parts of the west central Sudanic belt (see map, fig. 9 further in this book) can be linked convincingly to several expressions of the blues.

(2) Conversely, tonal-harmonic patterns in many traditions of Senegal and The Gambia, for example, on the *kora* (bridge-harp; cf. King 1972; Knight 1971, 1978), display heptatonism in combination with simultaneous sounds in open fourths and fifths. These traits are difficult to correlate with the blues.

(3) A meticulous survey on the provenance of Africans in colonial Louisiana carried out recently by Gwendolyn Midlo Hall (1992), who was working with French and Spanish language sources, has brought to light new patterns of slave trade history. While the importance of the Ile de Gorée as a springboard for the Atlantic slave trade remains undisputed, the story of the Bambara rice cultivators brought to Louisiana specifically for their technological expertise has opened up new aspects of the fine meshes and economics of the slave trade and its huge networks into the *interior* of the west central Sudan (cf. Hall 1992: 59, 121–23; on rice cultivation in colonial South Carolina see also Littlefield 1991).

The contrasts within the tonal universe across the savanna of west Africa have been researched in great detail by Junzo Kawada (1982, 1997), who distinguishes a "Hausa complex" as compared to a "Mande complex," delineating two major stylistic areas. "Mande complex" refers to people like the Malinke or Bambara speaking I.A.2 or Mande languages in Greenberg's classification (1966). "Hausa complex" refers to speakers of Hausa, a III.E. or Chadian language. Hausa includes more than 30 million speakers, and through trade the Hausa are scattered all across the west central Sudanic belt.

5 - Blues Recordings Compared with Material from the West Central Sudan

Like Oliver's recordings, some of my own from Nigeria, Togo and northern Cameroon since 1960 can be usefully compared with blues records, in spite of the *genealogical distance* that separates these traditions. I would like to cite the following examples from this material for detectable affinities.

Big Joe Williams, "Stack o'Dollars," CD, Blues Document Records, BDCD-6003, item 8. Guitar, one-string fiddle and washboard, recorded in Chicago. Original recording: October 31, 1935, Bluebird B 6231.

compared with

Meigogué with *gogé* (one-string fiddle), male, ca. 30 years old. Ethnic group: Hausa. Recorded by Gerhard Kubik in Yoko, Cameroon, February 1964. Language: Hausa. (see fieldnotes Orig. Tape R 30, G. Kubik 1964, Ph. A. Vienna).

Big Joe Williams was born in Mississippi in 1903. His recording "Stack o'Dollars" from 1935 can be compared with traditions of the western and central Sudan, especially in three areas: in vocal style by the abundant use of melismatic passages, the pentatonic basis of the pitch-lines, and his voice quality; in the instrumental realm by the use of a combination of stringed instruments including a one-stringed fiddle; and by the relative simplicity of the rhythmic structure. Both vocal part and instrumental accompaniment are also clearly based on a central reference tone that sometimes even assumes the quality of a bourdon resulting from the combination of voice and fiddle. European-style chord changes to subdominant and dominant chords are not used. This is particularly astounding when the singer begins line 2, where a subdominant chord might be expected. The central (tonic) tonality level is held throughout the piece and circumlocated by the melodic lines of voice and fiddle. The latter are also in a responsorial relationship with each other.

Meigogué, whose complete name was Adamou Meigogué Garoua—a name derived from that of his *gogé* (one-stringed bowed lute) and the town where he lived, Garoua, in northern Cameroon—was one of those itinerant Hausa musicians one can encounter in many parts of West Africa. He used to undertake frequent long journeys as a trader of various goods, to places such as Yoko in the central Cameroon grassland areas, where I recorded him in 1964. His companions on those journeys were the one-stringed fiddle and also a small oboe made from reed grass (cf. my various recordings, orig. tape R 30/items 5-7, side 1). His one-stringed fiddle had a gourd resonator covered with varanus lizard skin. The single string was wound out of horsehair. The string of the bow was made of the same type of hair. Characteristically, the skin covering the gourd had a circular sound hole, which—he told me—was for keeping "secret things" and money obtained from audiences. This compares to U.S. African-American (and southern European-American) fiddlers and guitarists who also often used to put money inside their instruments, and sometimes magical objects such as rattlesnake rattles, to make the strings sound more prominent through sympathetic vibration (cf. Evans 1972c; Klauber 1956: II.1240; and Jack Owens, Bentonia, Mississippi, July 15, 1971, interviewed by David Evans).

Meigogué's tonal material for the voice and his instrument is pentatonic, but in his shrill-timbred singing style he uses melisma extensively, including some microtonal shifts of the voice from the pentatonic skeleton, and lots of glissandi. Like the blues of Big Joe Williams, Meigogué's music is also based on the melodic circumlocation of a central tone that functions as a reference, sometimes even like a bourdon. Voice and fiddle part alternate, establishing a slightly overlapping responsorial structure; the fiddle part begins before the voice part has ended.

Meigogué's Hausa singing style is, of course, highly determined by the centuries-old cultural contact with the Arabic/Islamic world. The presence of the one-stringed *gogé*, with its history going back to the Maghreb (North Africa), is another testimony to these contacts. While the basic scalar framework used is pentatonic, the intonation of many tones both in the voice and the fiddle parts is wavy, bent, often approaching a tone from below before reaching maximum height, then quickly collapsing.

> Grinding song by a Tikar woman from Central Cameroon. Young woman. Rec. by Gerhard Kubik in Møŋbrã, half a day's walk west from Kong to Ngambe, Central Cameroon, 14 February 1964. Ethnic group and language: Tikar. Grinding stone for maize.

compared to

> Mississippi Matilda (Matilda Powell), voc., acc. Sonny Boy Nelson (Eugene Powell) and Willie Harris Jr., guitars. "Hard Working Woman," reissued RCA 07863 66719-2. Rec. New Orleans, La., 15 October 1936. Orig. recording Blue Bird B 6812.

The circumstances of my recording this grinding song in a village of the central Cameroon savanna are worth reporting. On a journey on foot for several days from Yoko to Ngambe through the thinly populated Tikar country, I reached, on the afternoon of February 14, 1964, the village of Møŋbrã. As my Tikar companion and I entered the village in the late afternoon I was suddenly attracted by the sound of a work song sung in solitude by a woman who was grinding maize on a stone. I could not photograph her, but while I hurriedly set up my tape recorder after introducing ourselves to her, I made a rough sketch of the scene and her equipment (fig. 8).

In contrast to the Hausa fiddle example, the song style of this woman represents an older, pre-Islamic West African tonality. There is no melisma. Its basic outline is in disjunct intervals, with falling melodic ductus of each line. The overall impression of the melody stunningly reminds one of the blues. In rhythmic organization her cycle of actions on the grinding stone covers 36 elementary pulses (4 times 9) for each line of the song. There are strong off-beat accents in the scraper-like grinding rhythm. These accents are placed so as to produce a *swinging* triple rhythm.

FIGURE 8. Field sketch of the grinding Tikar woman (Febr. 14, 1964, G. Kubik) with descriptive notes added:

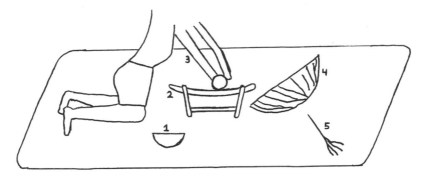

1 pot with unground
   maize grains
2 Flat, large grinding
   stone on a wooden stand
3 Hands of the woman holding
   stone ball for grinding

4 Basket into which the flour
   falls during the process
   of grinding
5 Small broom of straw
   used for brushing off flour
   from the stone, if necessary

The Tikar woman with her grinding stone sang a lament in the first person about the difficult circumstances of her life. Unfortunately I did not obtain her name before the continuation of our journey. Later I received the following rough French translation of her song lines from two of my Tikar-speaking informants, Michel Nyampang and Pierre Houmgblang:

J'ai eu une affaire à cause des hommes.

Si tu ne travaille pas tu ne peux pas manger.

Je pleure pour mon sort et pour ma vie.

Il reste un peu (encore un moment) et le monde va changer.

Je pleure pour le sort de mon enfant qui restera seul dans ce monde.

Il ne faut jamais oublier son fils dans ce monde.

Pour ton enfant, ne pense pas trop. Car il sera très malheureux, quand il n'aura
   plus personne pour lui.

Je vous dis la verité mes amis, n'oubliez jamais vos fils.

(Orig. Tape No. R 33/II/5, Ph. A. Vienna)

I have had a problem, because of men.

If you don't work you cannot eat.

I am crying about my fate and my life.

In a short moment the world will change.

I am crying about the fate of my child who will remain behind, alone in this
  world.

One must never forget one's son, as long as one is still around.

Don't worry too much about your child; no doubt he will be unfortunate once
  he will be left alone without anybody.

Friends, I tell you the truth, never forget your children!

(English translation G. Kubik)

The song text—and we can even judge this from the translation—consists
of various single lines of approximately identical length. Single-line ideas and
their variations in content and diction are joined by free association without
any particular order, certainly without any chronological order. In principle the
text is polythematic, but it does present a consistency of mood, and like blues
singers (Evans 1978b:443), she insists that she tells the truth.

The following transcription (ex. 8) will give an idea of the melodic lines and
their overall rhythmic structure. Exceptionally, the notes in the transcription
must remain without words, since I was unable to procure the original words in
Tikar from any informant in this remote part of Cameroon. The notational
system I am using here is identical with that used earlier in this book for the
Yoruba chantefable songs (see above).

Each text-line and its instrumental response, reinforced by the woman's accents during the action of grinding, covers 36 pulse units. As in the blues (cf.
Calt and Wardlow 1988: 87–93), the sung part covers a little more than the first
half of a line's pulse units, and is in itself bipartite. The Tikar woman mostly
ends her *impact* points on pulse 1 of bar 3; sometimes she triples it, ending on
pulse 3. Counting the durational values, one finds that the vocal line mostly
covers 22 elementary pulses out of 36, or 61.11 percent of the line. In the blues
the vocal usually occupies 10 of the 16 beats in a standard 4-bar line, or 62.5
percent of the line, almost identical to the percentage of the Tikar woman.

The melodic intervals are medium in size, and in contrast to the strongly

EXAMPLE 8

Melodic lines of a grinding song by a Tikar woman from Central Cameroon.
Elementary pulsation: 350 M.M.

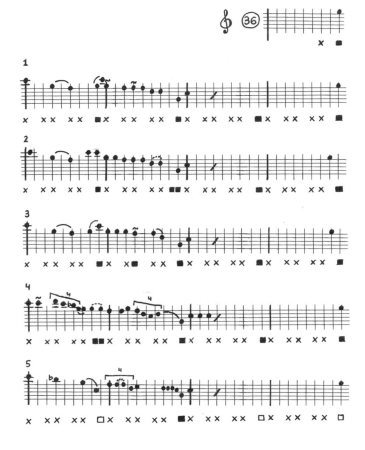

Line 6 and 7:   repetitions (not transcribed)

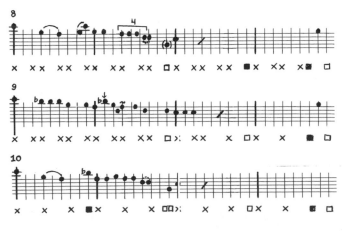

etc.

Islamicized Hausa style, pitch attack is straight, without any wavy approach or ornamentation. Rapid pitch sequences adhere to proportional divisions of the reference beat (marked by the grinding noises), either by three or by four. In spite of the absence of polyrhythm, the interplay between the Tikar woman's voice lines and her grinding action is rhythmically complex. It is a demonstration example for the subtle use of off-beat accentuation. The lack of a cinematographic record makes it impossible for me to analyze the movement patterns kinemically. Nevertheless, at least two forms of accent-producing variations in her grinding action can be distinguished by ear. One is the placing of accents within the scraping action itself, whose main beats are visualized in example 8 with the symbol x. The other is off-beat accents by actually *hitting* the grinding stone with her stone ball (indicated by a shaded square). This particular type of off-beat accent falls regularly on the ninth pulse of the four nine-pulse measures of each line. In view of the triple structure of the beat and the main accents of the woman's vocal line, it is precisely this one recurring accentuation that generates the incredible feel of swing in this work song.

It is interesting that in the same area many musical traditions are organized over a straight beat with this swing element: for instance, *timbrh* (lamellophone) music among the neighboring Vute (cf. recordings R 30/I, 1-4, Omaru Sanda, at Emtse, Cameroon). Swing with strong off-beat accents also steered another kind of work music I recorded in the same broad region among long established millet agriculturalists: the Chamba of northeastern Nigeria, at village Disol, in November 1963. Three women pounded millet in a mortar, each with one pestle; the combination was in interlocking style. Between their strokes, occasionally expanded by giving accents on the *rim* of the mortar, they produced a combination of sucking and clicking sounds with their mouths (cf. recording B 8609/Kubik, Phonogrammarchiv Vienna, and detailed description in Kubik 1989a: 80).

Most characteristic also in the Tikar woman's song is the fact that the singer always returns to a basic tonal center at the end of each line, just as in most blues. I have transcribed it as C, but there is a secondary tonal center as well, a fourth up from the bottom C, written as an F in my transcription. These two tones establish the basic reference frame for the essentially pentatonic melodic process. The scaffolding of this integrated system consists of the tones C, G, and F, which clearly establish the melodic framework. The tones D and B♭ (which can be called a blue note) are related to the C center. Due to the interference between the two centers C and F, an additional passing note appears transcribed as E. This may give the erroneous impression—if one indulges in a pitch-counting exercise instead of a *structural* analysis of tonal relationships— that the piece is hexatonic.

I see in the structural relationships outlined, and further discussed in a later part of this book, the survival of a probably ancient west central Sudanic stratum of pentatonic song composition among early millet agriculturalists (in spite of the fact that corn was already well established, replacing millet, in the area when I recorded her). This pentatonic system with two interrelated tonal centers, C and F, and their affiliated notes, G and B♭ respectively, is widespread also in northeastern Nigeria, and across the ancient east-west trade route from Lake Chad to the Nile valley (see the song "E Juba malek aleiy ana," which I recorded at Geigar, Sudan, in 1959. Cassette I, item no. 5, in Simon 1983). It is one of the pentatonic scales (among others) that can be encountered in the West African savanna traditions. I am not suggesting, of course, that it is only this particular tonal system that is continued in the blues. Blues is a merger of several pentatonic ideas, some with one, some with two tonal centers. Together they generated the pitch scaffolding found in the blues. (This will be disucssed further below.)

Mississippi Matilda's "Hard Working Woman" (1936) can be compared to the Tikar woman's performance, not only because of the topic of doing hard work, but also because the voice timbre of the two women is similar. By chance, Mississippi Matilda even starts her song with a phrase close in melodic ductus to that of the Tikar woman (see my transcription of her melodic line, Example 9), although she goes on to develop it in a different way.

Matilda's is a type of blues in a somewhat popularized idiom, suggested largely by the two-guitar accompaniment. It is this quality that provides perhaps all the essential stylistic differences between "Hard Working Woman" and the female Tikar grinding song. If we can abstract Mississippi Matilda's vocal line and its adjustments from the guitar accompaniment, then the parallels between the two female singers can hardly be overlooked.

The accompaniment to Mississippi Matilda is by two guitarists, her husband Eugene Powell and Willie Harris Jr., who work from the "standard" Western

EXAMPLE 9

Vocal line with text of the first stanza of Mississippi Matilda's "Hard Working Woman," Bluebird B-6812. Matilda Powell, vocal; Eugene Powell (Sonny Boy Nelson), guitar; Willie Harris Jr., guitar. Recorded at St. Charles Hotel, New Orleans, 15 October 1936. Reissued on Four Women Blues, RCA 07863 66719-2, track 14 (1997). (Author's transcription in relative notation.)

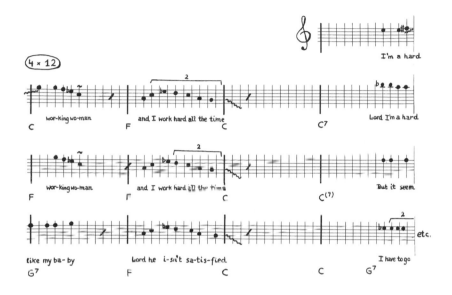

1. I'm a hard working woman and I work hard all the time.
   Lord, I'm a hard working woman and I work hard all the time.
   But it seem like my baby, Lord, he isn't satisfied.
2. I have to go to my work, baby, 'tween midnight and day.
   I didn't think my baby would treat me this-a-way.
   Go to my work, baby, 'tween midnight and day.
   I didn't think my baby, Lord, would treat me this-a-way.
3. Lord, I'm a hard working woman; Lord, I'm a common old rolling stone.
   Lord, I'm a hard working woman; Lord, I'm a common old rolling stone.
   And the way my baby treats me, Lord, I ain't gon' be here long.

Instrumental chorus
4. Now do you remember the morning, baby, you knocked upon my door?
   You told me, daddy, you didn't have nowhere to go.
   Can't you remember, you knocked upon my door?
   You told me, baby, you didn't have no place to go.
5. Lord, I'm a hard working woman, babe, and I work sick or well.
   Lord, I'm a hard working woman, Lord, and I work sick or well.
   But all I gets from my baby, hey hey, is a heap of hell.

Photo 15. "Mississippi Matilda" Powell, Chicago, Ill., February 8, 1972. (Photo: Steve LaVere—Delta Haze Corporation. Used by permission.)

chord sequence associated with the blues. Perhaps there is some urban and jazz influence. Eugene Powell was considered one of the top Mississippi blues guitarists in his heyday (early to mid-1930s), more or less superseded by the heavier, bluesier style of Robert Johnson and others. Matilda (1914–1978) was only semiprofessional, as was her husband Eugene. Basically she was a "hard working woman" who sang music on the side. The Powells also had several children (Eagle and LaVere 1972).

I tentatively suggest that the song style and high-pitched, mellow voice quality reuniting our Tikar woman with Mississippi Matilda would lend itself much more easily to accompaniment with the European I-IV-V harmony, including passing chords, than does the melismatic and declamatory Hausa style of Meigogué and its American extensions. I am thinking of a historical pattern of interaction, aware of the fact that contemporary urban blues singers such as B. B. King have developed a gospel-influenced singing style, sometimes called "soul blues," that is often extremely melismatic while based on I-IV-V harmonies.

If this observation is valid, it might bring surprising results when followed up systematically. It might be possible to correlate specific traits in the various forms of the blues, and to discover those within the total blues tradition that tend to be associated with one another easily to form *trait clusters*, as opposed to those which reject each other. That should give us a more sophisticated tool also for comparisons with African traditions. As it stands now, there are strong indications of at least two genealogical strands in the blues with regard to vocal style. One seems to perpetuate the melismatic *Hausa or Arabic/Islamic style*; the other could be called an extension of a pre-Islamic central-Sudanic pentatonic song-style stratum we might call the *Ancient Nigritic Style* (exemplified by the Tikar recording and many others from my fieldwork in northern and central Cameroon and northeastern Nigeria, 1963–64). This style seems to accommodate the Western tonic and subdominant chords with relative ease. Blues singers with a pentatonic melodic framework involving blue notes, but little melisma, seem to perpetuate this song-style tradition.

6 - Some Characteristics of the Blues

Rural blues in the Deep South is not a completely homogeneous tradition. Enough time has elapsed since pre-blues traditions crystallized into something toward the end of the nineteenth century that could be called "blues" to allow for early processes of *divergence* analogous to how a language splits into dialects, and subsequent processes of *convergence*, i.e., mutual influences and borrowings among the formerly divergent styles.

In a comparative study of hand postures and thumbing patterns of blues guitarists—from Henry Thomas, born 1874, to Robert Belfour, born 1940—Andrew M. Cohen has come up with the following revised delineation of *Blues Stylistic Regions*.

1. Eastern: I use this word as the equivalent of the more commonly used *Piedmont*, the rolling detrital hills that constitute tobacco country south and east of the Appalachians. We can expect black folk-blues guitarists from Delaware to Florida, east of a line connecting Knoxville and Atlanta and extending north and south from there, to extend their right thumbs when they play, and most of them play bass strings with an alternating thumb. A large majority of the black guitar players in the region play with their thumbs extended, as do most white guitarists in the region. The central part of this region—the Virginias and the Carolinas—is the part of the country where blacks and whites have lived side by side the longest. This fact may also help to explain why there is relatively more shared textual material in this tobacco country than in cotton country. . . .

2. Delta: The so-called Delta is not a delta at all but the lush swampy land, cleared of woods in the last century and a half, between the Yazoo and Mississippi Rivers from Memphis to Vicksburg. Not to be confused with the delta at the mouth of the Mississippi River below New Orleans, this patch of land is a part, but not all, of the hearth area of Mississippi's blues culture. As a stylistic region the Delta is much larger, encompassing the states of Mississippi and Alabama and extending to eastern Arkansas, west-

ern Tennessee, and northeastern Louisiana. In this region thumb use shows little overt patterning; instead thumbed notes are struck as needed within melodic guitar figures. I call this "utility-thumb" playing.

3. Texas: Another stylistic area can be identified between (roughly) Houston and Dallas and over to Texarkana, Texas, and Shreveport, Louisiana. . . . Most of what the Texas and northwestern Louisiana players do melodically (that is, on the treble side of the guitar) they do in conjunction with a "dead thumb," playing four beats to the measure on the same string. (Cohen 1992: 458–59)

From an Africanist perspective it appears that the Mississippi "Delta" (in Cohen's extended geographical sense of the term) is the most important core area for the more African stylistic traits in the blues. Africanists such as myself and Moya Aliya Malamusi, revisiting the area in August 1997, have had difficulty detecting *any* significant "European" musical components in this style, aside from the use of Western factory-manufactured equipment. For us, this observation includes chordal structures and preferences. After a joint visit with David Evans to bluesman Robert Belfour's present home in Memphis on August 1, 1997, Moya, himself a guitarist and one-string bass player—although rooted in a different tradition—made this comment: He said that what had struck him most was that at least in one of Belfour's tunings, the open tuning he called "Spanish" (high to low: E—C♯—A – F—A- -E), he would always let the fifth string vibrate unfretted. At the same time he would carry out elaborate finger-work on the upper strings. As a result the fifth string functioned like a drone, like a constant reference tone permeating the tonal-harmonic process. Here Moya had hit at the nerve center of Belfour's tonal-harmonic world, the world by implication shared with many others in the "Delta" or "Deep South" blues style, the presence of a *virtual bourdon* with a powerful central tonal gravity. Interrelated with this primary concept is the use of "riffs" (short repeated melodic-rhythmic figures) as a song's underlying building blocks (cf. Belfour's recordings on *The Spirit Lives On*, Hot Fox HF-CD-005).

It is, of course, natural for everyone to interpret a sound event in terms of the culture with which they are familiar. This is why Western-trained musicians will always detect European chord progressions in the blues, not only in those cases where their presence is obvious and intended, but also where there is evidently no such concept.

For certain, blues singers' first language is English—whatever variant that

PHOTO 16. Robert Belfour, whose individual style is strongly based on bourdon (single fundamental) reference tones on the guitar and a melismatic singing style, developed his music within the cultural mould of Delta blues musicians, Memphis, July 31, 1997. (Photo: Moya Aliya Malamusi)

may be (cf. Dillard 1972; Ferris 1974/75; Levine 1977d Leland and Nadine 1997 on the "ebonics" controversy)—not any African language. And yet there are specific intracultural musical and literary concepts, reflected in musicians' terminology, that researchers working from an emic standpoint (i.e., proceeding from categories conceptualized in the culture under study) will always try to take note of. (Cf. the works of Calt 1994; Evans 1971, 1981, 1982, 1994; and others.) By contrast, descriptions of the blues within the framework of European music theory will most often tend to distort these concepts. In a sense, one could with equal justification try to describe the blues in Chinese with the terminology of classical Chinese music theory. The results would be comparable in kind.

With this in mind, and all the precautions observed, I will try to arrive at some *etic*ally oriented descriptive formula—i.e., I will work out a comparative scheme using terminology that is as culturally neutral as possible, to cover in eleven paragraphs (*a* to *k*) a broad examination of the panorama of guitar-accompanied blues recorded throughout the twentieth century in the United States. For this purpose we have to split the tradition into single musical and literary traits, and interconnected trait clusters.

Blues shares with *other* African-American music many general characteristics inherited from one or another part of Africa, such as call-and-response organization, the "metronome sense," and so on. (See various summaries, e.g., Evans 1978, 1990; Kubik 1969, 1993; Kubik and Pinto 1994; Maultsby 1990; Oliver 1997; Ramsey 1957; Southern 1971; Waterman 1952, 1963.) These are not specifically discussed below.

Even in the absence to date of any large-scale systematic sampling of blues' stylistic characteristics, we can say with reasonable confidence that a large bulk of the blues tradition, as found especially in rural areas of the Deep South, displays combinations of any number, in any order, of the following traits:

(a) It is predominantly a solo singing tradition, with lyrics often standing in the first person. Related to this complex are the unaccompanied field hollers (cf. Courlander 1963: 80–88; James 1950. See also recordings in Botkin 1943; Stearns 1964; Lomax 1977; Evans 1978c). In Africa, I have repeatedly recorded parallels, for example among the Vute and Tikar of the Cameroon grassfield areas (cf. hollers and hunting shouts, recordings B 8662, in the Phonogrammarchiv Vienna, 1964/Kubik). Content and aesthetics of the blues' lyrics reveal many analogies to ideas and concepts in African cultures, including a "binary aesthetic terminology" (Evans 1978a; Thompson 1974, 1984), e.g., hot/cool, dirty/clean.

(b) Vocalists use a wavy intonation in many (though certainly not all) forms of the blues, with plenty of melisma, slurs, gliss tones, and timbre-melodic sequences that form the non-Western expressive repertoire of the blues. There is a particular concentration of the melismatic style in the rural Mississippi "Delta" and Texas regions, while it is less prominent elsewhere.

(c) In many blues there is a tendency toward, or predilection for, rather slow triple or swing tempos. Early in the twentieth century there was a general perception that blues was slow music, in contrast to nineteenth-century dance-related musical forms, and that it was associated with couple dancing, e.g., the "slow drag" (Evans 1982: 41–54). This is only a tentative generalization, and could well be nothing more than a repetition of early twentieth-century stereotypes. Certainly many blues pieces are fast, perhaps incorporating older patterns related to solo display dancing. There is a broad range of blues tempos, including slow pieces in a triple rhythm; but the average tempo, if there is such a thing, is undoubtedly slower than that of some nineteenth-century popular instrumental music played with fiddle, banjo, fife and drum, mouthbow, and so forth. But blues has shown enormous potential for tempo transformation.

(d) The relationship between the human voice and the melodic lines of instruments is mainly guided by the principle of unison or heterophony or a simple background drone/ostinato on the instrument. Also, in some cases the instrument drops out or plays only an occasional note behind the singing, coming back strong in the response. The latter is especially the case among Texas guitarists like Lightnin' Hopkins and Blind Lemon Jefferson. Vocal and instrumental lines alternate in call-and-response form. Some other guitarists, however, seem to have created *contrasting* vocal melodies and guitar parts (cf. Evans's discussion of Tommy Johnson's "Big Road Blues," Evans 1982: 268–77). In East Coast blues styles (cf. Cohen 1996) an alternating bass is often played with standard harmonic patterns—incidentally somewhat similar to some central African guitar styles (cf. videorecording, Kubik 1995). Western-type chords have been used variously in guitar and other accompaniments, but in defiance of these chords, vocal lines and melodic instrumental responses tend to pursue their own strategies, including the use of tones that cannot easily be accommodated within Western-style functional harmony. These have come to be called *blue notes* in the literature.

The simultaneous presence, even in some forms of New Orleans jazz blues, of virtually two different tonal systems—one serving as a reference grid for the "melodic" brass and reed instruments, the other for the chordal accompaniment (such as on a "vamping" banjo)—was already discussed in the late 1950s. Example 10 shows a passage by the clarinetist George Lewis in "Two Jim Blues," played in the key of B-flat, virtually neglecting the banjo's chord sequence. Blues guitarists also frequently perform this ubiquitous ragtime-derived chord sequence (A^7-D^7-G^7-C in relative notation) and sometimes insert it in the same place in the standard 12-bar scheme (measures 8–11), again without it necessarily being implied by the vocal line.

More recently, Thomas Brothers (1994: 490) has drawn attention to melodic anticipation of harmonic schemes in Louis Armstrong, e.g., "Big Butter and Egg Man" (1926), where "Armstrong's F chord comes a measure early, and as a result the phrase structure of the solo collides with the harmonic rhythm of the accompaniment." Brothers points out that such behavior serves "an African conception of syntax that involves two levels, a fundamental and a supplemental, with the supplemental moving in and out of agreement with the fundamental." These examples come from jazz, but comparable behavior is also found in the blues.

(e) Melodic lines in the blues' vocal part are often pentatonic, even when there is an underlying Western-style diatonic chord sequence suggesting tonic, sub-

EXAMPLE 10

Passage from "Two Jim Blues" (transcription from Blue Note, LP 1206, 1st chorus, bars 8 to 11). Illustration retranscribed in key of C from Kubik (1959a:450).

dominant, and dominant steps. However, pitch intonation within the pentatonic scheme demonstrates a broad *variation margin*, leading to the fact that, for example, a note in a C-based blues that is intoned as a slightly flattened *E* in the first line, may appear as an *E-flat* in the second line (with an underlying subdominant chord), without losing its tonemic identity. (See David Evans's "area" concept of blues notes, 1982: 24.) In many African musical cultures it has also been observed that two notes, even up to a semitone apart in repetition, are conceptualized by the singer as *one and the same toneme* (example: "Syelinga ne nkumijeli," Mpy m̄5 chantefable song, in Kubik 1994a: 198–99, 206–7, and CD, item 21). This variability concept has been retained in many blues. This explains the auditory tolerance of microtonal deviations from the pentatonic pitch framework in patterns of ornamentation. Such deviations can veil, but do not eliminate, the pentatonic scaffolding.

(f) Instruments suitable for individual or small-group music, such as guitar, fiddle, mandolin, mouth-harmonica, and piano, have played an important role in the rural blues tradition. Percussion instruments—if used at all—are simple in construction and performance technique, and either follow European models or

Some Characteristics of the Blues

Photo 17. The court music ensemble of the Lamido (Fulɓe ruler) of Toungo, with *ganga* bi-membrane snare drums, two *algeita* oboes and *gagashi* (long trumpet). The *algeita* still have the traditional funnel cut from a gourd, Toungo, northeastern Nigeria, November 25, 1963. (Photo: Author)

are utilitarian objects (e.g., the washboard) representing historical reinterpretations of African regional models (cf. Kubik 1959b; Courlander 1963: 204–20; Evans 1998b). Jug, kazoo, and other instruments sometimes used in early blues are played with the idea of motional and timbre-melodic patterns clearly inherited from specific African styles (cf. Kubik 1959b).

(g) Some Western factory-manufactured instruments are to be understood as "standing for" African instruments known in the remote past. For example, the central Sudanic *alghaita* oboe (cf. Kubik 1989a: 84–85 for its use in the court music of the Fulɓe *Lamido* of Toungo, Nigeria) has found an extension in certain blues harmonica performance styles, and in modern jazz most typically in some of

PHOTO 18. Napoleon Strickland playing harmonica with the technique of "cupping" the ear, near Senatobia, Mississippi, September 1970. (Photo: David Evans)

John Coltrane's timbre alternations and manipulation of overtones on the saxophone. The *alghaita* (sometimes pronounced *algeita*) came to the west central Sudan from North Africa centuries ago via the Saharan trading network. Its piercing, shrill tone quality and wavy intonation are echoed in some African-American traditions. In connection with blues harmonica styles one must also point to the technique of "cupping" one's ear, which is prominent in the west central Sudanic belt, especially among Fulɓe singers in one of their oldest vocal styles, called *daacol* (see pictures of the technique and text by Veit Erlmann in Kubik 1989a: 92–93). Characteristically this style is associated with cattle herding.

Blues harmonica has also incorporated elements of southeast and central African panpipes and whistle technique, especially the alternation of blowing and whooping (cf. Tracey 1970; Malamusi 1992, 1997 for descriptions of the technique in the lower Zambezi valley). Alternation between blowing and voice also marks the technique of single-note pipes such as *efu*, made by Mpy mɔ girls in the Central African Republic from a green, hollow branch of the papaya tree (recordings 1966/Kubik, orig. tape no. 97 at the Museum für Völkerkunde, Berlin). Central African adolescent traditions, such as the making and playing of monochord zithers (as in Gabon, Congo, southern Cameroon, southeastern Nigeria, etc.) characteristically with a slider, have survived in adapted and modified versions in the "jitterbug," "bo diddley," etc. (Evans 1970; 1998b).

Photo 19A. Baba Chale, at the age of 60, when we recorded him in the Lower Shire River area of south-east Africa. He was born in Tete, Moçambique, and had come as a refugee over the border to Ndamera (in Malaŵi). He told us in Chinyungwe: "I am tired; I would like to return to Tete." In front of his grass-thatched hut he played the *nyanga* (panpipe), as a soloist, in expert alternations between blowing, singing and whooping. Photo 19a has captured him the moment he was blowing, 19b the moment of whooping. Like many other men of his age he wore an old, thick army overcoat in the "chilly" morning hours of about 90 Fahrenheit. At Ndamera, on the Malaŵi/Moçambique border, May 1967. (Photos: Author)

PHOTO 19B.

(h) Complex Guinea Coast-style polyrhythm, and especially polymeter, characteristic of some music in the Caribbean and South America, is absent in the blues.

(i) Asymmetric time-line patterns also do not occur in blues.

(j) Equally significant is the absence in the blues of heptatonic parallel harmony.
*Hepta*tonic parallelism is characteristic of much west African coastal singing, for
instance among the Akan peoples of Ghana, the Baule of the Côte d'Ivoire, the
Bini (Ẹdo) and Ijesha/Ekiti Yoruba of Nigeria, and the Igbo and other southeastern Nigerian peoples. Parallelism does enter jazz- and pop-influenced blues in
horn sections and in cases where blues are sung in duet (e.g., Brownie McGhee
and Sonny Terry in a few examples) or by vocal groups (The Midnighters, Five
Royales, etc., and earlier groups from the 1920s). But this is a relatively minor

Some Characteristics of the Blues

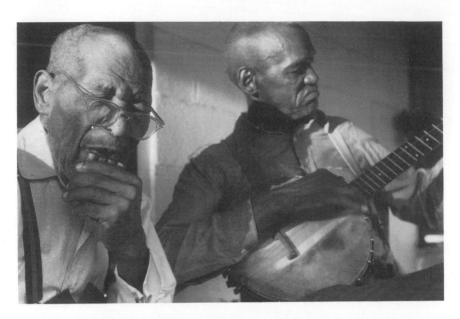

Photo 20. Sid Hemphill playing the quills (panpipes) with Lucius Smith playing 5-string banjo, Senatobia, Mississippi, 1959. Sid Hemphill, born 1876, was grandfather of blues singer and guitarist Jessie Mae Hemphill. (Photo by Alan Lomax. Courtesy of Alan Lomax Collection)

aspect of blues singing and playing and essentially represents an intrusion from other genres.

(k) Many blues have a three-line strophic form with the first line repeated, and the third introducing a new textual motif (conclusion). Each line by itself has a responsorial structure. However, the three-line form is not the only blues form; other forms exist (e.g., two-line, four-line, couplet plus refrain—see Dauer 1979), and also forms based on short cycles affiliated to cycles in African music.

Some of the traits outlined here seem to have gained more prominence in recent expressions of the blues; others seem to be on a fade-out. For example, cyclic structures relying heavily on the concept of the *riff*, using short repeated melodic-rhythmic figures on the guitar as the primary building blocks for the song, have been heard perhaps more frequently since the late 1940s, for instance in the blues of John Lee Hooker and Muddy Waters, than before (or perhaps have been more frequently recorded). Fred McDowell, Junior Kimbrough, R. L. Burnside, Jessie Mae Hemphill, and more recently Robert Belfour—all living within forty miles of one another in northern Mississippi and all recorded since 1959—demonstrate these trends. Another trait, extreme vocal melisma, can be observed, for example, in Jessie Mae Hemphill's singing (Evans 1998a).

Most of these artists display a tendency either to depart from the standard 12-bar blues chord sequence, or at least circumvent it in intriguing ways, for example by deleting the "major third" flavor from the tonic chord, which then sounds very close to the sort of central tonality found in Meigogué and other minstrels of the west central Sudan. Sometimes there are cyclic forms that are close to west African ostinato patterns, such as in the music for the *bolon* (bridge-harp of Guinée and neighboring areas; Charry 1994a) variously recorded by Gilbert Rouget in the 1950s. One track from Guinée published by Rouget displays a fabulous swing. It is particularly instructive for blues and jazz researchers investigating that phenomenon (cf. Rouget 1972, side A, track 4).

In all these cases it is, of course, difficult to determine to what extent such patterns represent a *continuous* tradition in Mississippi that might have been lingering in the memory of communities. Mississippi blues guitarists born in the 1890s and early 1900s (e.g., Charley Patton, Son House, and Skip James) sometimes used short cyclic forms, departing from the three-line formula. The local tradition seems also to be strongly influenced by riff-based fife and drum and perhaps even banjo music (cf. Evans 1978c; Lomax 1993). This suggests that in Mississippi it is probably essentially a continuous tradition. More recently, of course, some impact of Caribbean and even African influences through the mass media, or indirectly from blues-related styles like Rhythm and Blues, Soul, Funk, and so on that had absorbed these influences earlier, could have functioned as a reinforcement.

The vocal style of many blues singers using melisma, wavy intonation, and so forth is a heritage of that large region of West Africa that had been in contact with the Arabic-Islamic world of the Maghreb since the seventh and eighth centuries A.D. Cities such as Timbuktu and Gao grew up at the southern termini of the Saharan trade routes along the bend of the middle Niger River. Trade made possible the rise of powerful empires such as Mali and Songhai. In his "Cantometrics" scheme Alan Lomax (1968: 413) delineated those song style areas under the labels "Western Sudan (501)" and "Moslem Sudan (617)." These two song-style areas count among the strongest Arabic/Islamic influenced culture areas of Africa. The blues tradition, therefore, has incorporated the centuries-old impact of transculturation processes that took place between the Arab-Islamic world of North Africa and the autochthonous cultures of the Sudanic Belt. Many traits that have been considered unusual, strange, and difficult to interpret by earlier blues researchers can now be better understood as a *thoroughly processed and transformed Arabic-Islamic stylistic component*. What makes the blues different from African-American music in the Caribbean and in South America is, after all, its Arabic-Islamic stylistic ingredients.

These African song-style areas have their own history. Arabic-Islamic musical concepts were imposed on a local pentatonic stratum that had flourished perhaps for several thousand years in the pearl millet-growing savanna cultures of West Africa. The growing of millet was developed there between ca. 5,000 and 1,000 B.C. The Islamic influences spread across the region from the centers of trade and power, such as Timbuktu, and later the Hausa city states.

I am suggesting that many of the rural blues of the Deep South are *stylistically* an extension and merger of basically two broad accompanied song-style traditions in the west central Sudanic belt: (1) A strongly Arabic-Islamic song style, as found for example among the Hausa. It is characterized by melisma, wavy intonation, pitch instabilities within a pentatonic framework, and a declamatory voice production. All this behavior develops over a central reference tone, sometimes like a bourdon. (2) An ancient west central Sudanic stratum of pentatonic song composition, often associated with simple work rhythms in a regular meter, but with notable off-beat accents. This style reaches back perhaps thousands of years to the early West African sorghum agriculturalists, now scattered through the Sudanic Belt in remote savanna, often mountainous areas. This style has remained unaffected by the Arabic/Islamic musical intrusion which reached West Africa along the trans-Saharan trading routes, and subsequently spread from the early Islamic states, Mali (ca. 1230–1400 A.D.) and Songhai (ca. 1464–1600 A.D.) to the emerging Hausa city states and Fulɓe courts.

It is important to understand that across the west central Sudanic belt these two song-style traditions are *contrastive*. The Arabic-Islamic style from Mauritania to Lake Chad is urban in its genesis, is cosmopolitan, reflects social stratification, incorporates many bardic genres, and is accompanied with instruments that *often* (but not always) have a North African historical background. The "ancient Nigritic" style, on the other hand, is rural, is a part of the millet-agricultural life cycle, and, if accompanied at all, makes use of percussive devices that have a millenia-old history in the savanna. I became acutely aware of these contrasts during my research in northeastern Nigeria and the Adamawa plateau in Cameroon in 1963–1964. A comparison of Hausa and Fulɓe performances with those by villagers among the Chamba, Kutin, and Zanganyi illustrates these contrasts.

It is important to realize that the Arabic-Islamic song-style as perpetuated by Hausa itinerant musicians, Fulɓe and Hausa court music, and other traditions consists of a cluster of traits determining the *presentation* of a song, i.e., in a declamatory manner directed to some real or imaginary audience with whom the singer interacts with a lot of melodic ornamentation. It does *not* determine the type of *scale* used. Henry George Farmer (1955), in a letter to Hugh Tracey, made very clear that the Arabic-Islamic influence in the western and central Sudanic belt does not include transmission of the microtonal basis of Arabian art music. In the west central Sudanic historical scenario, the Arabic/Islamic way of declamatory articulation, raspy voices, and melisma was superimposed on *local scales*, mostly pentatonic, but in Senegal and parts of Mali and Guinée also heptatonic. Pentatonism, which is also found among the Berber people in the Sahel zone and the Sahara, is a deeply entrenched ancient presence in much of the area between Timbuktu, Lake Chad, and the Adamawa plateau. It is part of the "ancient Nigritic" song-style cluster.

Many people from small tribes in northern Nigeria and across the whole west African savanna were captured and eventually sent into slavery by their Hausa and Fulɓe overlords. Oral traditions about the slave trade were still alive in northeastern Nigeria as late as the mid-1960s, when I was doing my fieldwork. Blues, which in its genesis drew from a variety of vocal genres including work and cattle-herding songs transformed into field hollers, and string-accompanied minstrel traditions, owes its declamatory, melismatic articulation to the Arabic-Islamic song-style cluster, but its *pentatonic scales* ultimately to the "ancient Nigritic" song-style traditions. Blues that are closer in style to my recordings of the Hausa minstrel Meigogué perpetuate more of the former style, while blues that are closer to my recording of the Tikar woman's grinding song perpetuate more of the latter. Sometimes the "ancient Nigritic" element in the blues would seem to be vestigial, overwhelmed, or more or less fully absorbed into the Arabic-Islamic stylistic legacy, but it is unmistakable particularly in many scalar patterns.

forms of the blues in the southern United States we find a notable density of traits pointing to musical cultures in the west central Sudanic belt, that does not imply that the majority of the ancestors of creative blues musicians and their local audiences were deported through the infamous Ile de Gorée. In a group of people thrown together by the hazards of life, even one person is enough to transmit esoteric knowledge that might later become the property of a majority.

What probably happened in this process was that early in the nineteenth century one or another minority group among the African descendants in the Deep South gained prominence *culturally* over the others. Not for good, though; just for a while, until another juncture soon after the American Civil War, which marked the breakdown of the old social order, boosting innovation and cultural readaptation.

Therefore, the African stylistic allegiances of the rural blues as outlined earlier cannot tell us anything about U.S. African American mass genealogies. Culture is learned, and relearned, sometimes quite rapidly. Cultural goods also migrate from one segment of the population into another. At a favorable moment, a minority group makes a breakthrough to general popularity with its "own thing," based on inherited traditions. An initial minority culture can eventually become generalized, headed for cultural mainstream status.

From the musical database alone we cannot deduce whether a majority of the ancestors of those who created and perpetuated the blues originally came from places like Senegal, Mali, northern Ghana, northern Togo, northern Nigeria, and northern Cameroon. But that is of only peripheral importance, because others could have quickly learned from those who *did* come from there. Shared with others, their style could prevail. Under the circumstances of farm life in the nineteenth-century Deep South, one style cluster, with modifications, began to dominate, resulting in (among other things) the eventual development of the blues. Other style clusters were relegated to the background, retaining their potential for a breakthrough at some future opportunity. (That opportunity came in twentieth-century U.S. *urban* contexts.)

In culture contact situations it often happens that minorities win. Social pressure from a dominating culture can first push minority groups into encapsulation, resulting in the originally immigrant minority's retention of many of its cultural commodities including its "musical language." This can happen even at the smallest societal level, within families. At some later stage comes the breakthrough, the extrapolation of that "language" and its adoption by others. The cultural environment of the dominant group then gets flooded by the minority group's expressive style, eventually leading to cultural takeover.

Ironically, Charles Darwin's principle of "natural selection" and Herbert Spencer's "survival of the fittest" also work in culture contact situations as sociocultural processes of selection, although what constitutes the "fittest" is circumstantial. In other words, what survived as the "fittest" in the 1920s could be doomed under the circumstances of the 1990s. The chances of survival bear no relation to what observers would value as the "best." Scientifically, the selective scheme follows random patterns.

But culture contact is always competitive, a competition between traits and concepts. The likely scenario for the channeling of a west central Sudanic style cluster into what would be called the blues, therefore, is that the kind of socio-economic situation slaves of various genealogies encountered (second-, third-, and fourth-generation African descendants) boosted one or two African cultural extensions. They then found a better chance for imposing their peculiar artistic style on everybody. Obviously those African groups whose styles did not depend on percussion escaped the most severe forms of cultural repression. They were thus eligible to fill a vacuum. That happened to the style that can be heard across the west central Sudanic belt, with the exception of Hausa and Fulɓe court music with its rough marching-style drum rhythms (especially among the Fulɓe—cf. Kubik 1989a: 82–85), although the latter might have found an outlet in U.S. fife and drum music (see below). Those who carried on a strong tradition of unaccompanied solo song and the use of stringed instruments for the accompaniment of individual or small group music prevailed. The Protestant colonial mentality in the Deep South must have found those expressions less threatening than African community music with strange drum rhythms and massive gatherings.

For these reasons, stylistic traits from those African musical cultures with a predominance of soloist or stringed-instrument-accompanied vocal music had a better chance of survival on the plantations in the early nineteenth century; however, they survived in modified forms that would give both to the group itself and to outsiders the impression of successful acculturation, while remaining sufficiently different to confirm the "white" community's racist stereotypes of "the Negro" and his "natural ways." Moreover, western Sudanic stringed instruments could easily be modified to blend with European stringed instruments, such as the violin, the bandora, etc. In Virginia and the Carolinas the west central Sudanic plucked lutes mutated already during the eighteenth century to become early forms of the banjo. (On the banjo's history see in particular Epstein 1975 and Conway 1995).

But even in the Deep South, a remote echo of the louder musics of the west central Sudan is also perceptible. The harsh *ganga-algbaita* complex (Dauer 1985), oboes and long trumpet with drums, as in the Fulɓe and Hausa courts of Nigeria, has extensions in North America. Some of the concepts of this style were perpetuated by African-American musicians participating in local militias, and then after the Civil War by their descendants taking part in fife and drum bands playing for marching and dancing (cf. Evans 1972a).

The more intimate musical traditions of the West African savanna—minstrelsy, work music, story-telling, etc.—also had a stronger potential in southern United States plantation life to express the general mood of the captives. Instruments needed for such expression, and the experience of a certain vocal style, were still in people's memory. Environmental and social factors thus created a particular climate on the cotton and tobacco plantations that was conducive to these developments—promoting the west central Sudanic heritage, even if it was represented initially by only a minority of the slaves.

This is not to claim that everything in the African-American music of the Deep South is an extension of west central Sudanic cultural traditions, expanded by the absorption of European elements. Other African traditions, including those of minstrels from southeast Africa, for example, have also left their mark, though on a lesser scale. Their share can be assessed. One-stringed devices like the "jitterbug" and "diddley bow," surviving in the Deep South (Evans 1970) and discussed earlier, suggest by their organology and playing technique a background in some Benue-Congo (I.A.5) African cultures. The so-called "Spanish tinge" with its "additive" rhythms, characteristic of New Orleans, testifies to the proximity of the Caribbean. It is much less "Spanish" than it is a conglomerate of Guinea Coast and west central African rhythm patterns retained in the Spanish-speaking areas of the Caribbean. Influences upon the Deep South from Louisiana, whose musical cultures were much closer to those of the Caribbean in the nineteenth century and had a large share of Congo/Angola and Guinea

FIGURE 9. African areas from where principal traits that were reconfigured in nineteenth- and twentieth-century rural Blues have originated. (Map designed by G. Kubik)

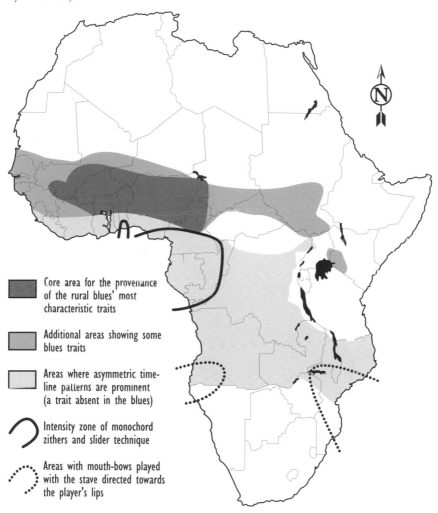

Coast west African elements, can also be felt in some idiosyncrasies within the blues tradition of the twentieth century.

In situations of population transplant anywhere in the world, we often get a picture of interaction that applies also to the United States in the nineteenth century: *one* stylistic cluster from a certain region survives in *one or two* particular genres (e.g., the blues), while another survives in a different one (e.g., the spirituals). The spirituals were a more or less tolerated outlet for community-based musical manifestations. Therefore it is not surprising that Western multipart hymn singing was quickly reinterpreted by concepts of *homophonic part singing* long established on the Guinea Coast and in west central Africa. Parallelism in fourths or fifths, forbidden in nineteenth-century European harmonic theory, crept into "Negro" singing (cf. Kirby 1930), while the blues remained unaffected by these concepts for a long time.

A pattern of evolution that can be observed in parallel instances from anywhere in the world is that at first the established culture, with all its expressions claiming to be superior, dominant, "high," or whatever, begins to open a "back door" for the alternative, even forbidden expressions of the other social stratum to come in. Here some of the members of the dominant culture's younger generation usually assume a catalyzing role. It is therefore no puzzle that secular song forms, hollers and lullabies "weird in interval and strange in rhythm" (as stated by Harvard archaeologist Charles Peabody in 1903), whose melodic materials eventually contributed to the genesis of the blues, remained underreported in the nineteenth century, even until after the Civil War "when slave songs were being collected and published by newly interested northerners," as pointed out by Harriet Ottenheimer (1987: 499). In spite of rising folkloristic interest in African-American expressions at that time, the virtual silence about secular song forms does not certify their nonexistence; rather, it shows how much the established culture tended to repress any awareness of the underground expressive forms. They were not reported, I believe, because they were among the most strikingly African, even more specifically west central Sudanic, expressive forms that had survived in the United States. Their carriers were people with a demonic reputation that made them extremely repulsive (cf. the Mandiŋ phobia across New World cultures). They symbolized the core of everything that the established elements of society were deeply afraid of, and had had such a hard time brushing away from their consciousness.

However, as we have learned from psychoanalytic theory, the repressed is at the same time fascinating. What one does not want to touch, even to know, even to admit the existence of, exercises a strange psychological pull. Ambivalence characterizes its reception, and normally it is then only a matter of time until some "back door" is left ajar to let the forbidden thing in—though somewhat dressed up, in a "socially acceptable" form.

It was not by chance, therefore, that the 1820s to the 1840s saw the rise of blackface minstrelsy (cf. Lott 1993). In theatrical performances, the "White Man" began to paint his face black, transforming himself into a "temporary Negro," and on stage he would act out much of what was unacceptable to his own fundamentalist Christian culture, or—more precisely—all that he had extracted from his own soul and projected outward upon the "Negro." As a blackened mask he could act out freely his dream fantasies. He could transform into a "Negro" and behave the way he had always desired without social sanctions from his community; and his audience could experience with him a long sought relief.

Thus blackface minstrelsy prepared the ground psychologically for the later ascendancy of ragtime, jazz, and blues. After some modest attempts by African Americans to reinstate African musical patterns by "ragging" the "White Man's" popular music of the day—leading to a substantial body of mostly original compositions to be played as written—a more faithfully African style cluster that was carried by a minority would eventually make a breakthrough to public awareness. Ma Rainey's fascination with the strange melodic patterns of the song of a poor girl who was hanging around Rainey's tent show (Work 1940: 32–33) symbolizes this passage of the early blues from a predominantly west central Sudanic minority culture on American soil to adoption by the more mainstream culture of the African-American theatre and show world of the day. Within a decade elements of the blues would show up in published sheet music and enter the world of mainstream *American* music and culture.

The later stages of the processes of cultural competition and takeover by minority cultures can also be studied. No doubt, there are always several intermediary stages. Recently, Lynn Abbott and Doug Seroff (1996: 402–3) have delineated some of the sociopsychological forces that steer human reactions in extremely stratified societies, in particular the artistic reactions of the lowest social stratum. It seems that the post-Civil War period in the United States generated an era of ambivalence and contradictory motivations in the various population groups that had come into closer contact. Eventually this resulted in *restatements* of what had survived more or less underground as the most intensive African cultural heritage.

Blues in its various twentieth-century expressions was shaped by the historical interaction of two separate impulses and the dynamic tension between them, all under the influence of a confounding outside force—commercialization in a racist society. The first impulse was to perpetuate the indigenous musical and cultural practices of the African-American folk heritage, which eventually formed the cornerstone of an independent black cultural heritage. The second, countering impulse was to demonstrate mastery of standard Western musical and cultural conventions. Through this impulse came the necessary formalizing structures, without which there could have been no composition, development, dissemination, and widespread popularization of ragtime, blues, and jazz. (Abbott and Seroff 1996: 402–3)

8 - Heterophonic Versus Homophonic Multipart Schemes

No serious student of African-American music will subscribe today to all-encompassing formulations such as that "harmony" in jazz and other African-American music is "European" in origin, while "rhythm" is "African" (i.e., a sort of pan-African hodgepodge). One still occasionally encounters the opinion, inherited from early twentieth-century writings, that "all African music was originally pentatonic" and that "the Portuguese brought heptatonic harmony to Africa," as I noticed to my surprise in the discussion following a lecture I gave to a scholarly circle in Chicago on August 20, 1997.

Harriet Joseph Ottenheimer (1992: 32) begins her "radical proposal" concerning the "Comoro Crossroads" of the blues with this statement: "Blues, for example, draws its harmonic structure from Europe and its melodic style from Africa." Even Thomas Brothers (1994: 479), whose thoughtful analyses of jazz improvisation provide ample evidence to the contrary, seems to feel the need to pay lip service to some of these stereotypes by elevating them in his introduction to the status of a "core of truth." It is at best a "grain of truth," in the sense that jazz and blues players certainly have a *sense* of I-IV-V based European-style harmony or other more complex derivatives. But the essence of this process is that they reinterpret and constantly convert it in ways that are based on unconscious African models. The same process occurred in twentieth-century developments of African popular music, with the result that, for example, the harmonic cycle C-F-G-F prominent in Congo/Zaïre popular music (cf. Kubik 1995, video *African Guitar*) simply cannot be defined as a progression from tonic to subdominant to dominant and back to subdominant (on which it ends) because in the performers' appreciation they are of equal status, and not in any hierarchical order as in Western music. In some forms of the blues—for example, much of Robert Belfour's and Jessie Mae Hemphill's music—Western-style harmony is even completely ignored or referred to only in the most perfunctory manner.

The popular belief that jazz and blues all inherited European harmony is kindled by authors who proceed from classical music theory. Using Western harmonic concepts as a blanket explanation for all the harmonic qualities in the blues, they fail to explore how the Western schemes are converted. Some jazz musicians have linked up with such perspectives—for instance, Charlie Parker when he stated in interviews that Arnold Schönberg was an inspiration to him. In the jazz world the identification of harmonic sequences in Western terminology has been elevated to "jazz theory," which is now required material for college students studying to be jazz musicians.

This is all the more surprising as the principles of several heptatonic harmonic traditions along the Guinea Coast and in west central Africa are well known (cf. Waterman 1952; Jones 1959; Kubik 1981, 1994a, etc.). Some of these principles persist in the structuring and approach to linear arrangements of harmony in New World styles, such as in vocal music (from the spirituals to the 1940s and 1950s vocal groups) and in instrumental settings like swing jazz (e.g., Count Basie, Jay McShann, and others) as well as in chord clusters and progressions of bebop.

As early as 1930 Percival R. Kirby was able to isolate in Negro spirituals at least one African-derived structural principle of counterpoint, comparing it to identical schemes in Nguni homophonic vocal harmony of South Africa (Kirby 1930, 1961; Kubik 1994a: 169–209). Kirby's was the earliest statement of what I later termed the "span process" or "skipping process" (cf. Kubik 1968: 29, 1994a: 174), a structural principle implying that usually one note of a given scale is skipped by a second singer to obtain harmonic simultaneous sounds in relation to the melodic line of a first vocalist. It gives the most varied results in African harmonic styles, depending on the type of scale underlying a tune—that is, the kind of tonal system to which it is applied. In this way it became possible to isolate an abstract structural idea behind some of the most diverse bi-part and multipart harmonic singing styles in Africa, a principle that has interregional validity and explains why in certain harmonic styles certain simultaneous sounds must follow each other, while some other progressions cannot occur (cf. fig. 11

below). A functional relationship between the type of tonal system and type of harmony was thereby detected, giving us by implication a formidable tool for identifying African-derived harmonic patterns in African-American styles (cf. my brief description of a guitar pattern of Bo Diddley perpetuating west central African mouthbow harmonies based on two fundamentals—Kubik 1993: 444).

Independently of the "skipping process" and other structural principles more recently uncovered (cf. Kubik 1994a: 210–48), multipart procedures in Africa can be broadly classified by form and patterning as (a) *heterophonic*, (b) *homophonic*, or (c) *polyphonic*. But here, as always in the study of cultural systems, we have to keep in mind that descriptions of African and African-American music with the vocabulary of Greek-derived terms such as "rhythm," "melody," and "harmony" (the "musical trinity," as Cajetan Lunsonga [1978: 72] expressed it sarcastically) are intrinsically flawed. We can attempt to *translate* African musical phenomena into these concepts for a foreign readership, but we have to recognize that they have no linear equivalents in African languages. Even phenomenologically, the Western categorizations do not match up with what they purport to describe, because there is also in most African styles, and by extension in African-American music, an acute awareness of timbre modification and timbre sequences, as a further dimension of musical structuring. As I have tried to point out in my analysis of drum patterns in Brazilian *batuque* (Kubik 1990), drumming in African and African-American styles is not just "rhythm"; it can be much better understood as timbre-melodic sequences. And a singer's or instrumentalist's melodic line is not just a set of pitch sequences, as Western staff notation will suggest, but more often—and particularly also in the blues—a delicate web of timbre-melodic and melodic-rhythmic patterns. In African stringed instrument traditions, for example, African musicians listen to the depth structure of the sound spectrum of a string; obviously, blues musicians "worrying" some notes are behaving in just this same way. Blues and jazz have inherited all these concepts, but in various combinations and reconfigurations testifying to the innovative character of African musical cultures in the New World.

Heterophony, the first of the three conceptual principles we have isolated above leading to simultaneous sound, is ultimately related to unison singing. Two or more people, or one vocalist with an instrument, perform the same melody more or less in unison, but the pitch-lines diverge slightly. An instructive example from the realm of blues is Robert Belfour's performance of "Poor Boy Long Way From Home" (CD *The Spirit Lives On*, LC 5740, item 1). Observe how the upper-string melodic guitar lines relate to the singer's voice.

In elaborate instrumental styles, heterophony is normally combined with *functional polyphony* that may be rooted in call-and-response schemes, for example, when different instruments such as a trumpet (playing the theme), a clarinet (with responsorial, commentatory, and embellishing function), and a trombone (providing a melodic-rhythmic bass line) interact like three drums in a Mozambiquan drum ensemble performing the *náwansha* dance (recordings Hillegeist/Kubik in 1962, Phonogrammarchiv Vienna). Such combination between heterophony and functional polyphony is also prominent in the blues, where the guitar can play sometimes in heterophony with or as a counter melody to the voice, at other times in repeated picking patterns, or in a persistent rhythmic note or chord, and so on (Cohen 1996).

Heterophonic styles do not necessarily exclude the use of chords even in the melodic lines. But in contrast to homophonic styles, such chords flash up as didactic accents not requiring a continuous linear development. They constitute *timbre-harmonic clusters* rather than functional chords. In the blues they serve to underline a point in a text or in an instrumental statement or a response. Out of many examples, I recommend listening to how Mose Vinson (b. 1917) responds to his vocal statements by throwing in sound clusters on the piano (cf. "Rock'n'Roll Blues," CD *The Spirit Lives On*, LC 5740, item 6). This implies that we have to reckon with *two genera* of chords in the blues: (a) Simultaneous sounds thrown in by the guitarist or pianist as timbre-harmonic clusters to set accents. These are not "resolved" and may occur as off-beat accents within single-note melodic lines to illustrate or comment upon the human voice. (b) Chords that are part of a *chord sequence* resolving into each other. These are often interpreted as chords in the Western sense, as they often serve to mark standard and expected harmonic changes within structural patterns (e.g., 12-bar AAB). Some blues artists use more of the first genus, some more of the second. The *share* of one or the other in an individual artist is a most important stylistic determinant.

These concepts of simultaneous sound characterize most of the Mississippi Delta blues style. Though the apparent "chords" in the guitar accompaniments are identified by researchers trained in Western musicology with the chord

Photo 21. *Functional polyphony* in a Mozambican three-drum ensemble. This group led by master drummer S. Venjiwa (center) used to accompany popular circle dances among the Ashirima of northern Mozambique, such as *náwansha*. The polyphonic network of timbre-clusters is created by the three drums rigorously adhering to their functions. The small *masha* (left) played with two sticks provides a high-pitched and extremely fast pulsation. The *mtíamu* (right) produces a complex cyclic pattern of several timbre-units. On the *joza* (center), the master drummer is free to develop elaborate variations and "speak" to the dancers. In his timbre-creating process he strikes different areas of his drum, using hands, and occasionally even an elbow. At settlement II, Mitukwe mountains, northern Mozambique, October 15, 1962. (Photo: Hillegeist/Kubik)

PHOTO 22. Mose Vinson, born in 1917, is one of the oldest piano-playing blues musicians still active. Born in Holly Springs, Mississippi, he eventually moved to Memphis but was only first recorded in 1953 by Sun Records. His characteristic left-hand solid beat which earned him the nickname "Boogie," his powerful voice, as if he were still in his prime, and his right-hand jagged timbre-melodic patterns interact like three "drums" transformed and united in his own body, Memphis, Tennessee, January 5, 1994. (Photo: Volker Albold)

symbols used in jazz, the underlying idea differs as much from that of Western chord progressions as it does from African homophonic multipart singing or its instrumental recastings. In addition, simultaneous sounds arising from a totally different process, not associated with production on a *single instrument*, occur sporadically in *ensemble* performances, such as between the three wind instruments in an early jazz ensemble or the Mozambiquan drummers cited earlier. These are neither functional nor commentative, but are generated by the interweaving linearity in heterophony and/or functional polyphony.

Another harmonic principle inherited from Africa, one that is particularly prevalent in the Mississippi Delta blues style, is the concept of *bourdon*, a term we use to designate the drone-like sound produced by sustained open-string techniques on guitars, lutes, and other string instruments, but also any continuous bass or basic tone that forms a keynote and sometimes is the fundamental of sound clusters derived from the natural harmonic series. The idea of the bourdon came to Africa through contacts with Asia, probably as early as the first millennium A.D., at first via the Indian Ocean trading network, then in the west central Sudanic savanna through trans-Saharan contacts with Arabic musical cultures. There is a hypothetical possibility that the use of the bourdon could have been present in the west central African sahel zone much earlier, entering the area from the Sahara through contacts with ancient Mediterranean and Egyptian music. At present it is particularly prominent in certain southeast African styles, as well as across the west central African Sudanic belt, and it lends itself easily to combinations with heterophony and functional polyphony. It can also accommodate the use of riffs—repeating short melodic-rhythmic patterns embedded in larger forms. But it is antipathetic to homophonic harmony as defined in African contexts.

In African *homophonic multipart styles*, whose remote history is sometimes rooted in the experience of mouthbow tunings with two fundamentals that are a whole tone apart, a group of people sings the same song together, rhythmically in line, with identical text for all participants, but each voice standing at a different pitch level. The voices often combine in parallel movement, but not necessarily. In areas of prominence of semantic and grammatical speech tones, as in most languages of the Kwa family (I.A.4) including Fanti, Twi, Yoruba, and Igbo, parallelism is the rule. If the tonality of the language is less all-embracing, contrary and oblique movement is frequent, as for example in eastern Angolan traditions (cf. LP double album, *Mukanda na Makisi*, MC 11, Kubik 1981).

By contrast, in African *polyphonic multipart styles* (see examples on the LP records Kubik 1989d and Kubik and Malamusi 1989) two or more singers—or, by extension, instrumentalists—would combine melodic-rhythmic lines that have different texts, are of different lengths, have different starting points, and interlock or interweave in one or the other way. Some authors—for instance, J. H. Kwabena Nketia (1962)—have termed such polyphony the hocket technique (from the European medieval "hoquetus"). This is an unfortunate choice of terminology, however, because it is unnecessarily cross-cultural, linking unrelated culture worlds, and it can be mistaken for an evolutionistic statement. Comparisons of this kind were common in the literature on African music during the first half of the twentieth century. A. M. Jones used to call the parallelism in fourths or fifths found in certain African multipart singing styles "organum" (Jones 1959), thereby conjuring up the European Middle Ages.

Multipart structuring in rural blues and early jazz—before the inception of the swing jazz era in the 1930s—was largely based on the concepts of *heterophony*, *functional polyphony*, and *timbre-melodic stringing*, rather than the concept of *homophony*. This identifies early jazz and blues as cultural strands different from spirituals, certain types of group worksongs, and Caribbean musical styles where homophonic multipart patterns are prominent.

In the face of incisive stylistic divisions across the hemisphere, we understand why, for example, the encounter in Accra in 1956 between Louis Armstrong and Ghanaian bandleader Emmanuel Tetteh Mensah, during Armstrong's West Africa tour, turned out to be a meeting of strangers. Both were at the time top personalities on the trumpet, and both had adapted their music to contemporary trends of the 1950s; but while Armstrong's jazz was essentially rooted in concepts of heterophony and functional polyphony, E. T. Mensah had processed the older Fanti, Twi, and other Guinea Coast heritage of tonality and parallel three-part harmony in his highlife music. He used his reed section to play in a set, an idea adopted from ballroom dance orchestras of the 1930s and early 1940s, but simultaneously this reed section represented melodic lines that could be sung traditionally by a Fanti group of vocalists. This is noticeable in many of Mensah's compositions, e.g., in "O hentse mi lo" (Decca Records, WAL 1002, I/3; see also Kubik 1989a: 164–65), demonstrating a characteristic southern Ghanaian homophonic style of harmony with specific sequences of three- to four-part simultaneous sound. The presence of a homophonic style of harmonic construction, as perpetuated in E. T. Mensah's highlife arrangements, originally within a non-modal heptatonic system, is attested for southern Ghana by the earliest written sources we know on Gold Coast music, such as Thomas Edward Bowdich's 1819 account with several notations of Asante and Fanti harmonic patterns (cf. discussion in Kubik 1989a: 33–34, 1997a: 85).

Many of the African harmonic traditions, especially some of those found along the Guinea Coast, as well as in Gabon, Congo, and Angola, were carried to places in the New World (cf. some of the 1950s recordings by Simone Dreyfus-Roche, LP *Bresil* Vol. 2, Contrepoint M.C. 20.138, Musée de l'Homme, Paris, for interesting examples from fishing songs on the shores of the Bay of Bahia).

Even in the United States, certain African tonal-harmonic templates have continued in the minds of African-American musicians as an inner reference grid that is sporadically activated for reinterpreting conventional Western chords in particular ways. While at the end of the nineteenth century one social class of musicians emulated European popular song forms and harmonic patterns in the process of creating ragtime piano and vocal quartet music, there was another social class on the plantations and in the urban back streets that was little affected by Western formal music education. Musicians from that mould remained faithful to tonal-harmonic principles inherited from one or another place in Africa, through enculturation processes within families and communities spanning several generations.

In all the Africa-derived procedures for creating multipart music, observers with a strong background in European music theory and little acquaintance with African music will tend to recognize the familiar chord progressions. But the same chords can also be looked at from a variety of African regional perspectives, and in this process they are quickly stripped of their Western functional or qualitative attributes such as "major," "minor," "diminished," "augmented," "dominant," "subdominant," and so forth. U.S. blues and jazz musicians often occupy a middle position. Neither African nor Western musicians, they have figured out ways to reconcile the African and Western concepts, sometimes using each for somewhat different musical statements (Berliner 1994).

We know from cognitively oriented research that identical phenomena are conceptualized in different ways by the adherents of different cultures. A bichord consisting of two simultaneous sounds that are 583 cents apart may be described as a diminished fifth (or, enharmonically, as an augmented fourth) by the adherents of one musical culture. But the same combination will be conceptualized by a Mugogo musician in central Tanzania as two distinctive "voices" (*sauti*), one smaller, one bigger, that are distinguished by their experimental location in different shapes of the human mouth. If this statement is translated into the language of acoustics, the two tones thus represent for a Mugogo musician the fifth and seventh partials of the natural harmonic series. An expert such as Hukwe Zawose (cf. recordings in possession of Philip Donner, Institute for Workers' Music, Helsinki) can actually reinforce them by purely vocal techniques. The latter has been called diphonic singing or "overtone" singing in the literature (Dargie 1991; Hai 1994).

African tonal systems are not uniform. There are several very different systems in use within the broad framework of tetra-, penta-, hexa-, and heptatonic resources. To someone familiar with African tonal systems, much of what happens in the multipart structuring of African-American music, including spirituals, blues, jazz, and rhythm and blues, rings a bell. When I listen to recordings in various African-American idioms, it is often as if signals flash up at various spots on the map of Africa. Sometimes a signal flashes up here, then there. And characteristically, there are areas in Africa where such signals flash up most frequently, and others where they almost never flash up.

Our approach suggests that we start off interpreting some of these African-American patterns in terms of sound-producing structures encountered in African cultures, and see where we arrive. For example, if parallel fourths appear in the brass or reed section of a 1940s swing band, Western music theorists might diagnose them as divergent from the classical rules of harmonic progression. However, we can look at the overall tonal contexts in which these progressions occur and sort out whether or not their formative principles perpetuate any of the known African harmonic traditions. Below I present five different harmonic schemes that are characteristic of different regional multipart singing styles in southern and central Africa (fig. 10a–e). The systems behind them can be cracked, if we link them to the scalar patterns from which they derive (fig. 11). All of them display the unmistakable fingerprint of the scalar skipping process.

These patterns can be explained. There is a reason why in example 10a (Swazi/Nguni) the chain of simultaneous sounds must be parallel fourths interrupted at one particular point by a major third bi-chord. We can also explain the origin of the Gogo progressions (fig. 10b), and we can discover why in the Nguni/Nyanja example (fig. 10d) there must be parallel thirds between the upper two voices and parallel fourths between the lower two. Observers looking at such progressions from the auditory standpoint of the Western tonal system might detect "blue notes" (E↓ and B♭). They might even feel compelled to describe this model (fig. 10d) as a progression from neutral third ($\frac{G}{E↓}$) to a minor third ($\frac{F}{D}$) and to a major third ($\frac{E}{C}$). The problem is that these categorizations simply do not work. If the observers were able to communicate with the singers, speaking their language, they would be surprised to hear that from their viewpoint the singers claim they are progressing in *identical intervals*. This fact suggests that in this particular tradition, E↓ and E are accommodated within the varia-

FIGURE 10A–E. Some characteristic multi-part progressions from Africa:

(a) Swazi / Nguni (South Africa)

(b) Gogo (Tanzania)

(c) Nkhumbi / Handa (Angola)

(d) Nguni / Nyanja (Malaŵi)

(e) Mpyɛmɔ̃ (Central African Republic)

*Music from these traditions can be heard on the following records: AMA—72, Swati, Songs with *makweyana* gourd bow, International Library of African Music, Grahamstown (South Africa); *Multi-part singing in East and South East Africa*, PHA LP 2, Phonogrammarchiv Vienna, text G. Kubik 1989; *Humbi en Handa Angola*, No. 9, Musée Royal de L'Afrique Centrale, Tervuren, Kubik 1973; *Opeka Nyimbo. Musician-composers from Southern Malaŵi*, MC 15 (G. Kubik/Moya A. Malamusi), Berlin: Museum für Völkerkunde 1989; Cassettes accompanying Artur Simon: *Musik in Afrika*, Berlin: Museum Für Völkerkunde, 1983; CD record accompanying G. Kubik (1994a): *Theory of African Music*, Vol. 1, especially items 13–21.

FIGURE 11A–E. Different African scales from which the harmonic patterns of fig. 10 are derived by the skipping process:

(a) Nguni (South Africa)

(b) Gogo (Tanzania)

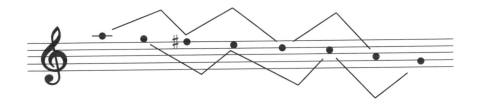

(c) Nkhumbi / Handa (Angola)

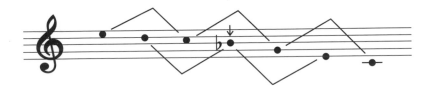

(d) Nguni / Nyanja (Malaŵi)

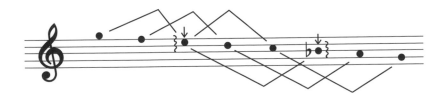

(e) MpyƐmɔ̃ (Central African Republic)

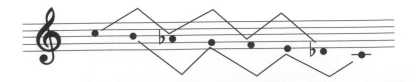

tion margin of what for the singers is *the same pitch*. The intonation actually chosen is circumstantial, a bit lower or a bit higher depending on the context.

Nor are the Nkhumbi/Handa (fig. 10c) and Mpyɛmɔ (fig. 10e) harmonic patterns any riddle, if one realizes that they derive from *two fundamentals* that are, in the first case, a whole tone apart (C → D), in the second a semitone (C → Db)). Above these fundamentals, Mpyɛmɔ vocalists in particular sometimes build lush "major sevenths." But the uniting factor in these different harmonic schemes is structural: the simultaneous sounds are always created by the scalar skipping process to different tonal materials. This is shown in fig. 11a-e.

There is even one rule of thumb for our research. Whenever Western music theoreticians find a harmonic pattern in jazz or blues to be strange or unusual (a common reaction to some of the guitar chords of Skip James, for example— cf. Calt 1994), it might indicate retention of one or another African concept. One could devise a "negative" test method for detecting Africanisms by registering the reactions of cultural outsiders. Whenever they use labels such as "strange," "unusual," "unorthodox," "deviant," "weird," "unstable," "uncertain," "idiosyncratic," "extreme," or even "fascinating," a signal flashes up somewhere on the map of Africa.

9 - The Blues Tonal System

Carl Gregor Herzog zu Mecklenburg and Waldemar Scheck (1963: 9) give an overview of the numerous theories by means of which Western musicians and musicologists from the 1920s to the 1960s tried to come to grips with a phenomenon in the blues that seemed to run contrary to all established harmonic rules of Western music: the "blue notes." By this term normally two tones are understood, variously written as B♭ and E♭ in relation to the Western diatonic scale based on C. These two notes seem to be notoriously unstable and somewhat superimposed on the Western major scale like "aliens."

In the literature blue notes have been described as "a microtonal lowering of the 3rd, 7th and (to a lesser extent) 5th scale degrees" (Robinson 1980: 812), and various theories for their origin have been proposed by such writers as by Winthrop Sargeant (1938), Ernest Borneman (1959), and Gunther Schuller (1968), all proceeding from the standpoint that the blue notes are "deviations" or "inflections" of *the* standard pitches (i.e., European diatonicism). More recently, Jeff Todd Titon (1977: 161, fig. 64) has suggested an "early downhome blues mode."

However, we who have worked in African cultures with the most diverse tonal systems cannot help but see the "inflections" on the other side. This impression is reconfirmed if we experimentally remove the blues' instrumental accompaniment, where it is based on tonic, subdominant, and dominant, or suppress its perception, and examine the singers' vocal lines in isolation, as if they sang without any accompaniment. Titon's (1977) transcriptions in relative notation (on C), omitting the guitar chords, are very useful in this context as a comparative database.

If we do this, it becomes clear that each vocal line is an integrated, patterned whole, without any particular tones having special status. In spite of their regular use for accompanying the blues and early forms of jazz, the three common Western chords appear to be the real "aliens," although blues and jazz musicians have for two or three generations now internalized them. And yet, musicians in the Deep South and even in many urban areas have never seemed quite comfortable with these chords. Mississippi bluesman Skip James's "Devil Got My Woman" (Paramount 13088, February 1931) is a testimony for a radically different approach, even in the early 1930s. More recently, these chords have often been replaced by bourdon-like recurring tones (e.g., various songs recorded by Jessie Mae Hemphill, Fred McDowell, R. L. Burnside, Junior Kimbrough, and Robert Belfour).

Even at the height of these Western chords' fashionable use, in the 1920s and 1930s when blues had come "to town" (cf. Mississippi Matilda's "Hard Working Woman" discussed earlier), the dominant chord at least was circumvented in some performances. And in the early 1940s, in bebop and thereafter, jazz quickly got rid of the simple chords with substitution chords, clustered chords, the simultaneous sounding of major and minor thirds, and the tritone intervals or flatted fifth chord (C-E F$\sharp$), by which a new tonal ambivalence was introduced while preserving tonality (i.e., a central tonal reference point) as such.

In my opinion, bebop brought jazz back closer to tonal concepts that even now prevail in certain African areas where so-called equiheptatonic tuning systems are found, notably in the Lower Zambezi valley (cf. a xylophone recording by Suze, double LP *Opeka Nyimbo*, Kubik and Malamusi 1989, item A 3), around Benin City, Nigeria, in southern Ghana, and in certain areas of the Côte d'Ivoire. The African distribution map of equiheptatonic tonal systems and associated nonmodal concepts of homophonic multipart singing involving "neutral thirds" includes many areas from which people were deported to the Americas (see my recordings from Angola, *Mukanda na makisi*, double LP, Kubik 1981; or Gilbert Rouget's *Pondo Kakou*, Musée de l'Homme, Paris, LP record MC 20141, item I 1). Equiheptatonic concepts must therefore have reached the New World African-American cultures during their formative periods. But what has remained of them? In Colombia and Ecuador, Lower Zambezi-type xylophones imported with Mozambiquans have survived to the present day in communities of African descent. In Central America, Congo xylophones have migrated into Amerindian cultures. In all these instances equiheptatonic and other tunings were soon adapted to the Western tonal system. Everywhere, factory-manufactured musical instruments tuned to the diatonic Western scale began within a few generations to erase from African-American musical cultures any concepts of equidistance. The same has happened from the mid-twentieth century on in African popular music, where the electric guitar has become a prominent and central instrument.

But equiheptatonic concepts have survived unconsciously and *do* find expression in New World African-American music, albeit indirectly. One of the signs of their hidden presence is a certain ambiguity toward diatonicism running through the history of African-American music in the United States. In equiheptatonic conceptualization, a major third and a minor third (in the Western tonal system) both fall within the margin of tolerance for deviations from the *equiheptatonic third* of 342.8 cents,* the "common" or "average" or "neutral" third. In heterophonic vocal styles these different thirds could be sung together or played together comfortably, since in the equiheptatonic system they represent *one and the same toneme.*

Some of this tonal ambiguity is found throughout jazz history and expressed in various ways on various instruments. It is almost certainly based on the retention and cultural transmission of auditory habits inherited from equiheptatonic mental templates prevalent in the African regions mentioned. But there are other African traditions of tonality that also contradict the Western scale, generating resistance in African-American musicians to the simple European chords they encountered among English-speaking settlers, especially in church singing.

Therefore, unilinear explanations of the "blue notes" as neutral thirds resulting from the projection of an (African) equiheptatonic scale upon the Western seven-note major scale seem to have led researchers astray. The idea of "neutral thirds" as such was launched by Erich Moritz von Hornbostel in relationship

---

*We express pitch intervals in cents, a system introduced by Alexander Ellis. The universal interval of the octave is assigned the value 1,200 cents. The semitone in the European tempered system, therefore, has the value of 100 cents. With this calibration established, any interval can be expressed. Thus the tempered major third (as on a piano) has 400 cents. But tempered intervals are quite artificial. The natural major third, as derived from the harmonic series, stands at 386 cents, the natural minor seventh at 969 cents (i.e., 31 cents lower than the tempered minor seventh on a piano). In African equiheptatonic systems the octave is divided by ear into seven approximately equal parts. This is a non-European example of temperature. Its standard interval is $1,200 \div 7 = 171.4$ cents, mathematically. Human auditory perception does not reach such a degree of accuracy. In practice the intervals will fluctuate between 160 and 180 cents. The equiheptatonic or "neutral" third is mathematically $171.4 \times 2 = 342.8$ cents. Again in practice it will fluctuate anywhere between ca. 320 and 360 cents.

to Faŋ tonal-harmonic patterns in Gabon, Equatorial Guinea, and southern Cameroon (Hornbostel 1913: 331–53). It was later perpetuated with explicit reference to the blue notes by Arthur M. Jones (1951: 9–10), Alfons M. Dauer (1955: V.6, 1958: 78), and myself (Kubik 1961: 55–56). In my own early article, originally written in 1959 (before my first African field experience), I spoke of the coexistence of two different tonal systems in archaic jazz, and compared the "blues scale" to tempered heptatonic scales as described by Hugh Tracey.

If the "origin" of the blue notes were to be found in African equiheptatonic tonal systems, the lower blue note would stand at roughly 343 cents from the basic tonal reference note (C in relative notation), i.e., about halfway between E♭ and E, while the higher blue note would stand at 1029 cents from the tonic, i.e., a tone somewhat higher than a B♭. For the lower blue note this estimate is fairly acceptable, but not for the higher one. To my knowledge, blues singers do not usually *sharpen* the B♭ toward B over a tonic chord. They only do this over a dominant chord, in which case this is simply the lower blue note (the "blue" third) transposed upward by a fifth. While the lower blue note can fluctuate between E♭ and E, or even gliss down to below a minor third, the higher blue note, in my experience, when sounded over a tonic chord, often flattens the B♭ to a value below the tempered tone of 1,000 cents.

The blue notes cannot derive unilaterally from equiheptatonic African tuning systems for yet another reason. Each tonal system has a sort of intrasystemic purpose. African equidistant scales are *tempered* scales that were developed on instruments such as xylophones and lamellophones. The idea behind them is to guarantee the identity of melodic patterns, when they are transposed through any step and in any direction of such scales. Modality, i.e., major/minor distinctions, would prevent the maintenance of melodic identity in transpositions.

The blues, on the other hand, are clearly entrenched in a permeating tonal reference basis. Only in bebop have tonal concepts reached a degree of relativism such that they often come close to African equiheptatonic ideas in spite of the Western tuning, and the perpetuation of a tonal center (albeit more vaguely conceived). Not by chance did the concept of the flatted fifth chord appear in bebop from 1940 on. The flatted fifth as such is often called "the third blue note." As a pitch-line phenomenon it was already prominent in blues singing, especially by Bessie Smith and other vaudeville blues singers of the 1920s, often used as a starting note in descending phrases.

The Blues Tonal System

The generalizing concept of "neutral thirds" in connection with the hypothesis of an equiheptatonic scalar framework as the "origin" of the blue notes is also incompatible with theories attributing a pentatonic origin to the blues' tonal system. In a paper called "Spatio-Motor Thinking in Playing Folk Blues Guitar," John Baily and Peter Driver restated the pentatonic position of earlier writers as follows: "Many blues melodies use a pentatonic blues scale with blue notes. This scale could be configured as root, neutral third, fourth, fifth, and neutral seventh. The neutral intervals are so-called 'blue notes,' somewhere between a minor and major third and minor and major seventh" (Baily and Driver 1992: 64). This would mean that for some unexplained reason such pentatonic scales were composed of three stable intervals and two unstable intervals "somewhere between" fixed pitches.

From a more evolutionistic outlook, Alfons M. Dauer (1955: V.6, 1958: 78) characterized "the west African tonality" as a system of absolutely fixed "main tones" (German: *Haupttöne*), i.e., root/octave, fifth, and fourth degrees, surrounded by diverse intermediate tones. He derived the notion of the blue notes from Guinea Coast *hepta*tonic systems, in which he saw a step in an evolutionary sequence. Believing that "African tonality was primarily based on pentatonic principles," Dauer held that coastal west Africans had "outgrown" pentatonism by tentatively adding two more notes, but still very unstable ones, in the two large gaps of the pentatonic scale. His model at least explains why (related to C) some more "stable" notes, such as D and A, also occur in the blues, and not only "root," "fourth," and "fifth" plus two more notes "somewhere between."

Dauer's idea was perhaps inspired by earlier evolutionistic ideas. One such pronouncement is by Annabel Morris Buchanan (1940) in her article on "a neutral mode" in Anglo-American folk music of the Appalachian mountains. In the tradition of anthropological theories of the early twentieth century, Buchanan projected a unilinear evolutionistic scheme upon her material, giving the diatonic scale the status of "completeness" (full) and "modernity." "These pentatonic modes have been in process of evolution for many centuries. Gradually the gaps began to be filled, with intervening notes added hesitatingly, sometimes wavering in pitch, until our full modern diatonic scale was reached" (Buchanan 1940: 79).

Dauer (1955: V.6) also proposed another, less well known hypothesis about the "origin" of the blue notes. Citing examples from the Twi language in Ghana, he stated that the "special character of the west African melodic third," which can appear either over the root or over the fifth degree, reflects the *mid tones* in speech patterns of west African tonal languages (notably of the Kwa [I.A.4] family).

The literature on the blue notes and their possible origins is abundant. Many of the hypotheses are clearly off track, while some others contain worthwhile hints and, in a sense, a grain of truth. I will now try to outline some of my own thoughts, using as a basis my field experience in west Africa and elsewhere. In no way do I claim, of course, to have found a Rosetta Stone. But I believe the exercise will be valid in itself on methodological grounds.

As a research strategy, one can first proceed from the simple, but cognitively relevant, axiom that intraculturally (i.e., for the performers themselves) the blue notes have no reality as separate conceptual pitch units. This is supported by the fact that Deep South blues singers themselves never talk about "blue notes" unless they have had some exposure to the jazz literature, have had Western formal musical training, or are influenced by fans from outside their primary community and audiences. In other words, "blue notes," or any other special type of note in relation to pitch, is not originally an intracultural concept. It seems the term was introduced by various jazz musicians and writers about jazz, who began to use it by the 1920s—perhaps even a bit earlier—in order to "explain" their music in Western terms (cf. Niles 1925).

Thus, the so-called blue notes are simply part of a blues singer's total pitch repertoire. Their existence as differential cognitional units is only generated through comparison with an extrasystemic parameter: the European diatonic scale. Some notes in the blues singer's repertoire of pitch patterns not coinciding with the Western scale are then called "blue."

The whole concept of blue notes therefore introduces an artificial split in the blues singers' pitch resources. Sounded against the notes of the Western scale, the blue notes may create tension, but here David Evans has warned that "from the point of view of the blues singer, of course, blue notes are not tension-producing per se but are rather a normal part of the blues scale" (1978b: 424).

Blues singers do, however, have concepts expressing microtonal pitch modifications. Lucid evidence is available, for example in Muddy Waters's discussion of pitch shading in Robert Palmer's book *Deep Blues* (1981: 102–4, 260). Muddy used this term to describe his singing, which Palmer adopted as the title of his book. Generally, Deep South blues singers speak of "worrying" or "bending" the notes of the voice or on an instrument such as a guitar (cf. Ottenheimer 1987: 497). These worried or bent notes are usually the third and seventh (and sometimes the fifth) of the Western diatonic scale.

David Evans suggested that blues musicians proceed from an awareness of *flexible pitch areas.*

In fact, "neutral" probably would best represent an *area* between major and minor where notes can be sung, rather than any specific point between them. Blues singers often waver at the third or seventh or glide from a lower to a slightly higher pitch. The lower part of the third and seventh areas tends to serve as a leading tone respectively to the tonic and fifth below, the upper part as a leading tone to the fifth and tonic above. (Evans 1982: 24)

"Pitch area" is, no doubt, an intracultural concept (though not expressed this way by blues musicians); but "deviation," i.e., from pitch units of the diatonic scale, is definitely not, at least not originally. Some blues musicians may have adopted the latter concept through acculturative processes, as they played such worried or bent notes on Western instruments (especially the piano). In such cases the worried notes might even be tension-producing. But this does not invalidate Evans's earlier statement (1978b: 424).

Here another crucial question comes up. What exactly is included by the expression "worrying the notes," for example, on a guitar by the use of certain finger techniques? Obviously, the term covers *both* the blue notes as an integral constituent of a non-Western blues scale, and various types of melisma (ornamentation). Some guitarists stretch the strings with their fingers. But which is a blue note and which is simply a "bent" note as an expression of a very melismatic style? Is Leroy Carr's vocal slide from (relative) F♯ upward into G at the start of his "Prison Bound Blues" (Vocalion 1241. Recorded in Chicago, 20 December 1928, transcription in Titon 1977: 92) evidence for the presence of a "third blue note," the flatted fifth, or is it simply an expression of his melismatic singing technique?

I have the impression that the concept of blue notes has been pushed too far in the recent literature. Traditionally, two blue notes, E♭ and B♭, were acknowledged. Then a third was added, F♯. But now it seems that there is also a "blue

A" (cf. van der Merwe 1989: 119, 127–28). Almost any note that is off-pitch from the viewpoint of the Western scale is qualified by some authors as a blue note. That stretches the concept too far, and we may end up at a point where the principle of deviation becomes paramount, any audible "deviation" from notes of the diatonic scale being called "blue."

There are several exceptional recordings by blues musicians using scalar patterns that suggest a radical departure from the diatonic scale. One is Mott Willis's guitar solo of "Riverside Blues" (recorded at Crystal Springs, Mississippi, 2 September 1970 by David Evans, discussed and transcribed in Evans 1982: 213–14). Willis plays blue notes between the major second and minor third (i.e., fluctuating around 250 cents from the tonal basis) and between major sixth and minor seventh (i.e., fluctuating around 950 cents). One could speculate whether perhaps some "memory" of an equi*pentatonic* scale from Africa might account for that. I would not categorically exclude that possibility, but equipentatonic scales are concentrated particularly in areas of Africa such as southern Uganda, from which no people were channelled into the Atlantic slave trade. An alternative assessment of Mott Willis's tune might perhaps be based on the fact that the interval distance between *his* two blue notes and the standard ones is identical: about 700 cents. So could it be a mere transposition?

Whatever may be lurking behind these uncommon pitch patterns, it is best not to widen the original concept of "blue notes" to the bursting point. The blues, not being a unitary or in any way homogeneous tradition, allows for a great number of individual styles. Here, the concept of *flexible pitch areas* is a useful antidote to the tendency in some of the recent literature to read meanings into minute pitch oscillations associated with a musical style in which melisma and microtonal fluctuations are habitual characteristics.

The concept of flexible pitch areas is also prominent in African musical cultures. Accounting for it, I coined the term "elastic scales" with reference to some tonal systems in central Africa (cf. Kubik 1970b: 18). In Zande harp music (Central African Republic) there is notable variation of the top pitch of the Zande pentatonic scale, referred to as *wili* and represented as an E in my transcriptions (cf. Kubik 1994a: 40, 101–5). Two Azande harp players I recorded, Bernard Guinahui and François Razia, who played harps tuned *in unison*, had on one particular occasion tuned those top notes at 734.5 and 711 Hertz respectively, which was $1334 - 1276 = 58$ cents apart! And they found the resultant friction comfortable (cf. Kubik 1994a: 110, and item 6 "Limbyayo" on the accompanying CD). Flattening the E even beyond a quarter tone is common with Azande harp players. Consequently, the harp patterns and singing of a musician like Raymon Zoungakpio (item 8 on the CD accompanying my book) will strike analysts as very bluesy, at least in the tuning he used on that day. On another day he could well have tuned that particular note a bit sharper, and identified it as the *same* tuning. The Azande speak a I.A.6 (Adamawa-Eastern) language and are settled in the central African savanna. Their territory is cut by the borders of Congo-Zaïre, Sudan, and Central African Republic.

Western categorizations tend to obscure the integrity of the blues singers' pitch resources and patterns. It is therefore necessary to abstract the vocal lines from their accompaniment by instruments tuned to the Western scale, and to look at the vocal lines and their tonal systems in isolation. The question of what the blue notes actually "are" can be reformulated to discover from what sort of tonal system the majority of singers in the rural blues proceed, and where that system originally could have come from.

This has been one of the tantalizing questions in blues research. But there are clues. One is that most vocal parts in the blues are either clearly pentatonic or proceed from expanded tetra-, penta-, or hexatonic frameworks, sometimes spread across the range of more than an octave, with circumstantial pitch modifications in adjustment to instrumental accompaniment. Another is the fact that the vocal lines superimposed on a guitar harmonic cycle, when it is in the three common Western chords, often circumvent those chords, most regularly avoiding the dominant, while the subdominant seems to be more acceptable. Even quite generally, the dominant chord is the least used in the standard 12-bar harmonic pattern, being found only in measure 9, sometimes in measure 10 (though usually replaced by the subdominant chord), and sometimes as a "turnaround" at the end of measure 12 to signal the coming of the next cycle. When the dominant chord does occur, it is usually "pulled" toward the subdominant (from measures 9 to 10 in the standard 12-bar form) or toward the tonic (after the "turnaround" in measure 12). In some other instances, musicians substitute for the dominant chord, as in "Two Jim Blues" by George Lewis (see Example 10) and in many recordings by Blind Lemon Jefferson, where he played a VI_7 chord at the beginning of the third line of a blues structure, followed in the next measure by a IV (subdominant) chord.

However, although musicians tend to circumvent, avoid, or quit the dominant *chord* quickly, as if it lacked oxygen, the fifth degree of the blues' tonal framework (up from the tonic) is a very important *note*, often "standing for" the dominant chord. A third clue is that all blues are based on awareness of a central tonality, a lingering basic tone to which virtually all vocal lines descend and regularly return, at least at the end of the third line. Shouldn't these be sufficient leads for musical detective work?

But if the blues really has so much in common stylistically with some of the musical cultures of the west central Sudanic belt, as discussed earlier, we should, as a next step, look at the tonal systems used in that region. According to A. M. Jones's "harmony map" (Jones 1959: 230) and the results of my own field work in some of these areas, particularly in northern Nigeria, northern and central Cameroon, the Central African Republic, and even the Republic of Sudan, most of this vast region from the Niger bend to Lake Chad, and beyond to the upper Nile River, is an area of pentatonic tonal systems. These are combined with unison singing (both in Arabic-Islamic and autochthonous styles), not excluding the occasional presence of rudimentary harmonic patterns in fourths, such as in the *batal* dance of the Chamba (northeastern Nigeria, rec. B 8599, Phonogrammarchiv Vienna/1963/Kubik). In western Nigeria, the pentatonic area extends as far south as the Ọ̀yọ̀ Yoruba; in Dahomey (Republique du Benin) and Togo it includes the Fõ, in Cameroon some "grassfield" peoples such as the Bamum, Tikar, Vute, and so on.

In the region outlined, pentatonic tonal systems are in no way uniform, however; they appear in a variety of shapes, mostly anhemitonic, i.e., without semitones and made up of major seconds and minor thirds. Most of them alternate between these two interval types within the octave layout, while others—under the impact of ornamental, melismatic styles from old contacts with North Africa—add a microtonal dimension to the pentatonic framework.

In some musical cultures of the west central Sudanic belt we find the idea of two tonal centers—a principal, basic one and a secondary one. Coolen (1982: 77) observed that that was the minimum in the *fodet* of Senegambia. The two tonal centers can be a whole tone apart, as in the Yoruba chantefable song "Baba ol'odo" (for transcription see Example 7), or they can form the interval of a fourth, with the secondary tonal center assuming a kind of subdominant flavor (e.g., the Tikar woman's grinding song, transcription in Example 8).

In the most western geographical Sudan (Senegambia, Mali, Guinea, etc.), we also often encounter heptatonic tuning systems with up to four shifts in the bichord progressions, such as, for example, in the music for bridge-harps (cf. Knight 1971, 1978; King 1972; recordings of *kora* player Sadjo Djolo from Guinea-Bissau, 18 May 1983, Orig. Tape A 175/Kachamba/Kubik, Museum für Völkerkunde, Berlin).

Contrasting with these musical cultures, some of the more eastern areas of the geographical Sudan display pentatonic traditions, often over a *single* tonal center that can be objectified as a persistent bourdon-like tone to which the musician and his voice constantly return (e.g., Meigogué, the Hausa *gogé* player—see above). This combination (of a pentatonic scale and bourdon-like center) contains for us important hints as to the remote history of the blues' tonality, because the blues—if abstracted from the Western-style chord accompaniment—also displays it in many of its manifestations. There is much to suggest that some of the early blues were based on a continuous bourdon-like tonal center without any notion of change between tonal steps, without any so-called "root progressions" to use John Blacking's term (Blacking 1959: 21). (See also transcriptions and videos compiled by Stefan Grossman, 1969, 1994.) Some early artists who sometimes performed pieces without progression between "degrees" were Charley Patton (Evans 1987b; Fahey 1970; Calt and Wardlow 1988), Robert Wilkins, Barbecue Bob, and Leadbelly.

For this reason I am reluctant to associate the remote origins of the blues with those stringed instrument traditions of the westernmost parts of Africa (Senegambia, etc.) where up to four tonality shifts can occur within a cycle. Some blues may have incorporated just one such shift, between the basic tonal center and a secondary center, a fifth downward (respectively, a fourth upward).

Tonal systems promoting the awareness of a basic tonal reference note are always indicative of a remote origin in the selective use of harmonics over a *single* fundamental. By contrast, where they include the idea of harmonic shift, tonal systems are often derived from the use of at least *two* fundamentals, such as are obtained on a mouthbow whose string is braced or stopped with a finger or stick (see my examples in an earlier chapter, figs. 10a, c, and e). This is the background to many of the harmonic structures found in the music of Gabon, Congo, Angola, and South Africa. There may also be retentions of this experience in some forms of the blues.

To understand harmonics-derived tonal systems—and they are abundant in Africa—it must be remembered that the notes of the natural harmonic series do not exactly correspond with the pitch values of the 12-note Western tempered scale. The B♭ of the natural harmonic series is 31 cents flat (969 cents), if compared with the tempered B♭ of 1,000 cents, and the E (386 cents) is 14 cents flat. The 11th partial at 551 cents is exactly halfway between a Western F and an F sharp. These are very audible differences (fig. 12).

FIGURE 12. The natural harmonic series from partial 4 to 11.

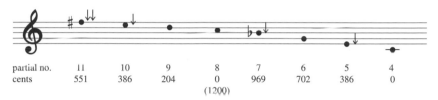

partial no.	11	10	9	8	7	6	5	4
cents	551	386	204	0 (1200)	969	702	386	0

The inspiration for harmonics-based African tonal systems, however, need not necessarily come from instruments, such as experiments with the stretched string of a hunting bow (like that of the Bushmen of southern Africa). It can also come simply from the formants of human speech. It is vowel formation that provides the key to understanding human discovery of speech-derived harmonics. A vowel is a *voiced* sound in which the air passes freely through the mouth or (in nasalization) through the nose. The difference between vowels is created by different shaping of the mouth as a resonance chamber, altered by movements of the tongue and shaping of the lips. Thus, each vowel has its own particular sound spectrum, it is defined as a difference in the selective reinforcement of harmonics; i.e., the vowel [a] differs from [u] by its harmonics, if sung to the same pitch. In Africa, not only multipart singing styles, but also *unison singing* can be based on scalar patterns generated by representations of speech-derived partials (harmonics) over a single fundamental.

Proceeding from this knowledge, I have developed a simple theory of the blues and about how scalar patterns from the west central Sudanic belt were perpetuated in the blues. First, the remote origin of these scales must be sought in speech. They do not derive from experimentation with instruments. Next, if such tonal systems are inspired by partials over a single fundamental, these partials must fall into the comfortable middle range of the natural harmonic series. Both postulates have the advantage also of explaining the presence of a single tonal center in many of the Sudanic styles *and* in the blues, since all partials-based tones sung by the performer reinforce the idea of their fundamental, and thereby the tonal center. The C in a blues written in the key of C, therefore, represents the fundamental of a harmonics-derived scale.

Pentatonic scales can arise from a number of primary human experiences, such as the transference of the interval of a fifth (originally also inspired by harmonics) through acoustic space, leading to a F-C-G-D-A chain. But some scales simply arise from the melodic use of a selection of the harmonic series that incorporates intervals neither too disjunct nor too narrow. The ideal harmonics-based pentatonic system over a single fundamental incorporates tones representing partials 4 to 9. Characteristically, it extends beyond the scope of a single octave, with its lower component forming a tetratonic pattern. From bottom to top the scale goes like this: C (0 cents)—E↓ (386 cents)—G (702 cents)–B↓♭ (969 cents)—C (1200 cents)—D (1200 + 204 cents) (see also fig. 12). This scale, if sung in descending order, sounds stunningly blues-like, though this is hardly the whole story.

Of course, there can be combinations of several of the basic scale-generating principles, because of age-old contacts between people. My theory then must also explain, in the present context, why pitch ambivalence occurs regularly at certain points of the blues scale. It is the lower blue note, between E and E♭, that seems to fluctuate the most, while the upper blue note (B♭), even if it is attained with a gliss, is intoned more firmly.

Something that is so trivial as to be hardly ever mentioned is the fact that men and women, boys and girls, mothers and children in a homogeneous community normally speak the same language. On different occasions they may, therefore, use the very same sentences with identical tonal inflections, but *each at their own voice level*. In many African cultures this idea is expressed in the designations given to the members of an instrumental set, or to playing areas on one and the same instrument, representing ranges of the human voice. These ranges are conceptualized as diverging by an interval of an octave (e.g., mother versus child; also sometimes mother versus father) or by a fourth or fifth (men versus women in general, boys versus girls, etc.). Azande musicians, for example, distinguish on their *kponingbo* log xylophones a tonal range called *ba-kponingbo* (father-xylophone) from another, higher range, called *na-kponingbo* (mother-xylophone). The two cheeks of their slit drums (*guru*) are called *nina* (mother) and *buba* (father) respectively (cf. Kubik 1994a: 106–8). In Fõ culture of Dahomey and Togo, the Guinea-type double-bell consisting of a big bell and a small one attached to it, is called *gakpāvi* (*ga* = metal, *kpā* = carry, *vi* = child), i.e., the metal carrying its child on the back, like a mother carrying her child (cf. Kubik 1989a). Yoruba musicians of southwestern Nigeria, Dahomey, and in the New World (Ortiz 1955; Pinto 1991: 181, 186, 207) cultivate the concept of a mother drum (*iya ilu*) within their *bàtá* and *dùndún* sets (the latter only in Africa, having not reached New World cultures until very recently, because they were introduced in Yoruba society only from the mid-nineteenth century on). Here the "mother" is not an oppositional category, but part of a hierarchical order of mother and "offspring." Among the -Nsenga of Zambia, one row of notes on a *kankobele* lamellophone represents boys, while another row represents girls. Each boy, says Marjorie Davidson (1970: 104), goes together with one girl. Characteristically, the sonic distance between the two is either a fourth or a fifth (cf. Kubik 1994a: 233–35). From the Mpyɛmɔ, settled in the southwestern corner of the Central African Republic, Maurice Djenda (1996: 13) reports the distinctions *mɔntumɔ* (child drum) and *nyaŋgɔ ntumɔ* (mother drum) for two drums of different size and tuning that are played together, the first with a "small" voice like a child, the other with a "big" voice like its mother. From African-American cultures we have a formidable testimony as to the retention of such concepts in a statement by New Orleans jazz drummer Baby Dodds reporting about the early drumming lessons he took from Walter Brundy:

He used to play with Robichaux and was a very good drummer. He was a reading drummer and that's what I wanted to learn—to read music. . . . Brundy taught me the fundamentals of reading music and I found out that everything I had been doing was wrong. He taught me that the right hand was "mammy" and the left "daddy," and I soon learned how to get my two hands working differently. This was, of course, after I mastered having both hands do the same thing. (Dodds 1992: 7–8)

Oppositional pairs such as father/mother, boys/girls, male/female, men/ women, and mother/child are regularly projected to express a dichotomy between higher and lower voice ranges. In some sub-Saharan musical cultures, sounds are even conceptualized as functional units within a larger set of consan-

guine or affinal family relationships (cf. Ngumu 1975–76 for xylophone terminology in southern Cameroon; and Malamusi 1992 for panpipe taxonomy in
Mozambique).

For now I will cite and discuss only one more example. It comes from within
the west central Sudanic belt, from an area understood as important for the
remote background of the blues. In November 1963, at Kontcha in the Adamawa
mountains on the northern Cameroon/northeastern Nigeria border, I recorded
two Kutin musicians playing two double bells (*toŋ ito*) in interlocking style.
The Kutin, like their neighbors, the Chamba and the mountain dwellers called
Zanganyi, are millet agriculturalists within what has been called the Ancient
Nigritic peoples (cf. Hirschberg 1988: 21). In the nineteenth century their home-
steads were raided by slave traders, and they were also subjugated by the Ful6e,
under whose Lamido (ruler) they have lived to this day in a state of virtual
serfdom. Each of the two players I recorded, Gonga Sarki Birgui and Hamadjam—observe their names in Fulfulde!—held his iron double-bell by its stem-
grip with the left hand, the bells' orifices directed toward his stomach (cf.
Kubik 1989a: 86–87). In his right hand each held one stick to strike the bells in
alternation.

The double-bells were both tuned at the interval of approximately a fourth.
Toŋ deni had the deeper voice, while *toŋ senwa* had the higher one. The task of
the higher bells was to provide a basic alternating-pitch beat, while the lower
ones were used to play interlocking variations. My measurements with a Korg
WT-12 tuner ascertained only rough fourths for the sound intervals within each
double-bell. But the musicians' tuning idea was unambiguous. The higher tone
of the *toŋ senwa* and the lower tone of the *toŋ deni* were meant to form the
interval of an octave (at 1,210 cents in my measurement), and each of them had
a "companion"—a fourth up or down. Bells are difficult to tune, and the mea-
suring apparatus is also confused by their rich overtone spectra. We do not
know how old these bells were. But the original blacksmith's intentions were
clear, and we can therefore present the bells' tunings as shown in Figure 13 (in
relative notation).

Remarkably, this is the pitch skeleton of "stable" tones Alfons M. Dauer
had postulated as underlying the pentatonic blues scale. It is also the tonal
scaffolding of the Tikar woman's grinding song (cf. transcription in Example 8,
this volume). But there is more to it. The two musicians (cf. rec. B 8910 and

Photo 23. The Kutin musicians, Gonga Sarki Birgui and Hamadjam, playing their two double-bells (*toŋ ito*). The four tones constitute a framework of "root," "fourth," "fifth," and "octave," considered by some researchers to form the scaffolding of stable "main tones" of the pentatonic blues scale (cf. fig. 13). At Kontcha, Adamawa mountains, northern Cameroon, November 1963. (Photo: Author)

8920, Phonogrammarchiv Vienna/1963 Kubik) also created timbre melodies by modifying the distance of the bells' orifices from their stomach. It is not easy to determine by ear which partials are thereby reinforced, nor would spectrograms be very conclusive. But even lower partials would give additional "shades" to each note.

Clearly the tuning of the two Kutin double-bells is not inspired by any intrinsic acoustic qualities of the bells themselves, but it is a projection of a tonal scaffolding associated in Kutin music with vocal ranges—i.e., the black-

FIGURE 13. Tuning of the Kutin double-bells *toŋ ito*.

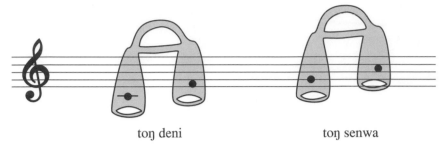

toŋ deni   toŋ senwa

smith tuned the bells so that the relationship between the central areas of adjoining voices, possibly male and female, would be reflected. Both ranges are conceptualized as identical, but each with a different tonal center. The tonal center of the voice represented by *toŋ deni* is written here as F, that of the *toŋ senwa* as C. The dependent tones derive from the third partials of the natural harmonic series, over fundamental F and fundamental C.

West central Sudanic concepts about gender (prior to Arabic influences) are based on analogy and internal identity. In music this is expressed by analogy between pitch ranges; for example, the tunings of the two Kutin double-bells are thought to be in identical intervals, but at different pitch levels. These pitch levels are not arbitrary, but a fifth apart, creating an octave frame between the highest and the lowest note of the four individual bells together.

Through overtone shading such a scaffolding can be expanded. If a scalar melody formed by *three* adjoining tones within the frame of a fourth, resulting in the descending melodic sequence C → B♭ → G, is sung by a woman, what will happen if a man wants to pick it up? As much as the lower Kutin double-bell is analogous to the higher one, so will a man imitate the melody at a lower level, according to the range of his voice; but he (like the woman) will also relate the pattern to the fundamental suggested by his own voice. That means that the melodic pattern will be composed of identical partials within his *own* voice portrait. Most comfortably, he might relate the pattern to a fundamental that is a fifth lower than that of the woman's voice, i.e., he might sing F → E♭ → C (descending) over a fundamental F, with the advantage that the two melodies will be connected in one common tone, C (which is the woman's fundamental), like the Cs on the two Kutin bells forming an octave.

Thus, if any scalar melody based on partials over a single fundamental is

"Female range"
partials-based scalar pattern
(over hidden fundamental C)

represents partial no.	8	7	6
speech-tones:	high	med	low

is transposed to "Male range"
(over hidden fundamental F)

represents partial no.	8	7	6
speech-tones:	high	med	low

transposed, maintaining not only its interval structure but also its implicated reference to a root (fundamental), the most likely transposition will be a fifth down (fig. 14a and b). Once established, this pattern can also be inverted: a fourth up gives the same tonal relationship.

Much solo vocal music from the west central Sudan can be described as based on a pentatonic scalar framework combining two identical harmonics-based tritone sections a fifth apart (at different octaves), sharing in one note

The Blues Tonal System

and thereby reinforcing the upper section's fundamental. Each section by itself also represents three speech-tone levels: high, mid, low. The upper section conforms to the voice level of a woman, the lower to that of a man (fig. 14a and b). The relationship can be reversed, "female" becoming male and "male" becoming female, resulting in a pattern in which the two scalar sections overlap: F—Eb—C—Bb—G. Each can also be expanded up by one more step in the harmonic series to include a tone representing partial 9 (fig. 15).

FIGURE 15. Integration of the three–note scalar pattern in Fig. 14a–b and expansion to include a note representing partial 9:

Cents:	204	0	969	702			
representing partial no.	9	8	7	6			

"Female" range over fundamental C

				204	0	969	702
				9	8	7	6

"Male" range over fundamental F

How the early millet agriculturalists in the Sudanic belt could have arrived at oppositional pairs in association with pitch ranges is, of course, an intriguing question. Marcel Griaule (1954), Griaule and Dieterlen (1950), and more recently Junzo Kawada (1982, 1997) have given some thought to the sound universe of the west African savanna peoples, especially the Dogon and various Mande-speaking groups, and how sound is related to mythology and to general cultural patterns. To follow this up in detail would go beyond the scope of this book. But pursuing our specific issues, we can now conclude that if in this broad Sudanic region any melodic patterns as shown in figure 14a appear in combination with a periodic return of the melodic lines to a sort of ground note or tonic C, then these three pitches cannot but represent a fundamental's eighth (at 1,200 cents), seventh (at 969 cents), and sixth (at 702 cents) partials. The Tikar woman's grinding song (see Example 8) shows such a melodic pattern in several places, and from the blues tradition there is also no lack of examples (cf. Titon 1977—specifically p. 67, "Dead Drunk Blues" by Lilian Miller; p. 97 and Example 11 below, "Mean Conductor Blues" by Ed Bell; p. 122, "Fo' Day Blues" by Peg Leg Howell; etc.). If, in addition, the three-note descending melodic pattern C—B↓♭—G (fig. 14a) also appears in transposition within the same song, as it does in some blues, we can assume that in such a case the system has begun to include a second fundamental functioning as a secondary tonal center (fig. 14b).

The reason for the vocal use of middle-range harmonics, rather than high-range partials (beyond partial 9), to form such melodic patterns is obviously connected with the sound spectrum of human speech and the tonality of the various languages spoken in west Africa. The good use of the set of three tones extrapolating the eighth, seventh, and sixth harmonics is that they are the minimal interval sizes accommodating speech-tone representation: high-mid-low in a tone language. As mentioned earlier, Dauer suspected as early as the 1950s that the "blue notes" conform with the mid-tones in speech patterns of west African tone languages (Dauer 1955: V.6). He had languages of the I.A.4 (Kwa) family in mind, but I.A.3 (Voltaic) and I.A.6 (Adamawa-Eastern) languages are also reasonable candidates.

While my illustrations (fig. 14a and b) suggest that some scalar patterns in the west central Sudan and in many blues are simply compounded of a three-note series (C—B↓♭—G) and its own transposition a fifth downward, each composed of three pitches, high, mid, and low as in a tone language, there are more subtleties to it. By singing the same pattern at different speech levels, the imaginary woman and her male partner in our scheme cannot avoid also becoming aware of the additional harmonics belonging to each fundamental. They swing along in the back of the mind, coloring the perception of the patterns actually sung. They include especially partials 5 and 9, besides 2, 3, and 4 up from the fundamental (fig. 16a and b).

Here we must remember again that the pitch values of harmonics-based tonal systems are (in part) very different from those of the 12-note Western tempered scale (cf. fig. 12 above). Therefore we cannot take the notes at their written face values; rather, we must observe their true pitch values expressed in cents. Once

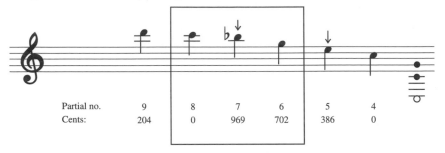

Partial no.	9	8	7	6	5	4
Cents:	204	0	969	702	386	0

"Male range" partials-based scalar pattern as in fig. 14b, with background interference
by other partials:

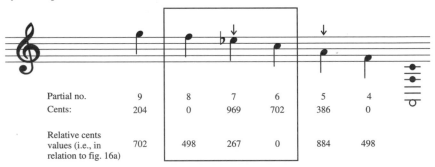

Partial no.	9	8	7	6	5	4
Cents:	204	0	969	702	386	0
Relative cents values (i.e., in relation to fig. 16a)	702	498	267	0	884	498

we have stayed clear of this trap, we can make an experiment. We blend and
integrate the two harmonics-based scales over fundamentals C and F as shown
in figs. 16a and b, and the surprising result is a combined model that encom-
passes the melodic repertoire of the blues (fig. 17).

Where this scale conflicts with the European scale can be seen by comparing
its cents values with those of the Western tempered scalar system: 0, 100, 200,
. . . up to 1,200 (octave). And since our merger model incorporates *eight* different
pitch values (without being "octatonic"), the Western diatonic scale only seven,
it is easy to reconstruct where they must have clashed. In culture contact, the
386- and 267-cents pitches were bound to mark off a *pitch area* assuming a vague
quality of "thirdness" in response to the Western scale. The nearest values in
the Western scale, i.e., major and minor third (at 400 and 300 cents), were
reinterpreted in that sense. One might think that the 267-cents value would have

FIGURE 17. Integrated model: melodic repertoire of the blues.

Cents values: 204   0   969   702   498   386   267   0   884   702   498

been more easily absorbed by and equated with the D, the second degree of the Western scale. But that could not have taken place for audiopsychological reasons. In the integrated model the D represents first of all the ninth partial over fundamental C. Even if it is transposed an octave downward, it is already "engaged," because it is one of the four tones—C, F, G, and D—that link the Western and the blues scale by congruence. Their cents values are compatible. It is also important to understand that the E 300 and E-267 pitch values constitute a frame. They are marginal values. The blue note will fluctuate with more frequency in the middle area between these two borderline values. This corresponds with the listeners' auditory impression that this blue note tends to range between 300 and 370 cents. A blue note below the "minor third" (300 cents) is found in the blues, but it is rare. The fact that the 267-cents value is just 63 cents from an octave-transposed D (at 204 cents—see fig. 18) may also have contributed to the fact that at least over the tonic chord singers avoid that threshold.

From Figure 18, we can deduce that if our west central Sudanic integrative model is projected upon the Western diatonic scale, the two spots where the ear will perceive the greatest difference are at -131 cents in the upper area (B♭) and -14 to -133 cents (fluctuating between the two values) in the lower area. These are the blue notes, and these are the closest rational values we can get for defining them. All the other notes in the two scales are close enough to each other to give an impression of identity.

My hypothesis about the origin of the blue notes, therefore, postulates that *many blues singers operate from a mental template (pitch memory) blending a pentatonic scale based on partials 4 to 9 with its own transposition a fifth lower. The resultant interference pattern functions as an overall framework for pitch perception in the blues,* with a central tonal reference note (tonic) representing the fundamental of the basic scale (C)

FIGURE 18. Integrated west-central Sudanic scalar model generating the blues' melodic repertoire (notes of fig 17 compressed into the range of one octave):

(Cents values of the blues' scalar pattern)

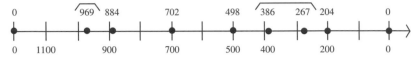

(Cents values of the western heptatonic scale in C major)

Differences between the two scales expressed in cents:

C	B		A		G		F	E	E	D		C
0	-131		-16		+2		-2	-14	-133	+4		0

and a secondary tonal center (F). This blues scale conflicts with the Western diatonic scale and its chords particularly in two places. It also conflicts with Western functional harmony in that the dominant chord is predictably the most difficult to accommodate in the blues, while the subdominant chord can be reinterpreted as a shift from the basic tonal center on C to the secondary tonal center on F.

In some parts of the eastern half of the west central Sudan *and* in the blues, vocalists proceed from an identical speech-based mental template that integrates two representations of the natural harmonic series (up to partial 9) at the distance of a fifth (702 cents) from each other (cf. the Kutin double-bell instrumentalization of the vocal ranges, shown in fig. 13). This can be compared to the blending of the voice ranges of a woman and a man, with the resultant interference pattern. It can also be visualized by two clock-faces turned against each other so that zero of one clock-face conforms with 702 on the other.

When such pitch memory is projected upon the Western diatonic scale, the two systems will be brought into alignment by the ear at points where they are congruent, the fundamental and the lower-partial derived degrees: fourth, fifth, and so on. Divergences will be perceived particularly in two places: at the B↓♭ of 969 cents, and the clustered E↓/E↓♭ pitch area fluctuating between 386 and 267 cents. The higher so-called blue note (B♭ 969 cents) will not pose any particular problem of accommodation within the Western scale, because it is close enough to that scale's own tempered B flat of 1,000 cents. Although a long way from C (at 1,200 cents), the blue note B↓♭ of 969 cents could not, therefore,

FIGURE 19. Mental template on which both west-central Sudanic tonal ideas and blues tonality appear to be based:

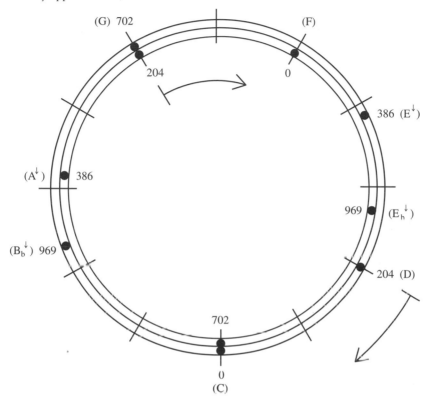

The number o indicates the system's two central reference points, C for the "female" series, F for the "male" series. From these tonal centers harmonics from partial 9 down to 4 are represented in counter clockwise order: 204 (partial 9), o (partial 8), 969 (partial 7), 702 (partial 6), 386 (partial 5) and o Cents (partial 4). The C-based series is represented by dots within the outer lane of the circular diagram, the F-based series by dots within the inner lane.

have created the need for a gap-filling intervening note during the process of encounter with the Western diatonic framework. But there is another, even more fundamental reason inhibiting pitch expansion. In all the scalar mental templates that we know from sub-Saharan Africa, the maximum number of notes within one octave is *seven*. This is one of the most resilient culture traits in the African and African-American culture worlds. New World reinterpretations of the Western diatonic or chromatic scales by people of African descent therefore tend to *restate* the penta-, hexa-, or heptatonic schemes of their former African home cultures. For example, in their encounter with the tempered Western scale incorporating twelve tones, the Africans in the New World reacted by *reinforcing the African pitch area concept*; e.g., two neighboring notes of the Western chromatic scale (as laid out, for example, on the piano) can at any time be compounded to form a pitch area, thereby preserving the penta-, hexa-, or heptatonic scalar templates inherited from Africa. Pitches that are equated within one of these pitch areas can also be substituted for each other. Such practice began with the development of the so-called "barbershop" harmony and the banjo chord sequences accompanying New Orleans jazz blues, such as: C C C C₇ / F Fₘ C A₇ / D₇ G₇ C C. Characteristically, the wind instruments often neglect them (cf. clarinetist George Lewis's phrases in "Two Jim Blues," Example 10, with a melodic C over the A₇ chord and a melodic F over D₇). The simultaneous use of notes within a pitch area is not felt as "dissonant." The underlying aesthetics continued through jazz history, reaching its culmination in bebop. Substitution chords in jazz often exist by virtue of the pitch area concept, historically one of the most decisive reinterpretive auditory reactions by people of African descent to the Western tonal system.

Thus, while the 969 cents blue note finds reasonable accommodation within the Western tonal system by equating it with the B♭ of the tempered scale (1,000 cents), the lower blue note tends to fluctuate (be "worried") considerably, because the Africa-derived mental template (figs. 18 and 19) allows for a 119-cents margin between *two different pitch values perceived by the singers as variants of one and the same toneme*. This explains why the lower blue note can fluctuate anywhere between the two values indicated, and why singers express this ambiguity by crossing that distance using glissando, wavy intonation, and so forth.

My model explains the following cognitional characteristics of blues tonality and audience reactions:

1. the pitch positions of the two blue notes in relation to the stable notes, i.e., why the blue notes are in precisely the locations they are along the scale.
2. why in many blues accompanied with Western chords, the progression from tonic to subdominant is taken with ease, but the dominant is often avoided, circumscribed, or totally neglected.
3. why the blue notes diverge from Western pitch expectations.
4. why in the blues there is a powerful central reference tone, a tonic or key-note

on which the last melodic text-line always ends. This trait is so universal that we find in Titon's (1977) transcriptions of forty-seven blues only two (nos. 9 and 43) that do not end on C (in relative notation). During the statement and repeated statement lines of the blues (i.e., the first two lines), the vocal parts may end somewhat more frequently on notes other than the tonic, especially on the third, fifth, or flat seventh—all parts of the tonic fundamental's overtone structure.

The scheme laid out in Figures 14–19 is theoretical, with the aim of reconstructing a possible evolutionary sequence. At the moment I am inclined to assume that the final step (so far) in that sequence was taken not in the west central Sudan, but in the southern United States. That a pentatonic scalar framework based on partials 4 to 9 began to be transposed regularly a fifth down (or conversely a fourth up) in one and the same song can be understood as an African-American innovation. In the west central Sudanic belt there are songs showing tendencies toward *transpositional shift*, but the secondary tonal center (on F) remains ancillary.

Here it is important to realize that we are dealing with depth structures. A mental template determining a scalar framework is not a song melody. Although blues melodies, vocal and/or instrumental, are sometimes transposed in part, the presence of a strong central reference tone acts as a counterforce tending to prevent it. Characteristically, the closest manifestation in actual sound of the idea of scalar transposition in the blues is the ubiquitous piano boogie-woogie walking bass line. That is where the structure in one or the other modifications comes to the surface.

Structure implies convertibility. I have explained above in theoretical terms that in the west central Sudanic context a pentatonic scalar framework is transposed down a fifth, from a "female" voice range to a "male" voice range. I also said that the pattern can be inverted and seen as transposed up a fourth from a "male" range to a "female" range. For this reason it is not surprising that the actual impression given by most blues is of transposition up a fourth, when the harmonic framework moves from tonic to subdominant. And the boogie-woogie bass line also usually moves upward a fourth, suggesting "male" to "female," rather than "female" to "male."

My integrated scalar model may have existed as a mental template in areas of the west central Sudan in the eighteenth century, but the particular expressions it assumed later are American. How and why this process occurred is open to speculation. One obvious possibility is that acquaintance with the Western concepts of tonic and subdominant and the use of Western instruments were the catalyst for this transposing idea. The African Americans' reactions were selective. Scalar templates based on the awareness of *two* tonal centers a fifth apart (in inversion, a fourth), brought along from the west central Sudan and other parts of Africa, eventually prevailed under the new stimuli. The tonal universe of the ancestors of the Kutin, Tikar, and other peoples of the west central Sudan was reinterpreted in the southern United States as a tonic/subdominant contrastive pair.

In the blues, men and women rarely sing together, except in certain early professional vaudeville teams. Therefore, it became the task of the solo blues singer (irrespective of gender) to express both scalar ranges reminiscent of the west central Sudanic dichotomy. This could even be one reason why there are *two* statements of the same textual line in the AAB blues, the genre's most common stanza form—the first statement at what might have represented the "female" scalar level, the second, repeated statement at the "male" level, or vice versa. Of course, it is very difficult to *prove* anything that is probably unconscious. But this would explain why certain tonal-melodic ideas inherited from the west central Sudan underwent the transformation they did in the southern United States. Conversely, no such development could have taken place in the west central Sudanic belt at the time in question, because any comparable acculturative stimulus was lacking.

There is ample evidence that the idea of melodic and/or scalar transposition as such by a fourth or fifth is common in Africa, and that it implies simultaneously the concepts of analogy and contrast. Harp tunings among the Azande can be transposed by a fourth downward, with some notes octave-displaced to retain the original pitch range in the transposition (cf. Kubik 1994a: 127–28). From further west there is more evidence. In some àló story songs I collected among the Ọ̀yọ̀ Yoruba of southwestern Nigeria, the melody of the chorus part alternates between two pitch levels that are a fifth apart, without any changes of text. In one song, "Ol'ọkọ́ d'èhìn" (Hoe seller go back), the chorus reacted to a change in the final tone of the leader's phrase by transposing its own phrase a fifth upward (cf. transcription in Kubik 1989b: 144–45). Other examples from my unpublished collection include the songs "Olómurọ̀rọ̀," "Jojoloro," "Oniràwé ma gbọna," and "Olu sin ma sin!" In all these cases, identical chorus text-lines within one and the same song were melodically transposed a fifth upward.

An ancient distribution area of such ideas seems to expand all across the west central Sudan, even as far as the Great Lakes Region of East Africa. From Buganda (Uganda) we have intracultural evidence for the existence of a concept of two analogous scales thought to stand a fourth apart. The tonal system in the ancient kingdom of Buganda was equi*penta*tonic, i.e., it had a standard interval of ca. 240 cents and fourths of 480 cents. Joseph Kyagambiddwa (1955: 20) informed us that in Buganda's court music this tonal framework was thought to embrace two oppositional ranges: *olutaamba olwa wansi* (the lower scale) and *olutaamba olwa waggulu* (the higher scale). A song would stand in one or the other. The two levels were a Kiganda fourth (i.e., ca. 480 cents) apart.

We do not know whether Kyagambiddwa's contrastive pair represents any remote historical influence upon Buganda from Nilotic musical cultures, but further east, among the peoples living in the vicinity of the Luo of Kenya (speakers of a II.E.1 Eastern Sudanic language), this seems to be the case; also among the Luhya and -Kuria who speak Bantu languages.

10 - The "Flatted Fifth"

There are many unusual scalar patterns in the blues, and some could perpetuate tonal concepts found in regions of Africa outside the west central Sudanic belt. One of the issues to be accounted for in any study of the origin of the blue notes is the so-called "flatted fifth" (cf. Schuller 1968: 51–52). It was only recognized as a blue note in the 1940s, but there is no doubt that it existed in some of the "early downhome blues" (cf. Niles 1949).

The flatted fifth is not part of my merger model. Does it represent a different strand in the blues tradition? After all, the two other blue notes are characteristic of the melodic repertoire in almost any blues that has been recorded, while the flatted fifth appears sporadically, e.g., in Bessie Smith, Ed Bell, John Lee Hooker, and others. It could even be that it became more common in the blues during the 1940s, after it had assumed a prominent position in bebop, a development which could have reflected back to blues singers such as John Lee Hooker.

Nevertheless, the flatted fifth, especially when used as a *starting note in descending phrases* (such as by Bessie Smith), or resolved downward in various other contexts, is to be considered a distinctive pitch value. Its melodic position within the singer's scalar pattern (disregarding the instrumental accompaniment) probably contains the clue for its genesis. The flatted fifth in the blues most often occurs as part of a *descending phrase*. In an *ascending phrase* sometimes the same singer would intonate a perfect fourth. This can be observed, for example, in Blind Lemon Jefferson's "See that My Grave Is Kept Clean." To me this suggests that the flatted fifth must be part of a descending scalar framework, blues scale, or whatever one might call it, while the movement upward from the basic tonal center to a perfect fourth is of a totally different nature, namely a progression *between tonal levels* and not between scalar steps. This would confirm what I have

Example 11

Ed Bell (vocal and guitar), "Mean Conductor Blues," Paramount 12546, Chicago, September 1927. Reissued on Document DOCD-5090, *Ed Bell (Barefoot Bill, Sluefoot Joe) (1927-1930)*. Bell plays the guitar in standard tuning, E position, but the actual sound is in the key of F♯, probably as the result of using a capotasta on the second fret. The piece has been transposed downward to the relative key of C in this transcription. Transcribed by David Evans.

1. That same train, same engineer;
   That same train, same engineer;
   Took my woman 'way, Lord, left me standin' here.
2. My stroller caught a passenger; I caught the mamlish blinds.
   My stroller caught a passenger; I caught the mamlish blinds.
   Hey, you can't quit me; ain't no need of tryin'.
3. Hey, Mister Conductor, let a broke man ride your blinds.
   Hey, Mister Conductor, let a broke man ride your blinds.
   "You better buy your ticket; know this train ain't mine."
4. I just want to blind it far as Hagerstown.
   Yeah, I just want to blind it far as Hagerstown.
   When she blow for the crossing, I'm gon' ease it down.
5. I pray to the Lord that Southern train would wreck.
   I pray to the Lord that Southern train would wreck.
   Yes, it kill that fireman, break that engineer's neck.
6. I'm standin' here looking up at the risin' sun.
   I'm standin' here looking up at the risin' sun.
   [If] Some train don't run, gon' be some walkin' done.

stroller—a rambler; in this case, the singer's woman.

passenger—a passenger train.

mamlish—an intensifying adjective of unknown etymology, having a meaning somewhat
   like "doggone."

blinds—the front of a railroad freight car; used in stanza 4 as a verb for hoboing.

Hagerstown—a town in western Maryland and important railroad junction, far from Bell's
   Alabama home.

Southern—name of a railroad line.

outlined above about a fundamental and a secondary tonal center in the blues.
The flatted fifth, however, does sometimes occur as part of an *ascending* phrase.
As a possible explanation of one such type of occurrence, David Evans has
proposed that the flatted fifth can function as "the blue note of the blue note"
(i.e., the third of the third). It seems John Lee Hooker often plays it this way,
moving from tonic to blue third and to blue fifth, as for example in his "Hobo
Blues" (Modern 20-663, rec. 18 February 1949) (D. Evans, personal communication, 25 June 1997).

Blue notes over roots other than the tonic *are* a reality. If Levester "Big
Lucky" Carter (b. 1920), in his song "Don't Be a Fool" (item 10, H.F. CD-005,
The Spirit Lives On, Hot Fox), raises his voice up to (relative) B♭ in measure 10,
then that is the "lower blue note" transposed up to an implicit "dominant" G
relationship.

Contrary to its name, the flatted fifth is not a flat fifth. It is an independent component of scalar patterns found in the blues. In the blues, G and the pitch area embracing ± F♯ are separate tonemes. This is obvious, for example, in the vocal part of Alabama bluesman Ed Bell's "Mean Conductor Blues."

The overall melodic vocal patterns in "Mean Conductor Blues" are pentatonic. Most striking is the fact that the intonation of the F♯ actually oscillates between this pitch value and F. From this behavior I conclude that F♯ and F are one and the same toneme in this singer's scalar panel. There is no need to distinguish gradations of a scale degree as separate notes.

From Ed Bell's "Mean Conductor Blues" I extract the pentatonic scalar pattern shown in Figure 20. Confirmation that this is indeed an independent scalar pattern comes from the fact that it remains unaffected by the guitar accompaniment. Although the melodic order of the notes is changed, as a scalar pattern it is maintained throughout the three text-lines of this blues.

FIGURE 20. Pentatonic scalar pattern in Ed Bell's "Mean Conductor Blues":

Ed Bell's guitar accompaniment in "Mean Conductor Blues" is a repeated cycle involving the tones C, E, F, G, and even D and A (absent in the vocal part). It contains *no* blue notes, and—characteristically—no changes into subdominant or dominant modes. Bell's riff-based guitar playing is merely a convenient sound background to a vocal melodic line that is virtually unrelated to it, except that both are connected by the keynote C.

What exactly is the tonal framework combining voice and guitar? Certainly, it is *no* merger scale. The clue to its structure lies in the oscillating quality of the F♯/F compound; the singer seems to aim at a value *between the two*. Such a value exists in African music. Tolia Nikiprowetzky (n.d.: 20) notates a flatted fifth in some Mauritanian modes that are based on Arabic antecedents. However, he does not explain its *systemic* function and exact cents values. In another area of millennium-old contacts between African and Arabic/Islamic cultures, northern Mozambique—off Kilwa Kisiwani and Mozambique Island—the flatted fifth also occurs as a melodic interval, for example in *takare* fiddle music. Interestingly, it appears in conjunction with another Asian import: the bourdon. This style is also shared by music played on the *sese* flat-bar zither, and it has radiated into other instrumental realms. In 1962, when researching xylophone traditions in northern Mozambique, I was startled by *mangwilo* log xylophone pieces all based on a persistent bourdon produced by two players sitting opposite each other and interlocking the same note with one of their hands. With the other they threw in chordal patterns, which to my surprise could be in any combination of notes on the xylophone, all sounding consonant. There was clearly one fundamental for the whole sound panorama. I then came to the conclusion that "the notes of the Mangwilo come very close to the location of some of the remoter upper partials of the natural harmonic series." I identified the six notes of one *mangwilo* I recorded as possibly representing partials 8, 9, 10, 11, 13, and 15 (Kubik 1965: 39). I have since restudied xylophone traditions in the area, reconfirming my analysis that their tunings are indeed based on the selective use of higher partials, although I now have doubts about the 13th and 15th. The 11th partial is definitely aimed at, and also represented in *vocal* music. Old-time songs of the Wakisi fishermen at Lake Nyasa in Tanzania include harmonic patterns incorporating a pitch that represents the 11th partial (recordings Kubik "Uyile" by two -Kisi girls, B 4851, April 1960, and *malimba* lamellophone played by Laurenti, B 7420, 1962/Hillegeist/Kubik, Phonogrammarchiv Vienna).

The 11th partial of the natural harmonic series is at 551 cents, just halfway between F and F♯ of the Western tempered scale. Seen from this angle, the five notes of Ed Bell's vocal scale in "Mean Conductor Blues" can be explained as representing the sector of the natural harmonic series shown in Figure 21.

The implications—theoretical, typological and historical—of these findings are enormous. One consequence is that in those blues where the melodic flatted fifth is an integral part of the scale used, it must form a pitch area together with

FIGURE 21. Graphic representation of Ed Bell's vocal scale in "Mean Conductor Blues":

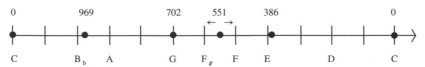

F, the fourth degree of the Western scale. But in this case, when F♯ and F are one and the same toneme, the F is often barred from assuming other functions. "Mean Conductor Blues" can serve as a good example. In the second and third lines there is no change to subdominant and dominant in the guitar accompaniment. The logic is that blues with an F/F♯ compounded toneme will tend to be more rigorously related to a continuous tonic through all twelve measures.

The typology of the blues includes several regional strands (Cohen 1996). One can also isolate different strands on the basis of the tonal system used. Preliminary work on this question has led me to suggest two such strands:

> 1. Blues based on a mental template integrating two simple pentatonic scales at the distance of a fifth, formed from representations of partials 4 to 9 (cf. figs. 18 and 19). This type embraces a subdominant tonality with the step from tonic to subdominant taken easily, while the dominant chord is largely circumvented. There are *two* fundamentals, C and F.
>
> 2. Blues based on a mental template defined by the constituent use of higher partials over a *single* fundamental. This blues scale seems to be based on the selective use of the harmonic series from the 6th to the 11th partial. If partial 9 (D) is omitted, a pentatonic character of the blues is retained, as shown in Figure 20.

I will not now expand this typology by adding other possible strands. They may or may not exist. There is probably no unitary theory to "explain" the "flatted fifth." Its origins might be traceable to multiple African sources, and consequently, it may function in the blues in various ways. In some blues it can be understood as a tone representing partial 11 transposed an octave downward. In others it may reflect a memory of Arabic/Islamic modes as they survive today in the west African sahel zone, notably in Mauritania (cf. Nikiprowetzky n.d.: 20, especially the pentatonic mode in line 5). In still other blues, as David Evans has suggested, the flatted fifth could be a blue third on top of a blue third. More functions are conceivable, and they are not mutually exclusive.

The "Flatted Fifth"

Part II

Return to Africa

Introduction

The most trenchant external influences on African music in the twentieth century were not European, as might have been expected in the face of colonial structures; instead they were African-American. These have included nearly every aspect of the New World music from the Caribbean and from South and North America. In the 1930s it was rhumba and some jazz-derived forms of ballroom dance music. Then came a wider range of Latin American and Caribbean styles—merengue, cha-cha-cha, pachanga, mambo, calypso, and so forth. From North America came swing jazz, then rock 'n' roll, twist, and soul, later superseded by Jamaican reggae. The distribution patterns of all these influences varied widely from area to area. While calypso from Trinidad and from West Indian emigrants operating in Britain had a strong impact on the Guinea Coast, Cuban son (in Africa generally called *rumba*) determined the creative output of generations of popular musicians in Congo/Zaïre. South Africa absorbed most of the North American cultural influences, especially after 1945, including bebop.

Today traces of all the successive waves of African-American music transmitted by the mass media can be found even in local traditions remote from the cities, in reinterpreted but still recognizable forms. Sometimes only a name survives, such as "blues" without any particular associations to blues music, but in a vague, general manner referring to styles of couple dances in bars that would once have been called *slow drag* in North America, or, more recently, *lambada* in Brazil. Latin American and other musical terms survive in the lexicon of musicians living in isolated rural areas of Africa. In the mid-1960s I was surprised that local musicians among the Vute of central Cameroon, playing a very swinging music on their *timbrh* raffia-made lamellophones (cf. recordings by

Omaru Sanda, B 8892–8896, Phonogrammarchiv Vienna, 1964/Kubik), classi-fied their dance patterns as *marenge* (clearly derived from "merengue"), *chacha*, and *contre-banjo* (pronounced in the French way). The music had nothing to do with Latin American patterns; it was based on duple-interlocking tone-rows, and the musicians themselves qualified *timbrh* music as "traditional."

In Yoruba-speaking southwestern Nigeria in the early 1960s, highlife musi-cians regularly absorbed scattered stylistic traits from jazz, even cool jazz, and integrated them into their expressive idiom. Roy Chicago's music could certainly not be described as a jazz derivative, and yet there are blue notes in the trumpet and saxophone parts, and "cool" jazz intonation and phrases—for example, in the alto saxophone solo in "Sere fun mi baby" (cf. *Roy Chicago and His Abalabi Rhythm Dandies*, Afro-Rhythm Parade vol. 5, Philips 420 011 PE, recorded 13 July 1961). Significantly, the saxophonist's blue-note phrases blend perfectly with the basically pentatonic flavor of the melodic outline of this Yoruba-language song, contrasting with the highlife-style chord progressions (example 12). In minute detail the melodic line of the saxophone solo unfurls the west central Sudanic integrative scale I described earlier (see figs. 15 and 17). This is not only an interesting testimony to its retention in an urban style; it also testifies to how this harmonics-based scale is reinterpreted by the underlying guitar chords. The G_7 guitar chord is totally neglected by the melodic line of the saxophone. While the blue note B♭ is clearly related to the C tonality of the first line, its transposi-tional counterpart, the E♭ relates to the F fundamental, also neglecting a G_7 chord. While jazz influence is obvious, the saxophone line is just as much a *fresh attempt* to accommodate the memory of a west central Sudanic tonality with guitar chords that emphasize the added sixth, seventh, and ninth. According to Nigerian musician and musicologist Bayo Martins (personal communication through Wolfgang Bender, Mainz), the saxophonist is probably Roy Chicago himself. In an attempt to give western Nigerian highlife a Yoruba authenticity, there is also a section in this song where the Western instruments fall silent and drummer Aramide Apolo (nicknamed Dr. Apolo) exercises speech patterns on the *dùndún* talking drum.

Several African musical traditions were thoroughly modified over the last half of the twentieth century through the absorption of selected traits from one African-American style or another. These include elements characteristic of the blues, although they reached Africa through filters, i.e., in various urban, popu-

Example 12

Blend of western Sudanic and blues scalar patterns through jazz influence in Nigerian highlife: the start of the saxophone solo in "Sere fun mi baby," by Roy Chicago.

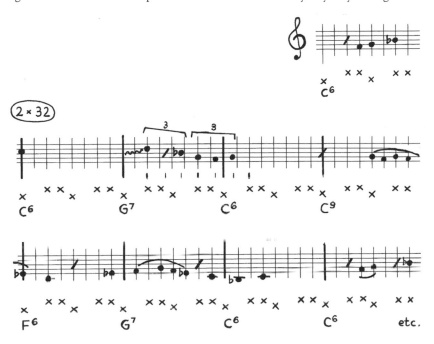

lar, and often commercialized African-American genres that had incorporated such traits earlier.

Between the two World Wars use of the common ballroom dance-band instruments of the 1920s had spread through practically every major urban center of colonial Africa, from Accra to Lagos, from Nairobi and Johannesburg. The British and Belgian territories were in the vanguard. Among these instruments were several models of the American banjo. They became common on the Guinea Coast, from Ghana to Nigeria and into Cameroon, and, of course, in South Africa (cf. Kubik 1989c on local developments in southern Africa). From the 1940s on, the banjo repertoire all along the coast of west Africa began to be based on those west African genres that had come to be called highlife; but the instrument was increasingly being used as a solo instrument, integrating the ever-changing international fashions, as they became accessible on phonograph records. In July 1960 I recorded in a Yaoundé township (Cameroon) a young man named Desiré, who was totally unknown to the mass media, and probably still is, but who turned out to be a formidable expert on his eight-stringed banjo. I have no photograph of Desiré, nor of his father Basil Fuda, whom he often mentions in his songs, but the instrument can be seen in the hands of a relative (photo 24).

In his songs "Cheri Margueriti" (rec. B 5114, Phonogrammarchiv Vienna, 1960/Kubik), "Ibaye, ibaye" (B 5115), and many others, Desiré had integrated both rock 'n' roll and contemporary highlife rhythmic patterns from eastern Nigeria, and molded them into a peculiar style of his own, heavily based on an age-old African technique for creating auditory illusions, i.e., patterns that are not played as such, but are constructed in the listeners' auditory perception by rearranging the total melodic input (cf. Kubik 1989b for a discussion of this phenomenon). Desiré's single-note banjo melodic lines, articulated with a fast-moving plectrum, were composed in disjunct intervals and in such an order that they would split up in auditory perception into two or three pitch-layers of conflicting melodic-rhythmic lines. Performed at incredible speed, the effect was as if more than one musician had played them.

Desiré's songs were cyclic, and often based on common highlife harmonic progressions, such as (relatively): C_7—$F_{(6)}$—G_7—C with their characteristic "blue" C_7 chord in transition to the subdominant with the added sixth. Otherwise Desiré's banjo songs were not particularly reminiscent of any form of the blues; his music was instead an original reconfiguration of highlife, some Caribbean, some jazz and rock 'n' roll elements. The language was a mixture of Nigerian/Cameroonian pidgin English, some French, and Etɔn, his mother tongue. Unfortunately, I have never met either him or his father again; nonetheless, Desiré's music is an instructive example of the creative reactions by a young west African in the late 1950s to the various influences from the record market, dominated at that stage by west African styles that had absorbed many African-American traits (cf. Bender 1991).

The word "blues" had already become current in many urban areas of Africa between the two World Wars. But in most cases blues remained nominal. By the mid-1950s a bit more of the blues form was imported with rock 'n' roll, and by the early 1960s with the twist. The CD *Pamap 102*, released by Wolfgang Bender and Günther Gretz in Frankfurt (1997), *Ngoma, Souvenir de l'indépendence*—a reissue of original NGOMA recordings from Leopoldville/Kinshasa—includes

Photo 24. The type of banjo played by the Yaoundé rock/twist and highlife soloist, Desiré; here held by a relative in the musician's absence. This is a so-called mandolin-banjo, with a string arrangement like that of a mandolin in four double-courses. In Yaoundé, quarters at mainroad Yaoundé-Obala, July 1960. (Photo: Author [Archive no. A 457])

the song "Seven O'Clock" in a 12-bar blues form by the group Musekiwa Isaac & Vedette Jazz, originally recorded in 1960. In "Seven O'Clock" the drummer plays typical rock/twist rhythms while the bass player clings to a Latin-American pattern. The song reveals its North American inspiration also by the fact that it is sung in some kind of English, and with a rough voice intonation (unusual for Congo/Zaïrean singers). Although it is difficult to find a particular American source for this item, it might well be a rearrangement in twist style of the 1955 Bill Haley hit "Rock Around the Clock."

This is an example of the many transient and quickly "fading" fashions that reached Africa in the latter half of the twentieth century, when phonograph records had become generally available and powerful radio stations such as Radio Brazzavillle were broadcasting to a large population. Anything that was on the world record market would become known almost instantly in Africa's urban centers, and would soon be picked up and "tried" by local musicians. But in order for any of the internationalized fashions to really take root, much more stimulus was needed, above all a favorable local audience reaction. In Congo/Zaïre, local audiences reacted extremely favorably to Cuban dance-band music by Xavier Cugat, Machito and His Afro-Cubans, and the eminent Johnny Pacheco (flutist from the Dominican Republic), and to hits such as Moises Simon's "El Manisero," composed in 1939 (Kazadi wa Mukuna 1992: 76). Anything else was doomed to become a passing pop fad. The situation was somewhat different on the Guinea Coast, and it was totally different in South Africa (cf. Ballantine 1993). Blues could not have become known directly in Africa between the two World Wars, because the so-called race records were targeted in the United States to specific American audiences, and were not exported to places around the world from which little revenue could be expected.

It is a fair estimate, therefore, that—apart from South Africa, where swing jazz and country and Western blue yodels had penetrated earlier—the rest of sub-Saharan Africa received its initial dose of blues-derived patterns and the 12-bar standard form only with rock 'n' roll from the mid-1950s, and with the twist dance craze between 1960 and 1963 promoted by Chubby Checker and others. This wave coincided with the independence declarations that were sweeping Africa in 1960. Not only in America did the twist have "liberating" effects, in whatever sense that can be understood; the fad assumed political importance in a number of urban African areas, including Kenya, where the twist craze found notable expressions (cf. Low 1982). On a general level, then, rock 'n' roll and twist implanted the seeds of blues patterns and forms in various places on the African continent, with markedly different prospects for their survival. In some places, these initial contacts were reinforced by soul music of the 1960s and 1970s, with the popular "Godfather of Soul," James Brown; in others lack of new input would stunt growth; while in yet other geographical areas the seeds have remained dormant, waiting for some future stimulus to activate them.

There are two prominent regions in Africa where elements of the blues have had a more profound impact: South Africa (after 1945) and—to a far lesser degree—the west central Sudan (from the 1970s into the 1990s).

11 - The 12-Bar Blues Form in South African *kwela* and Its Reinterpretation

South Africa was not a slave-raiding area for the New World labor market, and South African musical traditions therefore did not influence New World music before mid-twentieth-century contacts and exchanges (e.g., Louis Armstrong's adaptation of August Musurungwa's "Skokiaan" theme, the recording of "Wimoweh" by the Weavers in 1951 [Decca 27928]; the emigration to the United States of South African singers and instrumentalists such as Miriam Makeba, Dollar Brand, and others; and the touring of *mbaqanga* groups since Paul Simon's *Graceland* album—cf. Erlmann 1991). Influence in the other direction, however, had occurred much earlier. U.S. spiritual and harmony singing became known in South Africa in the last few years of the nineteenth century through the activities of the African Methodist Episcopal Church, through touring American minstrel groups (Coplan 1985: 39), and later the appearance of the Virginia Jubilee Singers in Cape Town and other places. All this influenced composers such as Reuben Tholakele Caluza, Alfred Assegai Kumalo, and many others (cf. Rycroft 1957, 1967, 1977, 1991 for a thorough assessment of the various Isizulu-language and other vocal styles). To this day, in South Africa and neighboring territories with a South-Africa-oriented educational system, late nineteenth-century Negro spirituals and some of their South African derivatives are standard teaching repertoire in many schools. Even in relatively remote areas of southern Africa, as on European-owned farms in Namibia, we recorded as recently as 1991 workers' choirs that had incorporated spirituals in their repertoires. One of these choirs, operating at the Ibenstein farm and carpet factory southeast of Windhoek, under the directorship of Frank Gebhardt, called itself The Weavers. Most certainly they had picked their name not only from their occupation but also from the name of the earlier American group, whose hit "Wimoweh" (itself inspired by *mbube* music) enjoyed wide distribution in South Africa. Their repertoire, however, was older. In the sample recorded they sing exclusively spirituals and gospel songs in English (cf. "Steal Away," "I'm Gonna Lay Down My Burdens," etc., rec. orig. tape no. 91/9, items 8-11, 25 October 1991, Malamusi/Kubik). The idea of teaching spirituals to "native" South Africans was originally promoted by the churches. It was rooted in the missionaries' belief in "innate" analogies between local and African-American choir traditions due to "race," and the assumption that Africans would understand Negro spirituals better than European hymns because both they and the African Americans were "black."

While biologically reductionist explanations of similarities in art—for instance, between U.S. American spirituals, gospel choirs, and South African choir music (*isicathamiya, makwaya*, etc.—cf. Erlmann 1994)—are not worth scientific attention, the similarities must be accounted for. Most twentieth-century South African innovations in music were stimulated by processes of diffusion from the Americas, and they unfolded their unmistakable characteristics as soon as the American styles had been processed on the basis of local musical traditions and South African languages. In the field of dance-band music, Christopher Ballantine (1993) vividly describes this interaction from the 1920s to the 1940s. Almost invariably, urbanized South Africans tried to emulate African-American musical fashions of the day but soon reacted by reinterpreting them heavily. During the 1920s and 1930s, the township dance music called *marabi* was the local proletarian undercurrent to the fashionable American dance-band music adopted earlier by the African bourgeoisie. Gradually, *marabi* concepts such as *cyclic short forms* (in contrast to strophic or chorus forms), inherited from older South African music, but with their root progressions "brushed up" by the use of chords from Western music, penetrated "concert and dance" music (Ballantine 1993: 11 ff.).

Peter Clayton (1959) and later Atta Annan Mensah (1971–72) talked about the "round trip" of jazz and its "homecoming." "Like a long absent virile traveler," wrote Mensah (1971–72: 124), "jazz returns to Africa as a full-grown art form nourished and revitalized, with new elements and new idiomatic expressions. In a sense, therefore, one may speak of the coming of jazz to Africa as a round trip."

The blues were one kind of African-American music that "returned" to Africa as part of a package of American musical traditions of the 1940s that had assimilated some blues elements. Not all were necessarily "virile." They included in particular the singing styles of Ella Fitzgerald, Lena Horne, and Billie Holiday, who served as models to emerging South African singers such as Miriam Makeba, Dolly Rathebe, and the Rhodesian-born Dorothy Masuka. (On the latter's musical fate, see Malamusi 1984.)

As already mentioned, North American traditions did not take root everywhere in Africa. For various reasons—stylistic, social, and so forth—Latin American genres were much more easily accepted, especially in central and east Africa, but also on the Guinea Coast, giving rise to innovative local styles. South Africa was the earliest and most notable exception to this rule, the only large area where North American genres would take root, from ragtime and spirituals of the early twentieth century to swing jazz, blues, and bebop (cf. Ballantine 1993, 1995a and b for a detailed account; also Roberts 1972; Coplan 1998).

There are many reasons for this. The social climate of an industrialized country, the only one in sub-Saharan Africa, with the record business in the hands of a minority that clung to U.S. fashions; the screening of American films after 1945 to local audiences in the townships (to an extent matched only in post-World War II Europe), and striking parallels between South Africa and the United States in the patterns of social stratification all played a role. Another reason why South African popular music absorbed jazz like a sponge can be found in the structure and stylistic profile of local traditions (see Alan Lomax's evaluation of the song-style area 511 *South African Bantu*, Lomax 1968: 314), which is different from other areas of Africa. Like U.S. music, it is characterized by the *presence* of the first three levels of subjective timing in African music (elementary pulsation, reference beat, and cycle—cf. Kubik 1994a: 42–46, and discussion earlier in this book), but by the *absence* of time-line patterns. Although off-beat phrasing of melodic accents is prominent in various forms of South African music, there is relatively little use of polyrhythm (except the 2:3 contrast inherited from Bushman music). In many areas—the Venda in northern Transvaal excluded—there is a notable absence of drums, and much music is rooted in the experience of partials-producing instruments such as musical bows, including unique developments (cf. the *igongquo* or *sekampure* friction chordophones—see Rycroft 1966, Dontsa 1997). Although of a different genesis, South African partials-based tonal systems (penta- or hexatonic) are compatible in a certain sense with U.S. African-American tonal traditions.

The concept "blues" in the sense of a slow-drag style of dancing with all its sensual implications became current in urban areas of South Africa just about the same time American jazz-based popular music swept Europe: during the 1920s. But American rural blues remained unknown there as in Europe, and even to most of the general public in the United States, until the 1950s. Christopher Ballantine's cassette of *marabi* dance-band recordings from South Africa during the 1930s, accompanying his book *Marabi Nights*, contains instructive examples of what dance-bands playing for the emerging African bourgeoisie were emulating in terms of various ballroom dances—the foxtrot, etc.—in the late 1930s, even including some echo of rhumba rhythms.

It was only during the 1940s that a different awareness of the concept of "blues" superseded the earlier ones; this time it was blues as a 12-bar musical form. And it was naturally among musicians that this new concept took root. The World War II period, and more intensively the first years after the end of the war in 1945, were notable for artistic departures, since many soldiers from South Africa and the neighboring countries to the north had returned to their homes with impressions of American music gathered in the Pacific and European war theatres. But even more important, a new postwar market for American films and jazz records gained momentum. Suddenly swing jazz was all around in Johannesburg and every other major South African city, with Count Basie, Lester Young, Cab Calloway, Glenn Miller, and others the leading stars, although none of them actually traveled to South Africa during the 1940s. Much of the impact came from the cinema. Young girls began to emulate Lena Horne's famous rendition of "Stormy Weather." Among many contemporary jazz films, Lester Young's *Jammin' the Blues* (Gjon Mili/Norman Grantz, 1944, 10 min.) was most certainly screened as a pre-program to full-length American evening films.

With swing jazz, and from 1946 on bebop as well, the 12-bar blues form became an important mold not only for jazz musicians who could afford pianos and saxophones, but down the social ladder to the poorest township adolescent, who was as much exposed to American cinema as the middle-class artist who took up jazz. Here again, it was not blues from the Deep South of the United States, a genre that remained totally unknown and which to this day has had very little, if any, impact on South African popular traditions. It was the 12-bar blues form in the Count Basie Orchestra, the Glenn Miller Orchestra, and other groups that began to be used as a scheme for local compositions, after a period in which the famous pieces heard on the soundtracks of popular films were simply imitated. It was instrumental blues and boogie-woogie as part of the repertoire of swing jazz orchestras that made a lasting impact.

From the mid-1950s on, when several original South African jazz-derived popular styles were already at the height of their popularity, rock 'n' roll, with its themes often based on the 12-bar blues form, acted as a further instigation. But even so, in popular South African music, the earlier, *cyclic forms* that were already present in *marabi* prevailed.

The story of jazz derivatives, incorporating some elements of U.S. American urban blues, really takes off by the mid-1940s. After much experimentation in the townships, insufficiently accounted for by contemporary writings, a singular event at the end of the 1940s gave a push to the rise and popular acceptance of local township jazz adaptations, as described by eyewitness David Rycroft, one of the first musicologists to pay attention to urban musical developments in that region.

A new music was started by South African township youngsters who had become exposed to 1940s American jazz records, particularly big band jazz presented by famous American band leaders such as Count Basie, Lionel Hampton, Woody Herman, Glenn Miller, Cab Calloway, and others. Trying to recreate the brass and reed sections of American swing orchestras, they began to use toy flutes that were cheaply available in markets, developing an ingenious new playing technique in which the embouchure was such that the mouth could function as a variable resonator. These so-called "pennywhistles," more correctly called cylinder flageolets because of their cylindrical bore, as opposed to the conical bore of the old pennywhistle (Kirby 1934, repr. 1965: 276), had been available in South Africa for a long time; but now, played with a new technique, they suddenly became popular among street youngsters. They played them either solo or in groups walking to bus stations, shops, markets, cafés, and other places of social gathering, showing off with the newest jazz tunes picked up from records. Characteristically, in the "white" areas of apartheid South Africa these boys found instant acclaim from onlookers and easily earned some needed pennies. At home, in the townships, the public reacted with mixed feelings, and professional musicians despised them, comparable perhaps to how W. C. Handy

(1970: 80–82) first reacted to poor blues-singing street musicians at the beginning of the twentieth century. The parent generation in the townships certainly enjoyed the boys' pennywhistle jazz—after all, they were playing precisely the music that had become for many a symbol of social advancement. But at the same time some looked down at these "dirty boys" with their torn clothes and their "primitive" substitute saxophones. While the pennywhistle players themselves were immersed in and captivated by their fantasy world of the cinema screen, identifying with their American idols, the parent generation hung on to "white" values, feeling ashamed of their offspring. This music had the stigma of gang culture, of poverty, lack of education, and the *tsotsi* (i.e., something like city-slicker's) world. Such associations haunted many middle-class South Africans in the townships and prevented early acceptance of this new music as an art form.

However, that was to change through commercial intervention. According to David Rycroft (1958: 55), pennywhistle playing gained general acceptance in 1950 "after the success of a locally made film called *The Magic Garden*, which featured a little penny-whistle boogie, played by a crippled boy." This film by Donald Swanson is a precious testimony to the history of jazz-related developments in South Africa. With an all-African cast and in spite of the somewhat thin story—money being stolen in a church; the fugitive thief digging a hole in somebody's garden and hiding it there—the plot is well developed, creating some very humorous episodes interspersed with local music. Not only is the film a testimony to township life of the period; its soundtrack gives a useful inventory of the kind of American music that had been assimilated by South Africans up to 1950. In it several jazz improvisations based on the 12-bar blues form can be heard on guitars and other instruments in a style inspired by Django Reinhardt, Count Basie, Lester Young, and other contemporary American performers. And then there is, in several scenes, a lone boy playing a metal pennywhistle, employing blue notes and a wide range of contemporaneous jazz expression. Local audiences in South Africa who saw this film reacted to it by *upgrading* the social status of that instrument and its performers, and all of a sudden a flood of youngsters in the townships began to buy and play pennywhistles for the purpose of recreating jazz.

That was the start of a new swing-based dance music, popularly referred to as "jive" in South Africa during those days, until someone within the entourage of the record companies, seeking a label, coined the term *kwela*. -*Kwela* is the stem of a verb in Isizulu and many other southern African Bantu languages, meaning "to climb," "to mount," "to ride." It saw limited use in musical contexts before the 1950s, but the label itself became well known when the record companies, discovering the new music in the streets, picked up the term. It became known worldwide in 1958 when one *kwela* tune recorded in South Africa, "Tom Hark," by the group Elias and His Zig-Zag Jive Flutes (Columbia DB 4109, 78 rpm), reached the top of the British Hit Parade list. This performance begins with a theatrical sketch featuring boys playing a forbidden dice game at a street corner in a South African city. At the appearance of the green police van, which was commonly referred to as *kwela-kwela* in the township jargon (see also Modisane 1963)—because the juvenile delinquents, when hustled in, had to "climb up"—one of the boys calls out: "Here comes the *kwela-kwela!*" The boys then hide their dice, pull out their flutes and begin to play "harmless" jive music (Rycroft 1958; 54, 56).

During the early period of *kwela*, around 1951, many groups used only one or two flutes and a guitar, as can be seen in another timeless cinematographic document, the South African-made film *Pennywhistle Boys* by Kenneth Law from around 1960 (16 mm, black-and-white, ca. 20 minutes) showing Robert Sithole, Joshua Sithole and Isaac Ngoma in Cape Town. But gradually, many groups added a one-string skiffle bass made out of a tea chest, designed to represent a jazz double bass. This instrument made them less mobile, but it was essential for the sound in the many shacks and "shebeens" (liquor-selling places) where *kwela* began to be performed for dancing.

The one-string bass used in *kwela* is an interesting blend of concepts and techniques derived from foreign inspiration (i.e., jazz performance) and from an age-old memory entrenched in many African cultures: the ground-bow. The latter was known among Bantu-language speakers of South Africa, but has only recently been documented in some detail among the Venda of northern Transvaal (cf. Kruger 1985, 1989). We do not know exactly when the first box bass made from a tea chest appeared in South African *kwela*, but it is most likely that this appearance either coincided with or was reinforced by the bass in British skiffle groups of the 1950s. South African soldiers could also have encountered it among American soldiers during World War II. Although in U.S. jive music of the 1930s and 1940s the one-string bass was used and could be seen on film, it is doubtful whether such films had become available in South Africa, and if so, whether they would have been much of an inspiration.

As always in the history of inventions, the story is complex. *Kwela* musicians, in their desire to represent the jazz double bass, no doubt drew upon the next best model available in foreign jazz-based music, the skiffle bass; but then something must have clicked in their minds: the new instrument was reminiscent of an old African instrument, vaguely remembered. In that sense, the *kwela* one-string box bass is as much a construction inspired by the bass in skiffle bands as it is a restatement of the idea of the ground-bow. In contrast to what happened in the New World (cf. the "mosquito drum" in Haiti mentioned in Courlander 1960), in South Africa the ground-bow did not "evolve" into the one-string bass—the model of the (foreign) skiffle bass reactivated the memory of the ground-bow. This is a pattern of reactions widely encountered in situations of culture contact. The *intent* may be to emulate a foreign status-enhancing

PHOTO 25. Clarence "Pops" Davis playing a one-string bass made from a washtub, Memphis, Tennessee, 1985. Davis, born in 1907, had been peripherally associated with the Memphis Jug Band in earlier years. He strikes the string with a thick stick. In some versions of his instrument he would run the string through a tennis ball that rests on the top of the inverted washtub and strike the tennis ball. This enables him to get a powerful sound without destroying the string or pulling it loose from the washtub. (Photo: Levester Carter)

PHOTO 26A. Ground-bow (*korongwe*) played by a boy of the Gbaya-Bokoto ethnic group, in a rural area of the Central African Republic. A can held by the boy's feet has one end of the string attached to it and serves as a resonator inside the pit. The boy strikes the string with his right index finger and stops it with his left hands. At Tugiritsa village, 6 km north of Carnot, on the road to Baoro, Central African Republic, June 1966. (Photos: Maurice Djenda)

fashion, but unconsciously this process reactivates something lost, a dormant knowledge that eventually invests itself in the new fashion. In many parts of Africa the association between tea-chest bass and ground-bow is quite real. When I traveled to Uganda in 1972 with the *kwela* group from Malaŵi discussed below, Luganda-speaking friends seeing our tea-chest bass immediately called it *sekituleghe*, which is the local name for the ground-bow.

PHOTO 26B.

Kwela as a new, original jazz offspring soon attracted "talent scouts" dispatched by the major South African record companies. The new music was then marketed under various names—"new sound," "flute jive," "pennywhistle jive," "kwela," "township jazz," etc.—but it was considerably manipulated in the studios, and its creators were recklessly exploited. For example, the one-string bass was regularly dropped, and replaced by a double bass played by a "professional" non-kwela musician permanently employed by the record company. The same applied to the percussion: a professional jazz musician usually accompanied the kwela groups with jazz drums. Lionel Rogosin's film Come Back Africa (1957) paints a merciless picture of apartheid South Africa in the 1950s, and it also contains several scenes of street-band *kwela*, very rarely heard on the commercial records.

PHOTO 27. The *kwela* band of Daniel Kachamba and His Brothers in Blantyre, Malaŵi, March 1967. With pennywhistle, guitar, rattle, and one-string bass this was a mobile group playing at street corners, in front of bars and at local dance parties in the townships. From left to right: Daniel Kachamba (guitar), Josefe Bulahamu (rattle), Donald Kachamba (flute) and Alfred Ombani (bass). (Photo: Author)

From 1958 on South African pennywhistle players used the flutes that were marketed by the Hohner company of Trossingen, Germany. Significantly, they had been developed for mass production from samples collected by a Hohner agent in Johannesburg from township youngsters who had made them locally.

Their rights to their designs unprotected by patent laws, those original designers will probably never be known. The Hohner flutes were available in C, B♭, and G. At the height of the *kwela* craze Hohner sold up to 100,000 specimens a year in South Africa alone (Kubik 1974: 31).

The Hohner flute has a cylindrical bore and six finger holes. In the manufacturing process a nickel-plated brass tube was sawed off and galvanized, then the head or "mouthpiece" was formed. An unprepared Western musician who has never seen *kwela* flute jive played would hold this flute with the embouchure of a recorder, i.e., in a straight direction with lips puckered. *Kwela* musicians developed a totally different approach. From the view of the player, the flute is rotated about 45° and in this position is pushed relatively deep into the mouth, pointing towards the inner side of the right cheek. An oblique head position results from this. The oblique embouchure guarantees that the edge and windway remain open between the lips of the player. The purpose of the deeper insertion of the flute is to obtain a full, round, and much louder tone, since the

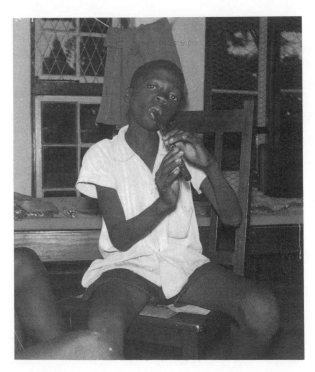

PHOTO 28. Fourteen-year-old Donald Kachamba was a superb jazz-style improviser, playing virtuoso runs on his Hohner B-flat flute. His inclined head position and characteristic embouchure are the hallmark of *kwela* flute playing technique. In Blantyre, Malaŵi, March 1967. (Photo: Author)

cavity of the mouth, as in the performance of the *umqangala* (mouthbow), becomes a variable resonance chamber (Kubik et al. 1987: 19).

But here too it was native concepts and techniques that blended with foreign models. The oblique head position and embouchure, as much as it may have roots in local techniques (though not necessarily local flutes, as claimed by some), was also inspired by characteristic attitudes of American saxophone players. Among these, Lester Young in particular was no doubt a model: South African youngsters not only imitated his playing posture, with the head and saxophone held obliquely; they also emulated his clothing style. On the pennywhistle, blue notes, jazz-type glides, and chromatic intermediate notes were achieved by various means: slight modification of embouchure, finger smearing, etc. Several types of trills were employed. Much of this technique can be studied in close-ups in a 1974 film by Donald Kachamba (E 2328, Encyclopaedia Cinematographica, Göttingen).

Kwela music is mostly based on short cyclic forms with four-segment harmonic structures, particularly (a) [C—F—C_4^6—G_7—] and (b) [C—C_7—$F_{(6)}$—G_7—]. These cycles, expanded and circumscribed by substitute chords, have continued into the more recent forms of South African popular music such as *simanje-manje* and *mbaqanga*. They should not be misinterpreted as "the three common chords." Rigid bass-lines give them a particular tinge, revealing that there is a hidden, non-European structural concept behind these chord sequences, with the third segment in cycle (a) appearing invariably as (what in Western music would be called) a $^6_4$ inversion of a triad. Occasionally, jazz-type chorus forms are also found in Kwela music, as well as 12-bar blues forms, for example in Lemmy Special Mabaso's "4th Avenue Blues" (Gallotone GALP 1246).

What came to be called "pennywhistle blues" was recorded on several occasions during the early 1950s. It included single or multiple flute performances in the 12-bar blues form in a slow, middle, or fast tempo, the latter sometimes patterned after Glenn Miller's "In the Mood" theme. This particular theme (cf. *The Glenn Miller Story*, LPM 9901, TELDEC) was very popular in southern Africa and elsewhere. It was recorded even in Namibia from a local group by the linguist E. O. Westphal (private collection, David Rycroft, Ashdown Cottage, Forest Row, England). It also appears in Lionel Rogosin's 1957 film *Come Back Africa*. The group that performs "In the Mood" there is not identified, but I remember that they adhered strictly to the 12-bar form of the main theme, and that they even proceeded to a second theme in the original Glenn Miller recording, although the guitarist misinterpreted one chord.

The 12-bar blues form was used by *kwela* groups such as the Solven Whistlers (cf. *Kwela with Lemmy*, Gallotone GALP 1246) and many others, besides the famous *kwela* stars, Lemmy Special and Spokes Mashiyane. A very attractive 12-bar blues is played with two flutes and guitar by Robert and Joshua Sithole in their film *Pennywhistle Boys* shot ca. 1960 in Cape Town by Kenneth Law.

Significantly, the South African blues derivatives are all based on American *urban* blues of the 1940s, and somewhat later on rock 'n' roll. The "pennywhistle blues" are all instrumental, as is most of *kwela* music. Jake Lerole was one of the early *kwela* musicians; he started to play pennywhistle in 1948 at the age of twelve. His music was based on *tsaba-tsaba* (a popular 1940s South African style), blues, and boogie-woogie. An example of the blues-based style is his 1952 recording "Blues Ngaphansi" (Allen 1995a: 3). He was unable to record blues-based forms again. Lara Allen, who recently researched the history of *kwela* in South Africa, writes that from 1954 onward producers refused to record anything but "four-bar cyclical sequences of primary chords topped with two or three melodies which repeated and alternated with each other. Blues and other American jazz forms were not accepted" (Allen 1995a: 3). In an interview for Allen, dated May 19, 1991, Jake Lerole reported that the record companies used to pressure musicians to "make something simple, just simple." When he tried to explain that such and such items were his own compositions, he was told to go to America and try to record his stuff there. Allen (1995a: 3) added: "The fact that two years earlier blues and boogie-woogie was not considered a financial risk, implies the workings of a shadowy insidious force: State ideology. . . . simple music was appropriate for the *Bantu*."

In a sense, this South African "state ideology" converged in time with a growing official and unofficial reaction against rock 'n' roll and rhythm and blues taking place in the United States during the 1950s, following an earlier reaction against bebop. It culminated in 1959 with the "payola" hearings in the U.S. Senate and the disgrace of several stars, including Jerry Lee Lewis and Chuck Berry. There were important differences, however. In contrast to apartheid South Africa, there was never direct government censorship or suppression of music in the United States, where the record industry was entirely privately controlled and infused with independent entrepreneurship. Also in contrast to South Africa, much of the reaction on musical grounds against rock 'n' roll was that it was *"too simple"* and that it was *"savage jungle music."* Behind all that was the fear that this "black" music attracted "white youth."

This is where the two scenarios are analogous in psychological structure. In South Africa the policy was that it should be *"simple"* in order *not* to attract "white youth;" that it should be confined to audiences in the "black" townships. With the dismantling of apartheid laws under the government of Nelson Mandela's ANC, a new interest in popular music of the 1950s can be felt everywhere in South Africa today (cf. my notes during my visit in September 1996). Musicologists and historians have begun to interview surviving musicians and even to reconstruct and revive some of the music. Lara Allen has tried to revive Jake Lerole's music at the Music Department of the University of Natal. She recorded one of Lerole's 1959 compositions called "Space Age," which was rejected at the time by the local record companies. She describes how startled the University's jazz students were at Jake Lerole's jazz-like music.

In the late 1950s *kwela* music spread to the states of the then Federation of Rhodesia and Nyasaland (1954–1963), now the independent countries of Zimbabwe, Zambia, and Malaŵi, where it put down new roots. During the 1960s it was developed particularly in Malaŵi by the musician-composers Daniel and Donald Kachamba (Kubik 1974; Malamusi 1994: 34–39). With some modifications and a broad panel of his own compositions, Donald Kachamba is one of the last surviving authentic representatives of the *kwela* tradition in southern Africa today. He has played flute since 1960, when he was seven years old and living with his parents and his elder brother in Harare, Zimbabwe. His elder brother, the late Daniel Kachamba, had started to play guitar and had bought Donald a flute and trained him. Even at fourteen he impressed audiences with his prolific flute solo variations (cf. the 16-mm film *Kachamba Brothers 1967*: Part I, "Where Can I Get Emery," a ten-bar rock blues. Copy deposited in the Center for Black Music Research, Columbia College, Chicago). Since 1972 he has been on concert and lecture tours in no less than 33 countries of the world, and has published LPs, films, and CDs. Among his most remarkable contributions as a composer are his multiple flute and guitar pieces recorded with a playback technique (cf. LP record A.I.T. GKA 01, Nairobi; CD record *Os Herderos da Noite*, Pinacoteca do Estado de São Paulo, 1994, item 20 "Sadya mbewa"; also Kubik 1979–80).

The demise of *kwela* in South Africa in 1964 was not voluntary. The powerful South African record companies no longer recorded it; they were anticipating a market that would give preference to loud music played with electrically amplified guitars. The new product was marketed under the label *simanje-manje* (Isizulu: "things of today") and the record companies often kept their own "professional artists" to promote it. It quickly gained popularity in the townships, where it was referred to as *mbaqanga* (= the homemade stiff porridge of millet or maize). From the 1980s on *chimurenga* (= liberation struggle) music in Zimbabwe succeeded in cutting out a significant market share for itself in southern Africa. With these new styles the awareness of the blues form receded.

Today, in the countries on the periphery of South Africa, one may encounter outstanding musicians playing in contemporary pop styles based on South African *mbaqanga* or Zimbabwean *chimurenga* music (cf. Bender 1991: 154–65) who have enormous difficulty even grasping the *idea* of the 12-bar blues harmonic sequence. I have had this startling experience while performing with various musicians in that region. The problem seems to be the long stretch on the tonic chord found in many blues, covering measures 11, 12, 1, 2 and 3 of the form. With no caesura marking the beginning of the blues' first line—unless, of course, there is a so-called "turnaround" on the dominant seventh at the end of measure 12—these musicians become disoriented. They seem to hear the *start* of the blues form at the beginning of measure 11 and then find the "non-ending" tonic chords very strange. A subdominant chord in measure 2, as is heard in some North American blues, would not alleviate the disorientation, because from their viewpoint it would actually stand in measure 4, isolated between C chords, and would therefore make no sense. Consequently, these musicians regularly miss the passage from C_7 to the two F measures of the second line by one measure in either direction, anticipating or delaying it, simply because they conceptualize this strophic three-line form in a way that is different from American musicians.

Eventually I discovered why this is the case. The problem actually arises from the fact that all these musicians think in terms of African short, cyclic forms. They perceive the transition from C_7 to F as analogous to the chord change from measure 2 to 3 in one of the two common *kwela* and *mbaqanga* cycles.

This is deceptively reconfirmed by the return to C after two measures of F and the start of the G_7 chord, even if it is followed—as it is in many blues—not by another G_7 but by a pull back into the subdominant F. They tend to perceive the transition from measures 9 and 10 to the tonic C as a point of *return to the beginning* of the cycle, and are perplexed that from here no less than five measures on C should follow before C_7 can be sounded again.

FIGURE 22. How some southern African musicians of the 1990s, unfamiliar with the 12-bar blues form, tend to reshuffle and reinterpret it in terms of a familiar eight-measure cycle with a "superfluous" four-measure extension.

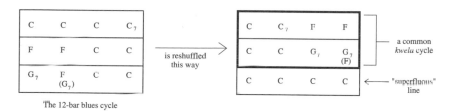

In the history of American music, incidentally, the 12-bar blues form has also perplexed composers. Some of the early U.S. piano rags that incorporated the blues form made analogous accommodations, often stretching it to 16 bars by repeating the last four bars, doubling it to a more "acceptable" 24 bars, or reducing it to eight bars by dropping the last four (cf. Berlin 1980: 154–60; van der Merwe 1989: 280–81, 285).

In southern Africa, the young Daniel Kachamba was confronted with this problem in the late 1950s, but he arrived at an ingenious solution: he reduced the 12-bar blues, which he had encountered in adaptations of "In the Mood," to a 10-bar form by cutting off two of the "superfluous" chords. Kachamba's blues then seem to be a typical *kwela* eight-bar cycle ending with a "coda" of two more bars.

The question, of course, arises: was it Daniel Kachamba's solution, or did he pick up the 10-bar mutation from someone else? The available sources from South Africa, audio and cinematographic documents from the *kwela* era, suggest that the South African musicians were faithful to the 12-bar form. But in the earliest period—before the ideological reversal discussed by Lara Allen

FIGURE 23. Daniel Kachamba's reinterpreted blues form: (10 bars).

C	C$_7$	F	F
C	C	G$_7$	F
C / F	C		

(above)—they were also forced into it. An illustration of the resulting products is perhaps the recordings "Zulu Rock" and "Zulu Roll" (composer Ngubane) on Troubadour AFC 491, described as "Jive." Both sides are instrumental performances in the 12-bar blues form with boogie bass figures. In a sense these musicians sound as if they were learning to navigate through the blues form; obviously they are having some difficulty with it, but not enough to throw them off seriously, or result in a major reinterpretation.

My guess is that the record company had played some rock 'n' roll records to them and told them to emulate this music without plagiarizing it, i.e., without violation of existing copyrights. That was normal practice in South Africa. In the studios producers often exposed local musicians to the latest "international" records, hoping that they would produce fashionable adaptations that would sell. It is understandable therefore that some were "navigating," but there were no choices: "learn it or perish!" They could not have tried to reinterpret the form itself (such as shortening it to 10 bars), because the producer would have quickly put in his veto!

The Kachamba brothers, on the other hand, were not subordinate to anybody. They were not in the service of any record company, so they were free to reinterpret the form according to their own ideas. This illustrates an important difference between the social setting of South African studio musicians, with all the constraints placed upon them, and street musicians on the South African periphery (but also in South Africa itself), and how the social environment can promote or inhibit nascent processes of reinterpretation.

I think it is possible, therefore, that the 10-measure blues form is Daniel Kachamba's own invention. Of course, he might have picked it up from some other, even unknown musicians in Rhodesia (Zimbabwe) who had arrived at the same compensatory solution to this cognitional problem. What is certain, however, is that Daniel Kachamba used the 10-bar form exclusively in all of his blues-based compositions, which he categorized (characteristically) as rock 'n' roll, thereby giving us a hint of the source of the 12-bar blues form he tried to emulate. Likewise, his younger brother Donald has used it in some of his own compositions, such as "I Was a Baby" (CD record *Concert Kwela*, Le Chant du Monde LDX 274972, 1994, item 11)—in a different rhythm. Daniel Kachamba pointed out that this fast, blues-based music was good for dancing during the dry season when it was cold. He compared the tempo of his rock 'n' roll to the revolutions of gramophone records, such as 78 rpm and 45 rpm, the latter being a very slow tempo. Jokingly he said that *his* rock 'n' roll had a speed of 82 rpm—a fictitious number that pleased him. The first 10-bar "rock 'n' roll" blues in his band's repertoire was the piece called "Chipiloni chanjamile," recorded in several versions in 1967. He told me (interview in Blantyre, March 1967) he had picked it up from a record by a Salisbury (Harare) group called Bogadi Brothers. He added that it was not very suitable for dancing, but rather for listening (transcription, example 13).

I have never been able to trace that particular record. "Bogadi" might even be a corrupt spelling of Bogart, as in the film actor Humphrey Bogart. A recording of "Chipiloni chanjamile" with text transcription is published on the *Daniel Kachamba Memorial Cassette*, ed. Mitchel Strumpf (1992). The last part of the text line "yu wa leti naaa!" is English (!): "You are late now!" The meaning of the other text parts, not in Kachamba's vernacular language, is obscure. *Chipiloni* is described by some informants as the name of a type of blanket, by others as the name of a company, and by Donald Kachamba (personal communication, 6 February 1988) as a type of millet beer that was sold in Harare.

After he had already presented six different versions of "Chipiloni" ("Chipiloni No. 1" to "Chipiloni No. 6") to the public, Daniel Kachamba composed, in late March and early April 1967, a piece based on the same form, but with a different melody and text:

> Anifa waiting for me! (4x through the chord sequence)
> I want to see you, dear Anifa! (Coda)
> (Recording: item D8, *Opeka Nyimbo*, Kubik/Malamusi 1989)

The 12-Bar Blues Form in South Africa kwela

Example 13

The vocal part of Daniel Kachamba's "Chipiloni chanjamile" (transcribed by author from live performances with the band in 1972).

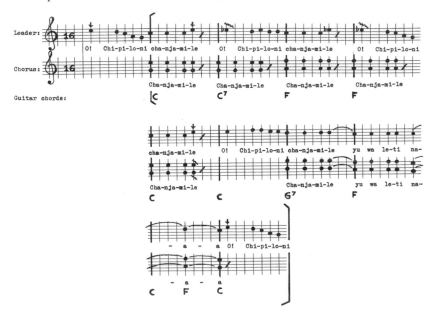

The final transformation of "Chipiloni" occurred to Daniel Kachamba in June 1967 (Djenda and Kubik, field notes 1967/Malaŵi). The new song, sung in Malaŵian township English to the words "We ka na get 'Emeri?" (Where can I get Emery) is one of the highlights of Daniel Kachamba's early career as a composer and performer. The piece was played with *kwela* instruments, Daniel on the guitar, Donald on the flute, Bulandisoni Kapirikitsa on the one-string bass, and the eight-year-old Moya Aliya Malamusi on the rattle. It is a fascinating jazz piece, coming from such an unlikely place as a village in southern Malaŵi, with the group developing a drive that is unprecedented in any other popular style of African music.

Luckily this piece was filmed in 16mm color, sync-sound, by Maurice Djenda and myself, putting on record what was always essential in Daniel's art: the integration of movement, sound, text and acting. The performance of "We ka na get 'Emeri?" opens up with the view of a lonely tea-chest (the one-string bass) standing in front of a hut, with strange flute sounds coming out of it. Daniel is seen rushing to it, knocking at the wood, then lifting the box, and there emerges the slim Donald playing flute. . . . The other band members run to the spot and the lively performance begins at high speed. The plot ends with Daniel, Donald, and Bulandisoni "kidnapping" the youngest band member, eight-year-old Moya, and carrying him away in the same box (Film: *Kachamba Brothers' 1967, Part I*, limited distribution).

It is probably merely coincidental, but perhaps there is also some deeper underlying analogy in the play of ideas, if we find that the theatrical gag of "emerging" from something on stage was used in U.S. show business from the early nineteenth century well into the twentieth. In the 1830s the "blackface" minstrel "Daddy" Rice used a midget partner who emerged from Rice's suitcase and danced "Jump Jim Crow" alongside Rice (Rourke 1931: 81). In the 1920s Ma Rainey reportedly emerged from inside a phonograph placed onstage, singing her latest blues record (Lieb 1981: 28–36).

Kwela is not the only genre in southern Africa that has incorporated elements of the blues. South African professional urban jazz from the 1940s on has used the blues form too. By the late 1950s and 1960s bebop, and especially hard bop, was already a tradition in Johannesburg clubs and elsewhere. Numerous recordings could be cited, but perhaps one published by the Jazz Appreciation Society, Johannesburg, in the 1960s (*Mankunku Jazz Show* JLP 01, Vol. 1) gives an idea. Groups such as the Soul Jazzmen from Port Elisabeth, the Jazz Faces Quintet, and the Lionel Pillay Trio are included. Lionel Pillay obviously trained his fingers on the music of Oscar Peterson. There are also esoteric forms of South African music displaying blues elements. In the 1960s the Malombo Jazzmen, using Venda drums along with factory-manufactured musical instruments, had absorbed blues elements on a more subtle basis (cf. LPs *Malombo Jazz Makers*, Vol. 2, Gallo Continental Records ZB 8162; *Malombo Jazz*, Gallotine GALP 1464). In 1964 they took First Prize at the National Jazz Festival in the Orlando Stadium, Johannesburg. The driving forces in this group were guitarist Philip Tabane and transverse flute player Abbey Cinti, then about thirty years old, who composed most of the pieces and wrote the arrangements. The formal basis of many of their pieces was the 12-bar blues, although Abbey Cinti often composed in 3/4 time or additive meters, a trait also found in several other contemporaneous jazz groups of South Africa, such as that of Gideon Nxumalo (cf. LP record *Gideon Plays*, JLP 02). By the mid-1970s a highly acclaimed jazz group incorporating Xhosa elements was The Jazz Ministers, led by Victor Ndlazil-

Photo 29. Johnny Mekoa (trumpet) and Victor Ndlazilwane (tenor saxophone), notable South African jazz musicians of the group The Jazz Ministers, during a public performance in the mid-1970s. (Photo reproduced from *The World*, Wednesday, November 19, 1975)

wane (photo 29). Some of his works were also performed by the legendary Hugh Masekela (cf. Nkosi 1966).

Blue notes are ubiquitous in South African popular music and have been the hallmark of *kwela*, *mbaqanga*, and choir singing since the 1940s and possibly earlier. Their use was exported into the neighboring countries to the north with migrant workers from those countries returning home, where their children would pick up the South African style and introduce it to their home schools, villages, and so forth. An instructive example of this transmission is the choir formed in 1967 by Elvis Viyuyu, seventeen years old (cf. Citumbuka-speaking parents), at Mlowe Primary School in northern Malaŵi. Elvis grew up in South Africa, where his father was working. He was there for fourteen years; practically all of his memory was South African with a strong Zulu cultural base. Returning to his nominal home country, he tried to implant his South African experiences there, obviously motivated by a strong desire to maintain his new identity. He trained his peers, and the outcome was a remarkable Zulu-style choir, although the texts had already become Citumbuka. In this music, the upper blue note

(B♭), as in much South African choir and pop music, was worked into a C₇ chord (Recordings orig. tape no. 102 at Mlowe, July 1967/Djenda and Kubik, Musikethnologische Abteilung, Museum für Völkerkunde, Berlin).

The ease with which the upper blue note (B♭) was accepted in South African music and that of the neighboring countries is due to its instant recognition as representing the seventh partial of the natural harmonic series. In the cultures of southernmost Africa with a strong Khoisan background this was predictable. The Bushmen discovered the natural harmonic series thousands of years ago, and among the Kalahari Bushmen (the !Ko) higher partials over a single fundamental are commonly used, for example, in the playing of friction chordophones such as the *sekampure*, or the tuning of the pluriarc (*tɔɔ*) (cf. results of the Namibia survey in Kubik and Malamusi 1991–93; Kubik 1994c). The historical and prehistorical Khoisan ("bushman" and "Hottentot") background of South Africa has had a profound effect on the musical cultures of Bantu-language speaking peoples who migrated to the territory during the first millennium A.D. Bushman background is felt not only in music, but also in languages, especially Xhosa, with no fewer than 2,395 words containing typically Khoisan click sounds. Of course, everyone remembers Miriam Makeba's famous "click song" and some of her other timeless recordings in Xhosa, for example "Pata-pata," touch-touch (REPRISE RA 0606).

The upper blue note B♭ together with its jazz-derived subdominant transposition has even penetrated the tunings of so-called traditional instruments in the region, whose performers had contact with the urban scene. In 1969, Hugh Tracey, Andrew Tracey, and I recorded at Marievale Mine, near Springs (South Africa), two Ndau mineworkers from Nova Mambone in Mozambique who played two *mbira* lamellophones together. Their music left us with a startling impression of blues melodic and harmonic patterns, the tuning and melodic patterns displaying the use of blue notes. Trying to figure out why that was so, I discovered that the melodic theme in a hexatonic (perhaps gapped heptatonic) scale was first presented at *tonic* level and then shifted to *subdominant* level, i.e., a fifth downward, within one and the same cycle. (Performers: Gombani Lange and Lucas Shishonge. Titles: "Temba kutsutsuma" [Trust is running away fast] and "Mwena kaji acitwa" [When a woman pounds]. Recorded 4 March 1969, MV 12 and MV 16, International Library of African Music, Grahamstown, South Africa.) It is certain that these musicians had exposure to South African

PHOTO 30. Xhosa singer Miriam Makeba with her group during a concert performance in Vienna, June 1990. (Photo: Moya A. Malamusi)

popular music; and yet the step they had taken, creating a tonal dichotomy by tuning their instruments so that their hexatonic scale (involving neutral thirds) would also appear in transposition a fifth down, demonstrates an analogy to what happened in the United States in the late nineteenth century (cf. Kubik 1969: 87).

Like commuters, blues elements are continually coming and going in southern African individual styles. Certainly, they are more than fading fashions. Actually they are deeply entrenched these days all across the region; and the word itself has the magic of serving as a label on many, often short-lived styles, whether they are based on the blues or not. No final assessment can therefore be given of a Zimbabwean female *mbira* (lamellophone) player of the 1990s, Taruwona Mushure, who has hit the headlines by declaring that she "recognized a connection between the blues and *mbira*" music. Consequently, she termed her style "mbira blues." Keith Goddard (1996: 81) has given this assessment:

The most daring artistically of today's *mbira* artists is probably Taruwona Mushure. She has recognised a connection between the blues and *mbira* and she terms her style "mbira blues." She sings in a tuneful, slightly mournful, ballad style and she superimposes these lines onto the traditional *mbira* texture provided by The Mujuru Boys, a branch of the famous Mujuru family. . . . the group consists simply of two *mbira*, *hosho*, *ngoma* (African drums) and voices. Her work has come under criticism, in particular from Zimbabwean men, because she sings to *mbira* in English, which many feel is disrespectful to the tradition. Taruwona also uses the medium of *mbira* to speak forcibly about the plight of women in Zimbabwe.

At last, ideology has captured the southern African region, and, as in the west central Sudan (see next chapter), and indeed throughout the world, local musicians, under the influence of popular journalism and the increased accessibility of such contents through TV programs, CD-ROMs, and so on, have discovered that it can serve self-promotion to "explain" one's music. Artists working for the international market—musicians, painters, and writers—have learned to package their products into sociocultural, sociopolitical, or historical theories. They no longer wait for art and literature historians or ethnomusicologists to do that job for them, explaining any meanings their art may transmit. From the moment the product is published, the artist is hard at work trying to determine its place in the history of art!

Some African touring artists of the late twentieth century have learned those tricks of the trade at a breathtaking pace. Involuntarily, however, they have thereby contributed to widening the social gap between themselves and the musical "have-nots" in the townships and villages. African artists with expensive equipment selling their music on the international market will often give their interviewers the impression that their products were something carefully calculated. They will also use the interviewer's sociological jargon, talking about liberation, resistance, protest, roots, power, identity, black consciousness, ethnicity, chords, blue notes, and the like. They will give the impression of *knowing* precisely what they are doing and *why*, and *how* their personal style came about, and how it compares to other styles. By contrast, township- or village-based African musicians with little inclination to theorize in a foreign language either lose access to the market or put themselves at the mercy of promoters sifting off most of their income.

The 12-Bar Blues Form in South Africa kwela

12 - Return to the Western Sudan

Since the 1970s some of the more recent developments in African American music in North America and elsewhere have radiated back to the western Sudan. In 1981 I was startled, during a visit to the "Conservatoire National" in Dakar, Senegal, to find an ensemble consisting of a brass section (trumpet and trombone), saxophone, piano, electric bass guitar, and jazz drums, playing in a style that came close to "Creole music" (cf. Borneman 1969 on that style) as found on some of the Caribbean islands and in Louisiana. A jazz-like shuffle rhythm was used, and blues tonality was unmistakable (Kubik 1989a: 191).

The region of the western Sudan is one of those areas in Africa where in some musical traditions we find *nonlinear off-beat phrasing*, i.e., a type of off-beat phrasing of melodic accents (cf. Waterman 1952 on the general term) where the accents are developed independently of the elementary pulsation (or regular division of the beat). They are not in a "ratio" with the pulse-line; on the contrary, they seem to fall irregularly in between, or their impact points are regularly retarded or anticipated. In jazz, a master of these techniques was trumpeter Miles Davis. In Africa, nonlinear off-beat phrasing probably has its origins in declamatory speech. It is common in several musical styles of the western Sudan (Senegal, Mali, Burkina Faso, etc.). Modern electric-guitar-based groups have revived this concept. The beat is temporarily suspended (though not lost) in the lead guitarist's perception, and for a short while the lead guitarist's melodic-rhythmic lines seem to be "floating." This floating quality is like that of a lead electric guitarist or harmonica player in contemporary U.S. blues, or a jazz soloist, especially in slow blues with a swing or triplet rhythm. From the west central Sudan we have an example recorded by Mose Yotamu in 1978 in the Côte d'Ivoire during a festival in which a Dyula dance band with electric guitars, drums, and other instruments gave a concert (Yotamu 1979, orig. tape no. Y6/I/1, November 1978, Archive of the Museum für Völkerkunde, Berlin). The lead guitarist displayed a harsh, expressive, blues-like style, changing his internal beat relationship during the performance. The Dyula are speakers of a I.A.2 or Mande language; the word simply means "traders" in the Mandiŋ language. Their history in Mali and neighboring countries goes back several hundred years.

These developments during the 1970s cannot be understood merely as borrowings from U.S. styles. Though my description of the guitar style in Yotamu's recording strongly suggests borrowing, that is but one side of the coin; the new music also reconfirms concepts and techniques that existed in the west central Sudanic style area long before any U.S. influences. All these developments have provided the turf for a new brand of more ideologically based, conscious developments in this region during the 1990s. The original suggestions arising from the results of researchers' painstaking reconstruction work regarding the "roots" of the blues eventually made their way back to the very region under consideration. Inadvertently, they had an effect on the behavior and tastes of individual musicians and audiences in Mali, Guinea, Senegal, The Gambia, and neighboring countries. Eric Charry, speaking of "The Grand Mande Guitar Tradition of the Western Sahel and Savannah," has published a detailed analysis of its history and its relationships with instruments such as the lute (*nkoni*), the bridge-harp (*kora*), and the xylophone (*balo*), the latter particularly in Guinea. He writes:

It is no coincidence that the Mande stars Salif Keita (from Mali) and Mory Kante (from Guinea) are both accomplished guitarists; it is the guitar that is the link between the ancient and the modern musical traditions that coexist and nourish each other in the Mande world. Most Mande guitarists are active players in an unbroken and still-vibrant tradition that goes back to the 13th century founding of the Mande, or Mali, empire. That tradition is primarily guarded by *jelis*, hereditary professional verbal/musical artisans. (Charry 1994b: 21)

Eric Charry's article, Samuel Charters's fieldwork in The Gambia and elsewhere in West Africa, and his follow-up book to Paul Oliver's 1970 publication (Charters 1982) rank among the most important sources for twentieth-century developments in this region. They also testify to how research results influence musicians. Just as Oliver's ideas were accepted in Paris at an early stage and diffused via radio programs and journalists' reports in French to Mali and Senegal, so also must Charters be considered responsible for having planted seeds, especially in English-speaking The Gambia. It is no accident that in 1992 The Gambia postal services issued a series of postage stamps called "History of the Blues." In the general realm of string-based traditions, Roderic Knight's work in The Gambia and elsewhere on the *kora* (bridge-harp), for which he invented a notation system (cf. Knight 1971), and on Mandinka drumming (1974), and his study of tunings and modes (1991) have been most influential in the region, with his didactic results adopted by schools.

The idea of associating The Gambia with African-American history was, however, implanted locally before Charters's research in that country, most probably following Alex Haley's visits and his much publicized Kunta Kinte story. By the late 1980s it had become a popular concept in audiences from Dakar and Banjul to Bamako and Paris—often via African expatriate musicians operating from Europe—that the "roots" of the blues, soul, and other African-American styles lay in the west African savanna. These developments converged with the need for new ethnic identities in the United States. In the ensuing processes of cultural revival, gaps in history were often filled with historical constructions. Alex Haley's *Roots* (1977) is one expression of this trend in popular narrative. Haley himself called his saga "faction" (cf. Morrow 1977: 52), i.e., fiction based on some sort of factual background. It is not surprising, therefore, that Paul Oliver's ideas of connecting the history of the blues to the west central Sudanic belt were eventually picked up by musicians from that region seeking their fortunes overseas, aiming at the broad market comprising Europe, the United States, and (to a lesser extent) west Africa.

From the 1970s on, some forms of urban blues in the United States, but particularly soul music, began to absorb traits from the music of the western Sudan, not directly, but through the filters of various American and European pop music genres. Certain aspects of the blues that had for years lurked on the fringe and in the shadows also began to emerge into mainstream acceptance, a process that culminated in the 1990s. John Lee Hooker probably led the way in the 1960s, and especially following his collaboration with the group Canned Heat in 1970. Fred McDowell had also been popular through recordings and on the concert and festival circuit in the 1960s and 1970s. R. L. Burnside began touring in America and Europe in the late 1970s, and Jessie Mae Hemphill in

1980. These market developments were by no means coincidental; they were a response to transformation in the auditory habits of the mainstream public of the so-called industrial world, making acceptable music that was stylistically closer to the west central Sudanic style world, by its use of cyclic form, a bourdon-like tonal basis, excessive melisma, and other elements.

At the same time, some blues records, but even more soul and rhythm and blues, eventually reached the towns of the western Sudan. Tours of blues artists sponsored by the U.S. State Department may also have had an influence (cf. Pearson 1990: 181–83). Memphis Slim, booked by his wife from Paris, also performed in west Africa. He even got a gig for fellow Memphis blues pianist Booker T. Laury in Cameroon in the early 1980s. U.S. Peace Corps members who acted as "folk musicians" in their leisure time might also have been a factor in spreading blues forms and techniques in remote areas of west Africa. In northern Nigeria and Gabon in 1963 and 1964 I met Peace Corps workers who interacted with local musicians.

While it is very difficult to sort out in detail all the contacts that might have occurred in a world with a dense global communication network, and airlines connecting New York with Dakar, Bamako, and Kano within a day, a reaction to this particular selection of American music and to researchers' suggestions was predictable. From the 1970s on, and increasingly in the 1990s, a slight, but consequential impact of U.S. blues on some west African griot traditions began to be felt, particularly among musicians who had actually traveled to the United States or Europe. One musician-composer, Ali Farka Toure from Mali—though not himself of any griot genealogy—had assimilated blues from the 1960s on and created a personal synthesis drawing upon American blues and local traditions. His recordings and personal appearances have been very successful in Western countries. Following the surge in the trade of art objects and handicraft products by Senegalese and Malian traders, who have crossed the Atlantic from Dakar since the early 1980s often on one-day missions to sell their products, the Dakar-New York axis has become increasingly important for trade in music as well. Performers of the *kora* (bridge-harp) have settled in cities like Chicago and become residents, interacting with the urban blues, soul, and rhythm and blues scene. These musicians often give public school programs, and they have learned to capture the local imagination by emphasizing the "roots" nature of their music.

These interactions have had a notable effect on audiences in the West, where the market is centered, but the effect on African audiences back home in Mali, Senegal, and so forth has been limited to sales of the pirate cassettes of such music there. If the songs are sung in any of the languages of the region, their positive reception is almost guaranteed, whatever American musical style might be emulated by local musicians: blues, soul, rap, and so on. Thus, the psychological basis for the acceptance of this new music is totally different in the United States and in Africa, serving the construction of quite different identities in the two places:

(a) in the United States, the construction of a *separate African-American identity* based on west African "roots" as a response to pressures by the mainstream U.S. American culture and to economic deprivation.

(b) in Africa, the construction of a *socially upwardly mobile class identity*, by adopting an American lifestyle and expressive repertoire ascribed to African Americans who appear to be economically advanced.

While African-American aspirations are often conditioned by literary notions about Africa, the griot musicians' response to America is much more pragmatic, taking a realistic account of market forces. To reach desirable economic goals many musicians will not balk at reconfirming their audience's stereotypes about Africans when touring Europe or America, thereby defending the small niche they have carved out in the worldwide entertainment market. Mostly these audiences have no firsthand knowledge of Africa, and their views are therefore based on popular writings and the mass media. In the 1930s Africa symbolized Tarzan's world, later the advance "from the Congo to the Metropolitan" (cf. Goffin 1944); then came the "roots" stereotype, the "liberation" syndrome, and more recently the transformation into "Positive Black Soul," as symbolized by the name of a Senegalese rap group of the 1990s (cf. rec. Island Mango 1995, SALAAM CO 524 167 2). At each juncture non-African audiences projected expectations about how Africans should behave onstage, if they were "genuinely African," and few successful groups touring the world have dared to contradict them.

The idea that the "roots" of the blues are to be found somewhere in Mali, Guinea, or Senegal made some trans-Atlantic careers possible. In America, Ali Farka Toure (photo 31) from Mali has earned for himself the title "Malian bluesman." He was born in 1939 at Gourmararusse, a remote village in northern Mali, and later moved to the area of the city of Timbuktu, that large trading city at the most northerly point of the Niger River that was part of the powerful Mali Empire from 1325 to 1433. (In the sixteenth century it was also one of the most important centers of Islamic scholarship in the western Sudan.) Ali Farka Toure spent long periods in Europe, though, most notably in France. In the 1960s he had heard John Lee Hooker and become intrigued by similarities between that musician's style and some forms of traditional music in Mali. Hooker, born in 1920, was experiencing an enormous resurgence of popularity in the 1960s and 1970s among European-American and European audiences, especially after his 1970 collaboration with the blues group Canned Heat (cf. *Hooker 'n Heat*, reissued in 1991 as EMI CDP-7-97896-2, 2-CD set). From the early 1960s on Hooker also performed a number of times in Europe and had LP releases on several French labels (cf. Herzhaft 1991).

Later, Ali Farka Toure aimed at creating a synthesis. Eventually, the mass media discovered him, and with the idea of the "roots of the blues in the western Sudanic belt" popularized in England and America, there was suddenly a market for selling Ali Farka Toure as "The Source," or the personified "Roots" of the blues. He first toured the United States in 1989. At least five CDs by the "Malian bluesman" have so far appeared: *Ali Farka Toure* (Shanachie, 1987), *The River* (World Circuit, 1989), *African Blues* (Shanachie, 1990), *The Source* (World Circuit, 1992), and *Talking Timbuktu* (Hannibal, 1994).

He describes himself ethnically as an Arma, a people that resulted from the intermarriage between Moroccan mercenary soldiers with speakers of Songhai in the sixteenth century. But he grew up at Niafounke, upstream from Timbuktu, interacting with peers from different ethnic groups. Toure apparently speaks and sings in eleven languages, underlining the eclecticism of his style; mostly, however, he sings in Songhai, a Nilo-Saharan (II.A) language; in Bambara (a Mande language, I.A.2), in Tamashek (the language of the Tuareg people, classed by Joseph Greenberg [1966] as a III.C or Berber language within the Afro-Asiatic super-family), and Fulfulde (a I.A.1 West Atlantic language). That astonishing linguistic panel, probably unattained by any other African musician, demonstrates Toure's capability to assimilate.

When Ali Farka Toure published one of his first LPs in 1977 (*Ali Toure Farka*, SONAFRIC SAF 50060), there was no talk yet in Mali about the "roots" of

PHOTO 31. Ali Farka Toure as shown on the cover of his first album, released in France in 1977, Sonafric SAF 50060.

the blues, which suggests that popular thought of this kind had not yet made it to center stage as a vaguely formulated sociopolitical idea. However, once it had become current in Western-educated circles in Timbuktu, as well as in Paris, the roots idea could be conveniently used as a marketing strategy for Toure's music. This occurred only during the 1980s. Bur it *is* significant, and confirms the thesis that he knew blues records before, that Toure starts off the very first song on that early LP, "Yer Sabou Yerkoy," with a 12-bar three-line guitar passage incorporating patterns drawn from blues. David Evans (letter, 15 July 1998) has provided the following analysis of this piece from the point of view of a blues researcher and guitarist:

This piece is performed in his favorite A position of standard tuning, in this case capoed up two frets to the key of B. Let us assume for the sake of discussion that it is in A. Toure uses the open fifth string (A) as a bourdon but occasionally briefly switches to the open fourth string (D). This parallels blues technique. There is, however, only minimal string bending and not the flexible blue note at the third (C-C#). Instead he plays the minor third (second string, first fret) and major second (second string open), the notes C and B. His guitar scale from low to high is A-B-C-D-E-G-A. On one occasion there is a hint of a C# (i.e., the major third), possibly a mistake in playing. There are more important (and deliberate) uses of the major seventh (G#) on the guitar, but as a leading tone to the tonic just above it, i.e., as a sort of grace note (ornamentation). In general, his playing is quite percussive, with frequent use of the techniques of "hammering" and sliding rapidly up to a note from one or two frets below. These techniques are common in blues guitar playing and may have reached Toure from the blues, reinforcing techniques of older Malian guitar styles or music played on unfretted stringed instruments. The introduction of this tune is quite interesting, because it could be viewed as *twelve bars* with an AAB structure. Bars 5-8 could be viewed as a variation of bars 1-4. In bar 9 there seems to be a tentative move to the "subdominant" note (D) as a second fundamental, without however abandoning the original fundamental note (A). The triple rhythm of the piece lacks the usual tension of a swing or shuffle rhythm in the blues. These characteristics and the prominent use of the "minor third" make the piece stand apart from traditional blues guitar playing, although the introduction perhaps shows the artist trying to come to grips with the 12-bar AAB form that he had probably heard in France. This piece doesn't appear to be based on any *specific* blues source. Each four-bar line is a *continuous* musical line, not a series of riffs, nor is it subdivided into statement and response in the manner typical of blues. As for the use of the "minor third," only Robert Pete Williams regularly featured it among the traditional blues guitarists. *All* others found the blue third *between* minor and major, often sounding it by bending a string upward or by wavering or sliding between minor and major. It's very unlikely that Toure ever heard Williams.

Arabic-Islamic singing techniques are a centuries-old heritage in Mali, and they persist in some of Ali Farka Toure's music. Many of the similarities actually perceived by listeners between his music and the blues are due to the fact that these techniques have been continued both in Mali and in the blues. That includes some of his guitar patterns, transferred from homemade instruments he played in his youth. The reviewer of the album *African Blues*, Dan Quellette, states quite correctly that Toure sounds "like a chanting Muslim muezzin at times" (Quellette 1990: 38).

Everyone is, of course, free to play the kind of music they like, and Ali Farka Toure's original interest in the blues is legitimate and perhaps an indication of personally felt cultural affinities. But the manner in which his predilections have been reinterpreted, and even exploited, is a long way from their original integrity and historical truth. Once the "Malian bluesman" label was established, it became clear that Toure, while on tour in the United States, had to live up to the associated expectations. This is not meant to question Toure's *artistic* achievements and his accomplishment of a synthesis. We are not concerned with art criticism here, but with the interplay of musical, social, and psychological factors in the rise of individual and regional styles.

While some of Toure's music is comparable, in a very broad sense, to the blues, it is uncertain to what degree his personal synthesis could be used to confirm pre-twentieth-century historical connections. In an apt statement, discussing Ali Farka Toure's interview by the British music critic Philip Watson for *The Wire*, blues historian Francis Davis (1995: 33–34) has said that "To make matters more confusing, African music is beginning to betray the influence of the blues. . . . Though the echo of Hooker's music in Toure's is often pointed to as evidence of Africa's influence on the blues, it's really the other way around."

One trait that distinguishes Toure's music from blues is the relative rarity of bending notes in his guitar playing, and there are also differences in his approach to rhythm, which lacks the double-triple ambiguity and accentuations responsible for "swing." (Cf. the Tikar woman's grinding song as an instructive example of swing from the broad west central Sudanic belt.) I myself find Ali Farka Toure's music only vaguely related to any type of blues. Vocally it is built upon a basic anhemitonic pentatonism, reminiscent of much Fulɓe (Fulani) music across the Sahel zone, without the tensions customarily created by blues singers. It is generally cyclic, lacking surprise off-beat accents, and quite often closer to a repeating litany than to the expressive world of the blues. Rhythmically, it stands much more in the Arabic-Islamic tradition than in autochtonous pre-Islamic styles of the west central Sudanic belt. And what might have escaped audiences in the concert halls of the West is that this music is pretty much on-beat; many times it even evokes the image of folk dances in 3/4 time, rather than anything like the subtleties in off-beat phrasing and swing common in the blues.

If comparison with African-American music is taken as a criterion of judgment, then many "traditional" musicians in Mali, Senegal, Guinea, and elsewhere can match his music—for example, Mamadi Dioubaté from the Mali ethnic group with his *seron* (19-stringed bridge-harp) displays qualities of rhythmic structure and accent distribution, with a rhythmic kink on the third pulse of a triple scheme that reminds one intensely of North American traditions. Independently of any "return" influences from jazz or boogie-woogie, which had not reached those areas at that time, this music displays stunning African-American characteristics. Dioubaté was recorded in Guinea by Gilbert Rouget and first published on Contrepoint (MC. 20.045, Musée de l'Homme, Paris) in 1952. Mose Yotamu's Dyula musicians too are in a general sense much closer to African-American traditions of North America than is Ali Farka Toure.

On Toure's CD *Talking Timbuktu*, American musicians such as blues guitarist Clarence "Gatemouth" Brown—who has had several concert experiences in Africa (I saw him in Dar es Salaam with his Gatemouth Express in 1976)—took the opportunity to jam with him. Here it is obvious that whenever one of the American musicians plays a solo, it is a venue for those traits (of blues and current pop styles) that are otherwise missing in Toure's own music. In addition, while his friend and producer Ry Cooder normally shows restraint in his guitar playing, others are less concerned about "hurting" Toure's style. Jim Keltner's drumming adds to this music precisely the kind of mainstream American beat that is incompatible with Toure's Mali-based style.

Paul Verna (1993: 82) has characterized Toure's music as a "stewpot of musical styles." Packaged into imaginative catchwords such as "African Blues," "Source," "Roots," and so on, it "has captured the hearts of American audiences." However, it has not captured the hearts of *all* Americans. Ninety-nine percent of rap fans probably have not even heard of Toure. And characteristically, Toure's popularity in the United States is almost entirely among European-Americans. This was predictable, because some of these audiences are motivated by an almost religious yearning for spiritual participation in the "roots of black music," a reaction that is to be understood psychologically as compensating for a feeling of "collective guilt" (e.g., the history of slavery). In other words, the same psychological situation that made it possible for the Kunta Kinte *Roots* TV series to strike a chord in the mainstream American unconscious also fuels the reactions to Toure *as a symbol*. By contrast, rap artists and their audiences obviously do not need that kind of psychological valve.

They have certainly not rejected blues in an ideological sense, expressing respect for all older forms of African-American music. But fashions have changed. In their "beats" they draw heavily from James Brown—whose music was largely a type of blues, renamed as "soul"—and "funk" styles of the 1970s, another very bluesy music, emphasizing riffs and prominent electric bass and percussion.

These recent blues derivatives have somehow eclipsed the earlier styles originated in the Deep South. For the broad, ethnically diverse American public this may have created the feeling of a vacuum. Acceptable musical kinship with the rural blues, particularly if such kinship came from an alleged "source" in Africa, could easily step in. Not surprisingly, Toure's Hannibal Records album *The Source* was able to stay atop the World Music chart for nine weeks in 1993.

Since Toure's debut the epithet "blues" has been increasingly used to package music from the west central Sudanic belt. Kanté Manfila & Kalla had some 1987 recordings released on a CD in Germany (by Popular African Music, Out of Africa Series OA 201, Frankfurt, marketed by World Circuit) under the title *Kankan Blues*. In this case the song has nothing at all to do with the blues. The person who actually "got the blues" was the recording engineer, who reports following Kanté Manfila to his unplugged village in Guinea, where he found that technology did not work to his satisfaction (see CD notes). Another CD set that came out in 1995, at the height of the current "African Blues" vogue, is called *Desert Blues—Ambiances du Sahara* (Network LC 6795), featuring several artists, including Ali Farka Toure with Ry Cooder, from countries such as Mali, Senegal, and The Gambia, but also Algeria, Morocco, Mauritania, Sudan, and Ethiopia. Just as the label "jazz" in central and southern Africa during the 1960s and 1970s (cf. OK Jazz, Bantou Jazz, etc.) was used for music and musical groups with no links to jazz, so the label "blues" now seems to assume a similar role for anything coming from the west central African savanna and sahel zone. This is a far cry from Paul Oliver's original ideas.

Summary and Conclusions

It is possible to delineate the panorama of the blues in its various strands in view of their foundations in the cultures of the western and central geographical Sudan, as well as other parts of Africa, emphasizing stylistic continuity and remote links with specific African genres and performance entities. However, it is not possible to adopt as an objective to "derive" blues directly from any single African tradition, because the blues' cultural genealogy stretches right across west central Sudanic and other African regional traditions, including minstrel music, chantefables, work songs, and children's music of the eighteenth century, and across a time dimension embracing several generations up to the late nineteenth-century rise of the blues in the Deep South of the United States. Earlier developments in proto-forms of the blues were probably as manifold as the abundant variety of individual expression and stylistic change the blues has shown in the United States from the late nineteenth century to the present. Blues is an African-American tradition that developed under certain social conditions on U.S. American soil, in the Deep South. It did not develop as such in Africa. And yet it is a phenomenon belonging essentially to the African culture world.

This latter fact is somewhat masked by blues' use of the English language (though considerably processed by African-American singers), European musical instruments, harmonic sequences, and strophic form, but all *modified and reinterpreted* to various degrees in particular cases, drawing upon African patterns, scalar templates, styles, and techniques. The use of rhyme and rough iambic pentameter verse suggests some background in the British four-line ballad form (cf. Evans 1982: 24–26 on this issue) and formal poetry probably learned in school, besides possible African strophic antecedents (cf. "Baba ol'odo," etc.) discussed earlier.

European elements, where they can be traced in the rise of the proto-blues forms, were first adopted, then considerably processed. This conforms with what we know generally about the psychology of culture contact, namely that in a stratified society, members of the lower classes first tend to identify with "upper class" values and traditions, trying to emulate them (cf. Kubik 1994b). Later, nourished by disappointment and feelings of rejection, unconscious memories of a totally different cultural heritage gradually gain the upper hand, infiltrate, and eventually *overturn* the accepted upper-class forms and modes of behavior. The result is a "proletarian" creative breakthrough, out of which something totally new emerges. This was so in the history of highlife in Ghana, for example. Not by chance was this new west African dance music called "highlife," because the initial model was the "high" life the local bourgeoisie displayed at their garden and dance parties, observable by the poor street children through peepholes in closed doors and walls. It was so in the *kwela* music of South Africa too, although in this case the "upper class" music to be emulated was not that of the Boers (Afrikaans-speaking descendants of the Dutch). Racial segregation and alienation was already too entrenched to have made that possible. The "high" music to be emulated was encountered in the dream world of Hollywood cinema productions and commercial records, and it was predominantly African-American.

These sociopsychological mechanisms tend to be invariables, like Werner Heisenberg's constant. Examples can be cited from other continents and cultures, and other times (see for example: Erdheim 1982; Alhadeff 1977; and generally on culture shock and ascribed identities, cf. Bock 1979, 1980; Michaels 1997). It can be argued in hindsight, therefore, that some African Americans in the nineteenth century would have started their artistic endeavors first by imitating the established musical and poetic forms of the day. In Africa too such imitations persisted until recently. In 1960 in Yaoundé, Cameroon, I recorded an old man reciting poetry in the German language (Cameroon was German-occupied until 1914), and I heard a guitarist in one of the townships who sang French-language ballads. He attracted large local audiences.

The important thing to understand here is that these processes are mere *stages* in a larger sociopsychological scheme. They do not stay put. In relatively short order, someone begins to modify the adopted forms by the power of his or her imagination and divergent cultural background, eventually finding acceptance with audiences who share the latter. Ragtime was heavily based on contemporaneous European forms inherited from marches, quadrilles, polkas, and so on. Their integration into New Orleans jazz first generated some modifications (cf. Jelly Roll Morton's account of the history of "Tiger Rag," in Morton 1938), until eventually the original European forms were abandoned.

Sometimes it happens that in the initial stages of a new artistic fashion only one or two traits can be discerned as coming from the culture that will eventually overturn the adopted expressive forms. For example, the relatively simple basic beat in the blues seems to be an early presence. It could not have been derived from European metrical schemes, with their preconceived accents. Characteristically, the blues beat is also found in work songs and some other music of the west central Sudan, often with considerable swing (cf. the millet-pounding performance of three Chamba women in northeastern Nigeria described earlier, rec. B 8609, at Disol, Nigeria, 1963/Kubik).

The blues tonality constitutes a further trait cluster that was probably present in the United States early on. It is also non-Western, most intensively so in the Delta blues styles and least so perhaps in blues from the East Coast region. In its west central Sudanic pentatonic origins, blues tonality is intrinsically speech-based, but it probably also incorporates traits from other, instrument-inspired African tonal systems using upper-range harmonics, such as I have suggested in my analysis of the "flatted fifth."

Several theories as to why the blues rose in the Deep South have been proposed by researchers. One is based on the reductionist view of U.S. African-American music in general that would characterize the blues as a type of music devoid of all the apparently prominent "African" musical traits (e.g., Guinea Coast polyrhythm, etc.). "Where Negroes were constantly in contact with whites who indoctrinated them with the feeling of the worthlessness of things African, and who resented African music, most of the more obvious African musical elements have disappeared, and Negro music is more European than African" (Waterman 1948: 26).

However, the explanation of New World African-American styles purely in terms of acculturative reductions does not work very well for the blues. Nobody denies that the factors outlined by Richard A. Waterman were important, but just as important is another kind of selective process within a social environment, namely the process that determines survival or disappearance of traditions by competition between the ethnically different African groups themselves. Thus, due to both the different ethnic composition of the people and a different social environment, the chances for survival of the various African musical styles were not equal in different parts of the New World. Acculturation, in this context, cannot be understood merely as adjustments to a foreign (European) culture that claimed superiority for itself. Contacts with a totally alien culture, whether forcible or by choice, sometimes lead to no borrowings at all. This is demonstrated, for example, by the virtually separate social existence of Indian and African community expressions in east Africa for more than seven decades. Blues historians and historians working on African-American music history have not yet reached a consensus on the degree and intensity of cultural interaction between Africans in the Deep South and European settler communities. My perception is that in many of its rural forms, the blues' depth structure is devoid of European elements. The use of guitars with factory-installed tunings and the I, IV, and V chords can be deceptive; they have also misled students of twentieth-century guitar-based traditions in Africa, who ended up calling them "Europeanized" or "hybrid" and who thought they were based on "the three common chords." What is rarely understood and accounted for in this context is the *cognitive hinge* of the matter. For the foreign observer the instrument and the chords are recognizably "Western," but for the native performer both may have totally different connotations and meanings.

I myself tend to emphasize that in the Americas traditions of different African ethnic backgrounds first passed through a period of competition between themselves, leading to victory by one or the other style or genre—whichever one proved adaptable to the new circumstances and had the potential for innovation. It could even be that on a microcultural level, i.e., within one and the same African musical style, a certain trait or cluster of traits received reinforcement under the new conditions, while others were suppressed. Obviously, conditions varied across the Deep South in human relationships, and this accounts in part for the great diversity of styles. If my sociopsychological model is correct, it would also appear that in those areas of the Deep South that show the least "European" and the most densely distributed "African" elements in the blues, such as the Mississippi Delta, African/European cultural segregation was particularly intensive, promoting greater resilience (cf. Cobb 1992).

Another common idea about African-American cultures (including the blues culture) was that acculturative processes tend to take place in "overlapping areas" of traits between contact cultures (Martin 1991)—that is, what is similar in the two cultures begins to merge easily. That may be so in those instances that represent a need for a common cross-cultural formula. Richard A. Waterman (1952) mentioned in this context the *general compatibility* of African and European scales, the existence of harmony, and so on. But culture contact situations also often create a desire in individuals to learn precisely what is unfamiliar and different in the other culture, to learn even about the most elusive and secret realms of the other's existence. In blues there is hardly any trait that could be explained as the result of "overlapping areas" between European- and African-derived traditions. Blues were not developed in consensus between "white" and "black" farmers. Blues expressed the African descendants' own concerns, and above all the concerns of individuals. As David Evans has said:

Folk blues do not deal with unique or remote experiences that only the singer could understand or with the experiences of people unlike the singer and his audience. These songs then serve as a means of self-expression for the blues singer but also indirectly for the audience around him. The blues singer becomes their spokesman, the organizer of their thoughts, opinions, and fantasies. (1978b: 443)

A recent version of the idea of "overlapping areas," although expressed in a different terminology, can be found in van der Merwe (1989). In a chapter called "The Old High Culture" (1989: 9 ff.) the author delineates a *Near Eastern style* in music whose origins go back to "musical trade between Egypt, Mesopotamia, and Persia from very early times." From there emerged, according to the author, what is now called an Arab/Islamic style whose distribution covers the Near East proper, the Maghreb, and parts of the Indian subcontinent. Van der Merwe stresses that the "Near Eastern singing style" along with certain instruments not only spread across the Sahara to the west central Sudan, but also in medieval times to Europe, where those Oriental influences linger on in the folk music of remote European areas like Scandinavia, Scotland, and Ireland (pp. 12–13). "These folk styles were taken across the Atlantic," van der Merwe writes (p. 13), "and the same poverty and inaccessibility that protected them in the old country continued to preserve them in such places as Newfoundland and the Appalachian mountains." Van der Merwe sees acculturation being facilitated to some degree between people of the west African savanna and rural Scottish-Irish settlers, because both represent, in his view, musical cultures with many residual Near Eastern traits.

It is worth noting that many Southerners of European descent, both the planters and the dispossessed "poor whites," were very early *attracted* to blues. Planters patronized it by hiring African-American musicians (cf. Handy 1970; Evans 1987b), and "poor whites" began trying to perform it (Russell 1970). Characteristically, they also had trouble with the 12-bar form, often reinterpreting it back in terms of Western models, a compelling indication of the 12-bar blues form's non-European background.

Essentially, blues was developed by interaction between African Americans of diverse cultural backgrounds about a generation after the nominal end of slavery. In relation to the white farmers' culture, especially in the Mississippi Delta, blues musicians were reclusive in the sense that the most successful of them were different from the ordinary stationary laborers, traveling freely and receiving payment on the spot for their services. Many were reclusive in other respects as well, being "hard to find" due to constant traveling and change of residence, or to residence in a remote habitation away from others. Ironically, this lifestyle—in a way recreating that of west central African itinerant musicians, traders, and praise-singers (cf. our Hausa lute players)—has paid off in securing for them a special social status. Through musical patronage they also often had more social access to members of the upper class and therefore more "privileges," such as riding in "white train cars" (during the segregation era) in order to entertain passengers, and even being served drinks.

Referring to my earlier characterization of culture contact situations as often stimulating a desire for learning, blues performers often, in fact, came to know something about "the most elusive and secret realms" of the European-Americans' existence, and were able to translate this knowledge to audiences within their original communities. David Evans has given a spectacular example of this process in his long essay on Charley Patton (Evans 1987b). While cross-cultural cognitive bridges did not really exist in the initial stages of the development of the blues, apart from the common understanding concerning tips for a performance, they began to be constructed clandestinely by both sides as soon as blues became generally known in the South as something special.

The people who were transferred from the Carolinas, Virginia, Georgia, and elsewhere to Mississippi and the other new southern territories during the first decades of the nineteenth century were carriers of a neo-African musical culture that presented a selection of traits from quite distinctive African regions. Under the new social circumstances, it then turned out that individual music had a better chance of survival in a social climate where the African community spirit had been targeted for suppression. The new forms also expressed the new mood. In this process culture traits from the west central Sudanic belt gained wide currency in rural areas of the Deep South, because they responded best to the new sociopsychological situation. Among the various new traditions that arose, one was the blues. The bearers of these developments, however, were probably a minority within the population of African descendants on the farms. But their stylistic seeds began to sprout, while other seeds were doomed.

Influences from Louisiana and the Caribbean did play some role during that period in the nineteenth century, and into the twentieth, and it is from here that stylistic patterns of another neo-African set (based on Congo/Angola and Guinea Coast music) had some impact in the Deep South areas. But in spite of these inputs, most of the blues tradition in the rural areas of Mississippi has prevailed as a recognizable extension in the New World of a west central Sudanic style cluster.

With the transformation from the 1910s onward of "country blues" into "urban blues" forms (Keil 1966), several new blues derivatives emerged in the cities. Eventually, blues completed what has been called the "round trip" (Mensah 1971–72) and radiated back to selected areas of Africa, where new derivatives emerged that addressed the concerns of Africans during the second half of the twentieth century.

Bibliography

Abbott, Lynn, and Doug Seroff

    1996   "'They Cert'ly Sound Good to Me': Sheet Music, Southern Vaudeville, and the Commercial Ascendancy of the Blues." *American Music* 14, no. 4 (Winter): 402–54.

Abrahams, Roger

    1992   *Singing the Master: The Emergence of African American Culture in the Plantation South.* New York: Pantheon.

Alhadeff, Gini

    1997   *The Sun at Midday: Tales of a Mediterranean Family.* New York: Pantheon.

Allen, Lara

    1995   "The Effect of Repressive State Policies on the Development and Demise of *Kwela* Music: South Africa 1955–65." In *Papers Presented at the Tenth Symposium on Ethnomusicology*, Music Department, Rhodes University, 30 September–2 October 1991. Grahamstown: International Library of African Music, pp. 1–4.

Ames, David

    1973   "A Sociocultural View of Hausa Musical Activity." In *The Traditional Artist in African Societies*, ed. Warren L. d'Azevedo. Bloomington: Indiana University Press, pp. 128–61.

Ankermann, Bernhard

    1905   "Kulturkreise und Kulturschichten in Africa." *Zeitschrift für Ethnologie* 37:1–132.

Baily, John, and Peter Driver

    1992   "Spatio-Motor Thinking in Playing Folk Blues Guitar." *The World of Music* 34, no. 3: 57–71.

Ballantine, Christopher

    1993   *Marabi Nights: Early South African Jazz and Vaudeville.* Johannesburg: Ravan Press.

1995a   "Fact, Ideology and Paradox: African Elements in Early Black South African Jazz and Vaudeville." In *Papers Presented at the Tenth Symposium on Ethnomusicology*, Music Department, Rhodes University, 30 September–2 October 1991. Grahamstown: International Library of African Music, pp. 5–9.

1995b   "The Identities of Race, Class and Gender in the Repression of Early Black South African Jazz and Vaudeville (ca. 1920–1944)." In *Papers Presented at the Eleventh Symposium on Ethnomusicology*, Department of Music, University of Natal, Durban. Grahamstown: International Library of African Music, pp. 6–11.

Baumann, Hermann, ed.

1940   *Völkerkunde Africas*. Studien zur Kulturkunde. Cologne: Rüdiger Köppe Verlag. Reprinted 1975–1979 as *Die Völker Afrikas und ihre traditionellen Kulturen*, 2 vols. Studien zur Kulturkunde, vols. 34 and 35. Stuttgart: Franz Steiner Verlag Wiesbaden.

Bender, Wolfgang

1991   *Sweet Mother: Modern African Music*. With a foreword by John M. Chernoff. Chicago and London: The University of Chicago Press.

Berlin, Edward A.

1980   *Ragtime: A Musical and Cultural History*. Berkeley: University of California Press.

Berliner, Paul

1993   *Thinking in Jazz: The Infinite Art of Improvisation*. Chicago: The University of Chicago Press.

Blacking, John

1959   "Problems of Pitch, Pattern and Harmony in Ocarina Music of the Venda." *African Music* 2, no. 2: 15–23.

Bock, Philip K.

1970   *Culture Shock: A Reader in Modern Cultural Anthropology*. New York: Alfred A. Knopf.

1980   *Rethinking Psychological Anthropology: Continuity and Change in Psychological Anthropology*. New York: W. H. Freeman.

Borneman, Ernest

1959   "The Roots of Jazz." In *Jazz*, ed. Nat Hentoff and Albert J. McCarthy. New York: Holt, Rinehart and Winston, pp. 1–20.

1969   "Jazz and the Creole Tradition." *Jazz Research* 1: 99–112.

Botkin, B. A.

1943   *Negro Work Songs and Calls*. LP with notes. AFS L8, Library of Congress.

Boucher, Jonathan

1832   *Boucher's Glossary of Archaic and Provincial Words. A Supplement to the Dictionaries of the English Language*. London: Black, Young and Young.

Brenner, Klaus-Peter

    1997   *Chipendani und Mbira.* Musikinstrumente, nicht-begriffliche Mathematik und die Evolution der harmonischen Progressionen in der Musik der Shona in Zimbabwe. Göttingen: Vandenhoeck & Ruprecht.

Broonzy, William

    1964   *Big Bill Blues: William Broonzy's Story as Told to Yannick Bruynoghe.* New York: Oak.

Brothers, Thomas

    1994   "Solo and Cycle in African-American Jazz." *Musical Quarterly* 78: 479–509.

Buchanan, Annabel Morris

    1940   "A Neutral Mode in Anglo-American Folk Music." *Southern Folklore Quarterly* 4: 77–92.

Cable, George W.

    1886   "The Dance in Place Congo." *The Century Magazine* 31 (February): 517–32.

Calt, Stephen

    1994   *I'd Rather Be the Devil: Skip James and the Blues.* New York: Da Capo Press.

Calt, Stephen, and Gayle Dean Wardlow

    1988   *King of the Delta Blues: The Life and Music of Charlie Patton.* Newton, N.J.: Rock Chapel.

Campbell, Randolph B.

    1996   "Slavery." In *The New Handbook of Texas*, vol. 5. Austin: The Texas State Historical Association, pp. 1081–83.

Carreira, António

    1979   *O Tráfico Português de Escravos na Costa Oriental Africana nos Começos do Séc. XIX (estudo de um caso).* Lisbon: Junta de Investigações Cientificas do Ultramar.

Charry, Eric

    1994a   "West African Harps." *Journal of the American Musical Instrument Society* 20: 5–53.

    1994b   "The Grand Mande Guitar Tradition in the Western Sahel and Savannah." *The World of Music* 3, no. 2: 21–61.

    1996   "Plucked Lutes in West Africa: An Historical Overview." *Galpin Society Journal* 49: 3–37.

Charters, Samuel

    1982   *The Roots of the Blues: An African Search.* New York: G. P. Putnam (Perigee).

    1993   *One-String Blues.* CD with notes. GDCD 6001. Gazell Records.

Clayton, Peter

    1959   Record sleeve notes to the LP *Something New from Africa.* LK 4292. Decca Records, London.

Cobb, James C.

    1992   *The Most Southern Place on Earth: The Mississippi Delta and the Roots of Regional Identity.* New York: Oxford University Press.

Cohen, Andrew M.

1996   "The Hands of Blues Guitarists." *American Music* 14, no. 4: 455–79.

Conway, Cecilia

1995   *African Banjo Echoes in Appalachia: A Study of Folk Traditions.* Knoxville: The University of Tennessee Press.

Coolen, Michael Theodore

1982   "The Fodet: A Senegambian Origin for the Blues?" *The Black Perspective in Music* 10, no. 1 (Spring): 69–84.

Coplan, David B.

1985   *In Township Tonight! South Africa's Black City Music and Theatre.* Johannesburg: Ravan Press.

1998   "Popular Music in South Africa." In *Africa. The Garland Encyclopaedia of World Music,* vol. 1. New York and London: Garland Publishing, pp. 759–80.

Courlander, Harold

1960   *The Drum and the Hoe: Life and Lore of the Haitian People.* Berkeley: University of California Press.

1963   *Negro Folk Music U.S.A.* New York: Columbia University Press.

Curtin, Philip D.

1969   *The Atlantic Slave Trade: A Census.* Madison: University of Wisconsin Press.

Dam, Theodore van

1954   "The Influence of the West African Songs of Derision in the New World." *African Music* 1, no. 1: 53–56.

Dargie, Dave

1991   "*Umnonqokolo*: Xhosa Overtone Singing and the Song Nondel'ekhaya." *African Music* 7, no. 1: 33–47.

Dauer, Alfons M.

1955   "Grundlagen und Entwicklung des Jazz." *Jazz Podium* 4: 7–8; 5: 5–6; 6: 7; 7: 7, 10; 9: 7–8; 10: 11–12.

1958   *Der Jazz: Seine Ursprünge und seine Entwicklung.* Eisenach/Kassel: Erich Röth.

1961   *Jazz—Die Magische Musik. Ein Leitfaden durch den Jazz.* Bremen: Carl Schünemann Verlag.

1964–65 "Betrachtungen zur afro-amerikanischen Folklore, dargestellt an einem Blues von Lightnin' Hopkins." *Archiv für Völkerkunde* 19: 11–30.

1979   "Towards a Typology of the Vocal Blues Idiom." *Jazz Research* 11: 9–92.

1983a   *Blues aus 100 Jahren.* Texte und Noten mit Begleitakkorden english-deutsch. Frankfurt am Main: Fischer.

1983b   "Mister Charlie—A Type of Chantefable-blues. In Commemoration of Samuel 'Lightning' Hopkins (1912–1982)." *Jazz Research* 15: 115–45.

1985   *Tradition afrikanischer Blasorchester und Entstehung des Jazz.* Beiträge zur Jazzforschung. Graz: Akademische Druk- und Verlagsanstalt.

Davidson, Marjory

    1970   "Some Music for the Lala *kankobele*." *African Music* 4, no. 4: 103–13.

Davis, Francis

    1995   *The History of the Blues*. New York: Hyperion.

Davis, John

    1803   *Travels of Four Years and a Half in the United States of America; During 1798, 1800, 1801 and 1802*. London.

Dias, Margot

    1986   *Os instrumentos musicais de Moçambique*. Instituto de Investigação Cientifica Tropical. Lisbon: Centro de Antropologia Cultural.

Dillard, J. L.

    1972   *Black English: Its History and Usage in the United States*. New York: Random House.

DjeDje, Jacqueline Cogdell

    1980   *Distribution of the One String Fiddle in West Africa*. Monograph Series in Ethnomusicology, no. 2. Los Angeles: Program in Ethnomusicology, Department of Music, University of California.

    1982   "The Concept of Patronage: An Examination of Hausa and Dagomba One-String Fiddle Traditions." *Journal of African Studies* 9, no. 3: 116–27.

    1984   "The Interplay of Melodic Phrases: An Analysis of Dagomba and Hausa One-String Fiddle Music." *Selected Reports in Ethnomusicology* 5: 81–118.

Djenda, Maurice

    1996   "L'importance de la fonction musicale pour la classification des instruments de musique en langage Mpyɛnɔ." *African Music* 7, no. 3: 11–20.

Dodds, Warren "Baby"

    1992   *The Baby Dodds Story, As Told to Larry Gara*. Rev. ed. Baton Rouge: Louisiana State University Press.

Dontsa, Luvuyo

    1997   "The Incredible Voices of Igongqo." *Symposium of Ethnomusicology* no. 14, Rhodes University, 1996. Grahamstown: International Library of African Music, pp. 7–80.

Eagle, Bob

    1993   (?) "Really the Roots of Rock." Unpublished typescript.

Eagle, Bob, and Steve LaVere

    1972   "Mississippi Matilda." *Living Blues* 8 (Spring): 7.

Edwards, Bryan

    1793   *The History, Civil and Commercial, of the British Colonies in the West Indies*. London: J. Stockdale.

Edwards, David "Honeyboy"

    1997   *The World Don't Owe Me Nothing*. Chicago: Chicago Review Press.

Ehret, Christopher

1981 "Languages and Peoples." In *Cultural Atlas of Africa*, ed. Jocelyn Murray. Oxford: Elsevier Publishers, Phaidon Press, pp. 24–30.

Epstein, Dena

1973 "African Music in British and French America." *The Musical Quarterly* 59, no. 1: 61–91.

1975 "The Folk Banjo: A Documentary History." *Ethnomusicology* 19: 347–71.

1977 *Sinful Tunes and Spirituals*. Urbana: University of Illinois Press.

Erdheim, Mario

1980 *Die gesellschaftliche Produktion von Unbewußtheit. Eine Einführung in den ethnopsycho-analytischen Prozess*. Frankfurt: Suhrkamp.

Erlmann, Veit

1991 *African Stars: Studies in Black South African Performance*. Chicago Studies in Ethnomusicology. Chicago: University of Chicago Press.

1994 "The Early History of Isicathamiya: An Interview with Thembinkosi Pewa." In *For Gerhard Kubik: Festschrift on the Occasion of His 60th Birthday*, ed. August Schmidhofer and Dietrich Schüller. Frankfurt: Peter Lang, pp. 193–217.

Evans, David

1970 "Afro-American One-Stringed Instruments." *Western Folklore* 29: 229–45.

1971 *Tommy Johnson*. London: Studio Vista.

1972a "Black Fife and Drum Music in Mississippi." *Mississippi Folklore Register* 6: 94–107.

1972b "Africa and the Blues." *Living Blues* 10 (Autumn): 27–29.

1972c "Delta Reminiscences: Floyd Patterson Interviewed by David Evans (Crystal Springs, Mississippi—August 31 and September 2, 1970)." *Blues World* 43 (Summer): 14–15.

1973 "Folk, Commerical and Folkloristic Aesthetics in the Blues." *Jazz Research* 5: 11–32.

1978a "African Elements in Twentieth-Century United States Black Folk Music." *Jazz Research* 10: 85–110.

1978b "Structure and Meaning in the Folk Blues." In *The Study of American Folklore*, ed. Jan H. Brunvand. Rev. ed. New York: W. W. Norton, pp. 421–47. 3d ed. 1986: 563–93.

1978c *Afro-American Folk Music from Tate and Panola Counties, Mississippi*. LP with notes. AFS L67, Library of Congress.

1981 "Black American Music as a Symbol of Identity." *Jazz Research* 13: 105–27.

1982 *Big Road Blues: Tradition and Creativity in the Folk Blues*. Berkeley: University of California Press.

1987a "The Origins of Blues and Its Relationship to African Music." In *Images de l'africain, de l'antiquité au XXe siècle*, ed. Daniel Droixhe and Klaus H.

Kiefer. Bayreuther Beiträge zur Literaturwissenschaft, vol. 10. Frankfurt am Main: Verlag Peter Lang, pp. 129–41.

1987b   "Charley Patton: The Conscience of the Delta." *The Voice of the Delta*, ed. Robert Sacré. Liège: Presses Universitaires de Liège, pp. 109–217.

1990   "African Contributions to America's Musical Heritage." *The World & I* 5, no. 1: 628–39.

1994   "The Music of Eli Owens. African Music in Transition in Southern Mississippi." In *For Gerhard Kubik, Festschrift on the Occasion of His 60th Birthday*, ed. August Schmidhofer and Dietrich Schüller. Frankfurt: Peter Lang, pp. 329–59.

1996   "Robert Johnson: Pact with the Devil." *Blues Revue* 21 (February/March): 12–13; 22 (April/May): 12–13; 23 (June): 12–13.

1998a   *She-Wolf*, Jessie Mae Hemphill. CD with notes. 6508, HighWater/HMG Records.

1998b   "The Reinterpretation of African Musical Instruments in the United States." In *The African Diaspora: African Origins and New World Self-Fashioning*, ed. Isidore Okpewho, Carol Boyce Davies, and Ali Mazrui. Bloomington: Indiana University Press.

Evans, David, and Volker Albold

1994   *The Spirit Lives On: Deep South Country Blues and Spirituals in the 1990s*. CD with notes. Kahla/Pfullendorf: Hot Fox Records HF-CD-005, LC 5740.

Evans, David, and Pete Welding

1995   *Bottleneck Blues*. CD with notes. TCD 5021, Testament Records.

Fahey, John

1970   *Charley Patton*. London: Studio Vista.

Farmer, Henry G.

1955   Letter to Hugh Tracey, African Music Society, Roodepoort, S.A. *African Music* 1, no. 2: 61.

Ferris, William R.

1971–72   Review of W. C. Handy, *Father of the Blues* (1970). *Jazz Research* 3/4: 257–58.

1973   "Gut Bucket Blues: Sacred and Profane." *Jazz Research* 5: 68–85.

1974–75   "Black Prose Narrative from the Mississippi Delta." *Jazz Research* 6/7: 90–138.

1989   "Voodoo." In *Encyclopedia of Southern Culture*, ed. Charles Reagan Wilson and William Ferris. Chapel Hill: University of North Carolina Press, pp. 492–93.

Finn, Julio

1986   *The Bluesman*. London: Quartet Books.

Floyd, Samuel A. Jr.

1991   "Ring Shout! Black Music, Black Literary Theory, and Black Historical Studies." *Black Music Research Journal* 11, no. 2: 267–89.

1995   *The Power of Black Music: Interpreting Its History from Africa to the United States.* New York and Oxford: Oxford University Press.

Garon, Paul

1971   *The Devil's Son-in-Law: The Story of Peetie Wheatstraw and His Songs.* London: Studio Vista.

1975   *Blues and the Poetic Spirit.* London: Eddison Press.

Gates, Henry Louis Jr.

1988   *The Signifying Monkey: A Theory of African-American Literary Criticism.* New York: Oxford University Press.

Gibbs, W. Wayt

1997   "A Matter of Language. The Popular Debate over Ebonics Belies Decades of Linguistic Research." *Scientific American* 276, no. 3 (March): 18–20.

Goddard, Keith

1996   "Reviews: *The Soul of Mbira* Twenty Years On: A Retrospect." *African Music* 7, no. 3: 76–90.

Godwin, Morgan

1680   *The Negro's and Indian's Advocate, Suing for their Admission into the Church.* London: F. C.

Goffin, Robert

1944   *Jazz from the Congo to the Metropolitan.* New York: Doubleday.

Graham, Richard

1994   "Ethnicity, Kinship, and Transculturation. African-Derived Mouth Bows in European-American Mountain Communities." In *For Gerhard Kubik. Festschrift on the Occasion of His 60th Birthday*, ed. August Schmidhofer and Dietrich Schüller. Frankfurt: Peter Lang, pp. 361–80.

Greenberg, Alan

1983   *Love in Vain: The Life and Legend of Robert Johnson.* Garden City, N.Y.: Doubleday.

Greenberg, Joseph H.

1966   *The Languages of Africa.* Research Center for the Language Sciences, Indiana University. Bloomington: Indiana University Press.

Griaule, Marcel

1954   "Nouvelles remarques sur la harpe-luth des Dogon." *Journal de la Société des Africanistes* 24: 119–22.

Griaule, Marcel, and Germaine Dieterlen

1950   "La harp-luth des Dogon." *Journal de la Société des Africanistes* 20: 209–77.

Grossman, Stefan

1969   *Delta Blues Guitar.* New York: Oak Publications.

1994   *Legends of Country Blues Guitar.* 2 videos, 1 hour/color. Sparta, N.J.: Vestapol Productions 13003 and 13016.

Gushee, Lawrence

    1994   "The Nineteenth-Century Origins of Jazz." *Black Music Research Journal* 14, no. 1: 1–24.

Hai, Trân Quang

    1994   "Le chant diphonique: Description historique, styles, aspect acoustique et spectral, demarche originale, recherches fondamentales et appliquées." *EM—Annuario degli Archivi di Etnosmusicologia dell'Accademia Nazionale di Santa Cecilia* 2: 123–150.

Haley, Alex

    1977   *Roots: The Saga of an American Family.* New York: Dell.

Hall, Gwendolyn Midlo

    1992   *Africans in Colonial Louisiana: The Development of Afro-Creole Culture in the Eighteenth Century.* Baton Rouge: Louisiana State University Press.

Handy, William Christopher

    1949   *A Treasury of the Blues.* With an Historical and Critical Text by Abbe Niles. New York: Charles Boni.

    1970   *Father of the Blues.* Ed. Arna Bontemps. New York: Collier Books (Macmillan).

Harris, Marvin

    1968   *The Rise of Anthropological Theory.* London: Routledge & Kegan Paul.

Heide, Karl Gert zur

    1994   "Who was the Leader of Charles Bolden's Orchestra?" *New Orleans Music* 5, no. 2 (December): 6–10.

Herskovits, Melville J.

    1938a   *Acculturation: The Study of Culture Contact.* New York: J. J. Augustin.

    1938b   *Dahomey, An Ancient Kingdom.* 2 vols. New York: J. J. Augustin.

    1941   *The Myth of the Negro Past.* Boston: Harper & Brothers.

Herzhaft, Gérard

    1991   *John Lee Hooker.* Paris (?): Éditions du Limon.

Hirschberg, Walter

    1988   "Altnigritische (Altsudanische) Kultur." In *Neues Wörterbuch der Völkerkunde,* ed. W. Hirschberg. Berlin: Dietrich Reimer, p. 21.

Holloway, Joseph E., ed.

    1990   *Africanisms in American Culture.* Bloomington: Indiana University Press.

Hornbostel, Erich Moritz von

    1913   "Musik." In Günter Tessmann, *Die Pangwe,* vol. 2. Berlin: Wasmuth, pp. 320–57.

Howard, Joseph H.

    1967   *Drums in the Americas.* New York: Oak Publications.

Howe, George

    1890   "The Last Slave Ship." *Scribner's Magazine* 8: 124.

Irwin, John Rice

1979   *Musical Instruments of the Southern Appalachian Mountains.* Norris, Tenn.: Museum of Appalachia Press.

Jabbour, Alan

1993   "The Fiddle in the Blue Ridge." In *Blue Ridge Folk Instruments and Their Makers*, ed. Vaughan Webb. Ferrum, Va.: Blue Ridge Institute, pp. 28–32.

Jahn, Janheinz

1958   *Muntu. Umrisse der neoafrikanischen Kultur.* Düsseldorf and Cologne: Eugen Diederichs. English translation 1961, London: Faber & Faber.

James, Willis Laurence

1950   "The Romance of the Negro Folk Cry in America." *Phylon* 16: 15–30.

Jamison, Kay Redfield

1995   "Manic-Depressive Illness and Creativity." *Scientific American* 272, no. 2: 46–51.

Jones, A. M.

1951   "Blue Notes and Hot Rhythm." *African Music Society Newsletter* 1, no. 4 (June): 9–12.

1954   "African Rhythm." *Africa* 24, no. 1: 26–47.

1959   *Studies in African Music.* 2 vols. London: Oxford University Press.

Jones-Jackson, Patricia

1987   *When Roots Die: Endangered Tradition on the Sea Islands.* Atlanta: University of Georgia.

Katz, Bernard, ed.

1969   *The Social Implications of Early Negro Music in the United States.* New York: Arno.

Kawada, Junzo

1982   (1988) *L'univers sonore de la savane.* 2 cassettes with a book of commentary. Tokyo: Hakusui Sha.

1997   "Les deux complexes de la culture sonore en Afrique occidentale: Le complexe mande et le complexe hausa." In *Cultures sonores d'Afrique*, ed. Junzo Kawada. Tokyo: Institut de Recherches sur les Langues et Cultures d'Asie et d'Afrique, pp. 5–49.

Kazadi wa Mukuna

1992   "The Genesis of Urban Music in Zaire." *African Music* 7, no. 2: 72–84.

Keil, Charles

1966   *Urban Blues.* Chicago: The University of Chicago Press.

King, Anthony

1960   "Employment of the 'Standard Pattern' in Yoruba Music." *African Music* 2, no. 3: 51–54.

1972   "The Construction and Tuning of the Kora." *African Language Studies* 113: 113–36.

Kirby, Percival R.

1930   "A Study of Negro Harmony." *The Musical Quarterly* 16: 404–14.

1934   *The Musical Instruments of the Native Races of South Africa*. London: Oxford University Press. 2d ed. 1965, Johannesburg: Witwatersrand University Press.

1961   "Physical Phenomena Which Appear to Have Determined the Bases and Development of an Harmonic Sense among Bushmen, Hottentot and Bantu." *African Music* 2, no. 4: 6–9.

Klauber, Laurence M.

1956   *Rattlesnakes: Their Habits, Life Histories, and Influence on Mankind*. 2 vols. Berkeley: University of California Press.

Knight, Roderic

1971   "Towards a Notation and Tablature for the Kora, and Its Application to Other Instruments." *African Music* 5, no. 1: 23–36.

1974   "Mandinka Drumming." *African Music* 7, no. 4: 24–35.

1978   *Kora Music from The Gambia Played by Foday Musa Suso*. LP album with notes. 8510, Folkways Records, New York.

1991   *Vibrato Octaves: Tunings and Modes of the Mande Balo and Kora*. Baltimore: Sempod Laboratory, Department of Music, University of Maryland, Baltimore County.

Koelle, Sigismund Wilhelm

1854   *Polyglotta Africana: or, A Comparative Vocabulary of Nearly Three Hundred Words and Phrases in More Than One Hundred Distinct African Languages*. London: Church Missionary House. Re-edited by P.E.H. Hair and D. Dalby, Sierra Leone, 1963.

Kruger, Jaco

1985   "The State of Venda Chordophones: 1983–1984." In *Papers Presented at the Fifth Symposium on Ethnomusicology*, Faculty of Music, University of Cape Town, 30 August–1 September 1984. Grahamstown: International Library of African Music, pp. 8–12.

1989   "Rediscovering the Venda Ground Bow." *Ethnomusicology* 33, no. 3 (Fall): 391–404.

Kubik, Gerhard

1959a   "Archaischer und moderner Jazz." *Neue Zeitschrift für Musik* 9, no. 120 (September): 448–51. Complete version printed in *Jazz Podium* 10, no. 2 (1961): 54–56.

1959b   "Das Jazzinstrumentarium." *Neue Wege* 15, no. 147 (October): 9–10.

1960   "Musikforschungen in Ostafrika." *Jazz Podium* 9, no. 4: 57.

1961a   "Spuren des Blues. Ein Bericht aus Nigerien." *Jazz Podium* 6, no. 3: 157–60.

1961b   Review of Jahnheinz Jahn, *Muntu* (1959). *Black Orpheus* [Ibadan, Nigeria] 9 (June): 63–65.

1965 "Transcription of *mangwilo* Xylophone Music from Film Strips." *African Music* 3, no. 4: 35–51. Corrigenda in *African Music* 4, no. 4 (1970): 136–37.

1968 *Mehrstimmigkeit und Tonsysteme in Zentral- und Ostafrika.* Austrian Academy of Sciences. Vienna: Hermann Böhlaus Nachfolger.

1969 "Afrikanische Elemente im Jazz—Jazzelemente in der populären Musik Afrikas." *Jazz Research* 1: 84–98.

1970a Review of Paul Oliver, *Savannah Syncopators. Jazz Research* 2: 164–66.

1970b *Natureza e estrutura de escalas musicais africanas.* Estudos de Antropologia Cultural, vol. 3. Lisbon: Junta de Investigações do Ultramar.

1972 "Oral Notation of Some West and Central African Time-Line Patterns." *Review of Ethnology* 3, no. 22: 169–76.

1973 *Humbi en Handa–Angola.* LP record and booklet no. 9. Tervuren: Musée Royal de l'Afrique Centrale.

1974 *The Kachamba Brothers' Band. A Study of Neo-Traditional Music in Malaŵi.* Zambian Paper no. 9. Lusaka: Institute for African Studies, University of Zambia.

1979 *Angolan Traits in Black Music, Games and Dances of Brazil: A Study of African Cultural Extensions Overseas.* Estudos de Antropologia Cultural, vol. 10. Lisbon: Junta de Investigações Cientificas do Ultramar.

1979–80 "Donald Kachamba's Montage Recordings: Aspects of Urban Music History in Malaŵi." *African Urban Studies* 6: 89-122.

1981 *Mukanda na makisi: Circumcision School and Masks.* Double album. Museum Collection MC 11. Berlin: Museum für Völkerkunde.

1982 *Musikgeschichte in Bildern: Ostafrika.* Leipzig: Deutscher Verlag für Musik.

1983 "Kognitive Grundlagen der afrikanischen Musik." In *Musik in Africa,* ed. Artur Simon. Berlin: Museum für Volkerkunde, pp. 327–400.

1986 "Afrikanische Musikkulturen in Brasilien." In *Brasilien,* ed. Tiago de Oliveira Pinto. Mainz: Schott, pp. 121–47.

1987 "Das Khoisan-Erbe im Süden von Angola. Bewegungsformen, Bogenharmonik und tonale Ordnung in der Musik der !Kung' und benachbarter Bantu-Populationen." In *Musikkulturen in Africa,* ed. Erich Stockmann. Berlin: Verlag Neue Musik, pp. 82–196.

1988a "Àló–Yoruba Chantefables: An Integrated Approach towards West African Music and Oral Literature." In *African Musicology: Current Trends. A Festschrift Presented to J. H. Kwabena Nketia,* ed. Jacqueline Cogdell Djedje and William G. Carter. Vol. 1. Los Angeles: University of California, African Studies Center & *African Arts Magazine,* pp. 129–82.

1988b Review of "*Cuyagua*—a film by Paul Henley, Granada Centre for Visual Anthropology, University of Manchester, U.K., 1977." *Yearbook for Traditional Music* 20: 255–57.

1989a   *Musikgeschichte in Bildern: Westafrika.* Leipzig: Deutscher Verlag für Musik.

1989b   "Subjective Patterns in African Music." In *Cross Rhythms. Papers in African Folklore*, ed. Susan Domowitz, Maureen Eke & Enoch Mvula. Vol. 3. Bloomington: African Studies Program, Trickster Press, pp. 129–54.

1989c   "The Southern African Periphery: Banjo Traditions in Zambia and Malaŵi." *The World of Music* 31, no. 1: 3–29.

1989d   *Multi-part Singing in East and South-East Africa.* Selected recordings of the East Africa Expedition of Helmut Hillegeist and Gerhard Kubik, 7 August 1961–10 January 1963. PHA LP 2. Vienna: Phonogrammarchiv of the Austrian Academy of Sciences.

1990   "Drum Patterns in the 'Batuque' of Benedito Caxias." *Latin American Music Review* 11, no. 2: 115–81.

1991   *Extensionen afrikanischer Kulturen in Brasilien.* Aachen: Alano.

1993   "Transplantation of African Musical Cultures into the New World." In *Slavery in the Americas*, ed. Wolfgang Binder. Würzburg: Königshausen & Neumann, pp. 421–52.

1994a   *Theory of African Music*, vol. 1. International Institute For Traditional Music, Berlin. Wilhelmshaven: Florian Noetzel.

1994b   "Ethnicity, Cultural Identity and the Psychology of Culture Contact." In *Music and Black Ethnicity*, ed. Gerard Béhague. New Brunswick, N.J.: Transaction Publishers.

1994c   "Namibia—Survey 1991–1993 Gerhard Kubik/Moya A. Malamusi. Landesweite Bestandaufnahme von Musiktraditionen und Oralliteratur." *EM—Annuario degli Archivi di Etnomusicologia dell'Accademia Nazionale di Santa Cecilia* 2: 209. Synthesis in Italian by Giorgio Adamo.

1995   *African Guitar.* Solo fingerstyle guitar music, composers and performers of Congo/Zaïre, Uganda, Central African Republic, Malaŵi, Namibia and Zambia. Audiovisual field recordings 1966–1993 by Gerhard Kubik. Sparta, N.J.: Stefan Grossman's Guitar Workshop.

1996   "West African and African-American Concepts of *vodu* and *òrìṣà*" In *African-Caribbean Religions, Part 2: Voodoo*, ed. Manfred Kremser. Vienna: Wiener Universitätsverlag, pp. 17–34.

1997a   "Multipart Singing in Sub-Saharan Africa: Remote and Recent Histories Unravelled." *Symposium on Ethnomusicology* no. 14, Rhodes University, 1996. Grahamstown: International Library of African Music, pp. 85–97.

1998a   "Intra-African Streams of Influence." In *Africa: The Garland Encyclopaedia of World Music*, ed. Ruth Stone. Vol. 1. New York and London: Garland Publishing, pp. 293–326.

1998b   "Central Africa: An Introduction." In *Africa. The Garland Encyclopaedia of World Music*, ed. Ruth Stone. Vol. 1. New York and London: Garland Publishing, pp. 650–80.

Kubik, Gerhard, assisted by Moya Malamusi, Lidiya Malamusi, and Donald Kachamba

1987   *Malaŵian Music: A Framework for Analysis*, ed. Mitchel Strumpf. Jointly published by the Centre for Social Research and the Department of Fine and Performing Arts, Chancellor College, University of Malaŵi, Zomba.

Kubik, Gerhard, in cooperation with Moya Aliya Malamusi

1989   *Opeka Nyimbo*. Musician-composers, southern Malaŵi. Booklet accompanying the double album MC 15 (Museum Collection). Berlin: Museum für Völkerkunde, Musikethnologische Abteilung.

Kubik, Gerhard, and Tiago de Oliveira Pinto

1994   "Afroamerikanische Musik." In *Die Musik in Geschichte und Gegenwart*, vol. 1, A–Bog. Kassel: Bärenreiter, pp. 194–261.

Kyagambiddwa, Joseph

1955   *African Music from the Source of the Nile*. New York: Praeger.

La Vere, Stephen C.

1990   *Robert Johnson: The Complete Recordings*. Booklet notes. CBS Records, Columbia, New York.

Leland, John, and Joseph Nadine

1997   "Education: Hooked on Ebonics." *Newsweek*, 13 January, pp. 50–51.

Levine, Laurence W.

1977   *Black Culture and Black Consciousness: Afro-American Folk Thought from Slavery to Freedom*. Oxford: Oxford University Press.

Lieb, Sandra

1981   *Mother of the Blues: A Study of Ma Rainey*. Amherst: The University of Massachusetts Press.

List, George

1973   *Cantos Costeños: Folksongs of the Atlantic Coastal Region of Columbia*. LP with notes. EST-8003, Ethnosound Records.

Littlefield, Daniel C.

1991   *Rice and Slaves: Ethnicity and the Slave Trade in Colonial South Carolina*. Urbana: University of Illinois Press.

Lomax, Alan

1962   *Folk Songs from the Ozarks*. Album no. 25006, Prestige International Records, New York.

1968   *Folk Song Style and Culture*. Publication no. 88. Washington, D.C.: American Association for the Advancement of Science.

1977   *Roots of the Blues*, LP with notes. NW 252, New World Records.

1993   *The Land Where the Blues Began*. New York: Pantheon Books.

Lornell, Christopher

1981   "Why Blacks Sing the Blues: Cedar Grove and Durham, North Carolina in the 1930s." *Jazz Research* 13: 117–27.

Lott, Eric

1993   *Love and Theft: Blackface Minstrelsy and the American Working Class.* New York: Oxford University Press.

Low, John

1982   "A History of Kenya Guitar Music 1945–1980." *African Music* 6, no. 2: 17–34.

Lunsonga, Cajetan

1978   "Music Education in Africa and the Africanization of Other Subjects." *Review of Ethnology* 5, nos. 9–10: 65–76.

Lutero, Martinho, and Carlos Martins Pereira

1981   "A música tradicional em Moçambique." *Africa* 11: 79–88.

Malamusi, Moya Aliya

1984   "The Zambian Popular Music Scene." *Jazz Research* 16: 189–98.

1990   "Nthano Chantfables and Songs Performed by the *bangwe* Player Chitenje Tambala." In *African Languages and Music: Contributions in Honour of David Kenneth Rycroft,* ed. Rosalie Finlayson. Special issue, *South African Journal of African Languages* 10, no. 4: 222–38.

1992   "Thunga la Ngororombe—The Panpipe Dance Group of Sakha Bulaundi." *African Music* 7, no. 2: 85–107.

1994   "Rise and Development of a Chileka Guitar Style in the 1950s." In *For Gerhard Kubik. Festschrift on the Occasion of His 60th Birthday,* ed. A. Schmidhofer and D. Schüller. Frankfurt am Main: Peter Lang, pp. 7–72.

1996   "Stringed Instrument Traditions in Southern Malaŵi." *African Music* 7, no. 3: 60–66.

1997   "Two panpipe ensemble traditions." *Kalinda.* The Newsletter of Afro-Caribbean and U.S. Black Music Interconnections (published by CBMR, Chicago), Fall, pp. 22–24.

Martin, Denis-Constant

1991   "Filiation or Innovation? Some Hypotheses to Overcome the Dilemma of Afro-American Music's Origins." *Black Music Research Journal* 11, no. 1 (Spring): 19–38.

Martinez Suárez, Juan de Dios

1994   *Las Barbúas.* Maracaibo: Colección Lago de Maracaibo.

Maultsby, Portia K.

1990   "Africanisms in African-American Music." In *Africanisms in American Culture,* ed. Joseph E. Holloway. Bloomington: Indiana University Press.

Mecklenburg, Carl Gregor Herzog zu, and Waldemar Scheck

1963   *Die Theorie des Blues im modernen Jazz.* Strasbourg and Baden-Baden: Heitz.

Mensah, Atta Annan

1971–72   "Jazz—The Round Trip." *Jazz Research* 3/4: 124–37.

Merriam, Alan P.

1953   "African Music Reexamined in the Light of New Material from the Belgian Congo and Ruanda Urundi." *Zaire* 7, no. 3: 244–53. Reprinted in *African Music Society Newsletter* 1, no. 6 (September): 57–64.

Merwe, Peter van der

1989   *Origins of the Popular Style: The Antecedents of Twentieth-Century Popular Music.* Oxford: Clarendon Press.

Michaels, Benn

1997   *Our America: Nativism, Modernism and Pluralism.* Durham, N.C.: Duke University Press.

Minton, John

1996a   "West African Fiddles in Deep East Texas." In *Juneteenth Texas. Essays in African-American Folklore.* Publications of the Texas Folklore Society, vol. 54, Francis Edward Abernethy, Senior Editor, Carolyn Fiedler Satterwhite, Assistant Editor. Denton: University of North Texas Press, pp. 291–313.

1996b   "Houston Creoles and Zydeco: The Emergence of an African American Urban Popular Style." *American Music* 14, no. 4 (Winter): 480–526.

Modisane, Bloke

1963   *Blame Me on History.* London: Thames and Hudson.

Morrow, Lance

1977   "Living with the 'Peculiar Institution'." *Time,* 14 February, pp. 52–53.

Morton, Jelly Roll

1938   Interviews with Alan Lomax at the Coolidge Auditorium, Library of Congress, Washington, D.C. 12 May–14 December. Recordings located in the Library of Congress's Folk Life Reading Room, AFS nos. 1638–1688; 2487–2489.

Mourão, Fernando A. A.

1980   "La contribution de l'Afrique Bantoue à la formation de la société brésilienne: Une tentative de redéfinition méthodologique." *Africa* [São Paulo] 3: 1–17.

Multhaupt, Tamara

1989   *Hexerei und Antihexerei in Afrika.* Munich: Trickster.

Ngumu, Pie-Claude

1975–76 "Les mendzaŋ des Ewondo du Cameroun." *African Music* 5, no. 4: 6–26.

Nikiprowetzky, Tolia

n.d.   *Trois aspects de la musique africaine: Mauritanie, Sénégal, Niger.* Paris: Office de Cooperation Radiophonique.

Niles, Abbe

1925   "Blue Notes." *The New Republic* 45: 292–93.

1949   "The Story of the Blues." In *A Treasury of the Blues*, ed. W. C. Handy. New York: Charles Boni, pp. 9–32.

Nketia, J. H. Kwabena

  1961   *African Music in Ghana.* Accra: Longmans.

  1962   "The Hocket Technique in African Music." *Journal of the International Folk Music Council* 14: 44–52.

Nkosi, Lewis

  1966   "Jazz in Exile." *Transition* 24, no. 1: 34–37.

Oakley, Giles

  1976   *The Devil's Music: A History of the Blues.* London: British Broadcasting Company.

Oliver, Paul

  1969(1975) *The Story of the Blues.* Radno, Pa.: Chilton.

  1970   *Savannah Syncopators: African Retentions in the Blues.* New York: Stein and Day.

  1972   "Some Comments: African Influence and the Blues." *Living Blues* 8 (Spring): 13–17.

  1973   "Echoes of the Jungle?" *Living Blues* 13 (Summer): 19–34.

  1989   "Blues." In *The New Grove Dictionary of Music and Musicians.* Vol. 2. London: Macmillan, pp. 812–19.

  1990   *Blues Fell This Morning: Meaning in the Blues.* Rev. ed. Originally published 1960. Cambridge: Cambridge University Press.

  1997   *Conversations with the Blues.* 2d ed. New York: Cambridge University Press.

Ortiz, Fernando

  1952   *Los instrumentos de la musica afrocubana.* Vols. 1–5. Havana: Dirección de Cultura del Ministerio de Educación.

Ottenheimer, Harriet Joseph

  1987   "The Bardic Origins of the Blues." *The World & I* 2, no. 11 (November): 492–503.

  1992   "Comoro Crossroads: African Bardic Traditions and the Origins of the Blues." *Human Mosaic* 26, no. 2: 32–38.

Ottenheimer, Harriet, and Martin Ottenheimer

  1982   *Music of the Comoro Islands: Domoni.* Ethnic Folkways Records FE 4243. Folkways Records and Service Corp., New York.

Palmer, Robert

  1981   *Deep Blues.* New York: Viking Press.

Parrish, Lydia

  1942   *Slave Songs of the Georgia Sea Islands.* New York: Creative Age Press.

Peabody, Charles

  1903   "Notes on Negro Music." *Journal of American Folklore* 16: 148–52.

Pearson, Barry Lee

1990 *Virginia Piedmont Blues: The Lives and Art of Two Virginia Bluesmen.* Philadelphia: University of Pennsylvania Press.

Pinto, Tiago de Oliveira

1991 *Capoeira, Samba, Candomblé: Afro-Brasilianische Musik im Recôncavo, Bahia.* Berlin: Museum für Völkerkunde.

Pollak-Eltz, Angelina

1977 "Las máscaras." In *Actes du XLIIe Congrès internationale des américanistes.* Paris: Société des Américanistes.

1979 "*Devils* and *Devil* Masks in Venezuela." In *Ritual Symbolism and Ceremonialism in the Americas: Studies in Symbolic Anthropology,* ed. N. Ross Crumrine. Occasional Papers in Anthropology, No. 33, Museum of Anthropology, University of Northern Colorado, Greeley, pp. 80–88.

Prévos, André J. M.

1996 "Religious Words in Blues Lyrics and Titles: A Study." In *Saints and Sinners: Religion, Blues and (D)evil in African-American Music and Literature,* ed. Robert Sacré. Liège: Societé Liègeoise de Musicologie, Etudes & Editions 5, pp. 313–30.

Quellette, Dan

1990 "Ali Farka Toure. African Blues." Review in *Down Beat,* August, pp. 37–38.

Ramsey, Frederic Jr., and Charles Edward Smith

1957 *Jazzmen.* London: Sidgwick & Jackson.

Roberts, John Storm

1972 *Black Music of Two Worlds.* New York: Praeger. Reprinted 1973, London: Allen Lane.

n.d. *Songs the Swahili Sing.* Album and liner notes. Original Music OMA 103, New York.

Robinson, Bradford

1980 "Blue Note." *The New Grove Dictionary of Music and Musicians,* ed. Stanley Sadie. London: Macmillan.

Rouget, Gilbert

1972 *Musique malinke: Guinée.* 12″ LP. Vogue LDM 30113.

1982 "Cithare et glissando: Nouvelles données sur le chromatism au Bénin." *Revue de Musicologie* 68, nos. 1–2: 310–24.

Rourke, Constance

1931 *American Humor.* New York: Harcourt, Brace and Co.

Russell, Tony

1970 *Blacks, Whites and Blues.* New York: Stein and Day.

Rycroft, David

1957 "Zulu Male Traditional Singing." *African Music* 1, no. 4: 33–36.

1958	"The New 'Town Music' of Southern Africa." *Recorded Folk Music* 1: 54–57.
1966	"Friction Chordophones in South-Eastern Africa." *Galpin Society Journal* 19: 84–100.
1967	"Nguni Vocal Polyphony." *Journal of the International Folk Music Council* 19: 89–103.
1977	"Evidence of Stylistic Continuity in Zulu 'Town' Music." In *Essays for a Humanist: An Offering to Klaus Wachsmann.* New York: The Town House Press, pp. 211–60.
1991	"Black South African Urban Music Since the 1890's: Some Reminiscences of Alfred Assegai Kumalo (1879–1966)." *African Music* 7, no. 1: 5–31.

Sargeant, Winthrop

1938	*Jazz: Hot and Hybrid.* Revised and reprinted as *Jazz: A History.* New York: McGraw-Hill, 1964.

Schuller, Gunther

1968	*Early Jazz.* New York: Oxford University Press.

Simon, Artur, ed.

1983	*Musik in Afrika.* Berlin: Museum für Völkerkunde.

Sloane, Sir Hans

1707	*A Voyage to the Islands of Madera, Barbados, Nieves, S. Christopher and Jamaica, with the Natural History of the . . . Last of These Islands.* London: Printed by British Museum for the author.

Southern, Eileen

1971	*The Music of Black Americans: A History.* New York: W. W. Norton.

Spencer, Jon Michael

1993	*Blues and Evil.* Knoxville: University of Tennessee Press.

Stearns, Marshall W.

1964	*Negro Blues and Hollers.* LP with notes. AFS L59, Library of Congress.

Strumpf, Mitchel, ed.

1992	*Daniel Kachamba Memorial Cassette.* With booklet by Gerhard Kubik. Zomba: Department of Fine and Performing Arts, University of Malaŵi.

Summers, Lynn

1971	"African Influence and the Blues: An Interview with Richard A. Waterman." *Living Blues* 6 (Autumn): 30–36.

Thompson, Robert Farris

1974	*African Art in Motion.* Los Angeles: University of California Press.
1984	*Flash of the Spirit: African & Afro-American Art & Philosophy.* New York: Vintage Books.

Titon, Jeff Todd

1977	*Early Downhome Blues: A Musical and Cultural Analysis.* Urbana: University of Illinois Press. 2d ed. with a new Foreword by Alan Trachtenberg and a

new Afterword by the author, Chapel Hill: University of North Carolina Press, 1994.

Tracey, Andrew

1970   "The Nyanga Panpipe Dance." *African Music* 5, no. 1: 73–89.

Turner, Lorenzo D.

1949   *Africanisms in the Gullah Dialect.* Chicago: University of Chicago Press.

Verna, Paul

1993   "Toure's Music Journeys from African 'Source'." *Billboard*, 30 October, pp. 82–84.

Vlach, John Michael

1978   *The Afro-American Tradition in Decorative Arts.* Cleveland: The Cleveland Museum of Art.

Waterman, Richard A.

1948   " 'Hot' Rhythm in Negro Music." *Journal of the American Musicological Society* 1: 24–37.

1952   "African Influence on the Music of the Americas." In *Acculturation in the Americas*, ed. Sol Tax. Chicago: University of Chicago Press, pp. 207–18.

1963   "On Flogging a Dead Horse: Lessons Learned from the Africanisms Controversy." *Ethnomusicology* 7: 83–87.

Wegner, Ulrich

1984   *Afrikanische Saiteninstrumente.* Berlin: Museum für Völkerkunde.

White, George R.

1995   *Living Legend: Bo Diddley.* Chessington, U.K.: Castle Communications.

Whitefield, George

1740   *Three Letters from the Reverend Mr. G. Whitefield. . . .* Philadelphia: B. Franklin.

Wieschhoff, Heinz

1933   *Die afrikanischen Trommeln und ihre außerafrikanischen Beziehungen.* Stuttgart: Strecker & Schröder.

Winans, Robert B.

1990   "Black Instrumental Music Traditions in the Ex-Slave Narratives." *Black Music Research Journal* 10, no. 1 (Spring): 43–53.

Work, John W.

1940   *American Negro Songs and Spirituals.* New York: Bonanza Books.

Yotamu, Moses

1979   "My Two-Week Fieldwork in Ivory Coast—A Preliminary Report." *Review of Ethnology* 6, nos. 21–24: 161–92.

Index

Artists and authors

Abbott, Lynn, 103

Akiskal, Hagop S. and Kareen, 40

Albold, Volker, 18, 110

Alexander, John Milton, xiii

Allen, Lara, 174, 175, 177

Ames, David, 23

Ankermann, Bernhard, 68

Apolo, Araniide (Dr. Apolo), 156

Armstrong, Louis, 86, 112, 161

Baba Chale, 90

Baby Dodds. *See* Dodds, Warren "Baby"

Baily, John, 122

Ballantine, Christopher, 162, 164

Barbecue Bob, 128

Bastin, Bruce, 33

Baumann, Hermann, 68

Béhague, Gerard, xvii

Belfour, Robert "Wolfman," xv, xvi, xvii, 38, 82–84, 92, 106, 108, 119

Bell, Ed, 146–47, 149–50

Bender, Wolfgang, xvii, 156

Berliner, Paul, xvii

Berry, Chuck, 174

Birgui, Gonga Sarki, 132–33

Blacking, John, 128

Bo Diddley, 63, 107

Bogart, Humphrey, 179

Borneman, Ernest, 51, 52, 118

Boucher, Jonathan, 8–9

Bowdich, Thomas Edward, 112

Boyce, R. L., 52

Brand, Dollar, 161

Broonzy, William (Big Bill), 42

Brothers, Thomas, 86, 105

Brown, Clarence "Gatemouth," 195

Brown, James, 160, 196

Brown, John Henry "Bubba," 40, 41

Brown, Robert (Washboard Sam), 39

Brundy, Walker, 131

Buchanan, Annabel Morris, 16

Buford, Jimmie, 52

Buis, Johann, xvii

Bukka White. *See* Booker T. Washington White

Bulahamu, Josefe, 171

Bunch, William, 24

Burnett, Chester (Howlin' Wolf), 38

Burnside, R. L., 92, 119, 188

Calloway, Cab, 164–65

Caluza, Reuben Tholakele, 161

Campbell, Randolph B., 47

Carr, Leroy, 124

Carreira, António, 13

Carter, "Big Lucky," xvii, 148

African ethnic-linguistic designations

Song titles index

Index

General Index

AAB form (of the blues), 42–43, 46–50, 176–80

AB-plus-refrain form, 50

absence of drums, 51

additive rhythms, 100

African drum from Virginia, 7

"African roots," 4, 21

African song-style areas (Lomax), 94

Afro-Asiatic languages, 60

Afro-Latin music, 51

algeita (alghaita), 88–89

àló, 43–46, 144

alter ego, 40

Amerindian population, 12

Ancient Nigritic Cultures, 68

Ancient Nigritic song-style cluster, 95

Ancient Nigritic Style, 81, 94

Anglo-American folk music, 16

anti sorcery, 34

apala, 46

Appalachian mountains, 12, 15, 16, 30

Arabic (language), 61

Arabic-Islamic influences, 46, 93

Arabic-Islamic musical intrusion, 94

Arabic-Islamic singing techniques, 193

Arabic-Islamic style, 80

Arabic-Islamic stylistic component, 94

Arabic-Islamic world, 72, 93, 94

arhoolies, 26

Asante *apentemma*, 7

asymmetric time-line patterns, 51, 54–55, 58, 63

Atlantic seaboard states, 12, 47

Azande harpists, 24

ba-kponingbo, 130

ballroom dance-band, 157

ballroom instruments of the 1920s, 157

balo, 187

bamboula, 51

bandore, 8

banger, 9

bangwe, 30–32

banjer, 8

banjo, 8, 16, 25, 47, 65, 93, 157–59

Bantu languages, 49

bardic style (East African), 48

bardic tradition, 50

bàtá, 131

batuque, 107

bebop, 106, 119, 121, 163, 181

benta, 17

Benue-Congo (I.A.5) languages, 26, 54, 60, 62

big band jazz, 165

binary aesthetic terminology, 85

"birthplace" hypothesis (of the blues), 49

Black-American English, 66

blackface minstrelsy, 65, 103

blue devil, 29

"blue note of the blue note, the," (Evans), 148

blue note(s), xvi, 78, 86, 114, 118–51, 156

Blues characteristics, 82–96

Blues (core area of African or origins), 101

blues' cultural genealogy, 197

blues form, 41

blues harmonica, 89

blues lyrics, 28

Blues recordings compared with material from the West Central Sudan, 71–81

Blues Stylistic Regions, 82–83

blues texts, 29

blues tonal system, xvi, 118–51

"bo diddley," 16, 89

Bogadi Brothers, 179

bolon, 93
"bones" (concussion sticks), 58
boogie-woogie, 33, 143, 174
bourdon, 83–84, 110
bowed lute(s), 7, 47, 65, 72
Brazilian samba, 4
bridge-harp, 7, 69, 93, 188, 195
British four-line ballad, 197
buba, 131

call-and-reponse (concept, form, organi-
    zation), 50, 85–86
"calques" (Coolen), 67
calypso, 27, 155
canebrakes of Texas, 20
"canned heat," 40
carángano, 17
cattle pastoralists, 66
cha-cha-cha, 155
cha-cha-cha-cha, 55
chacha, 156
"chacta," 51
Chadian language(s) (III.E.), 70
chantefables, 27–28, 30, 45
chimurenga, 176
chipendani, 12, 14
chord sequence, 108
Christianity (Christian beliefs), 23
Civil War, United States (1861–65), 29, 47,
    98, 100
"clave," 57
Cleveland Museum of Art, 62
cognitive hinge, 200
"collective guilt" (feeling of), 195
Comoros islands, 49
"Concert and Dance," 162
contre-banjo, 156
convergence (processes of), 82
"cool" jazz intonation, 156
cord-and-peg tension, 7

cotton gin (old), 13
cotton plantation, 47
"counjaille," 51
Count Basie band, 43
Count Basie orchestra, 165
court music (Fulɓe and Hausa), 95, 99
Creole song, 51
Cuban clave pattern, 57
cultural comprehension test (Kubik), 46
cultural invariables, 57
cultural underground currents, 97
culture shock, 48
"cupping" the ear, 89
cycle, 43, 53–54, 58, 92, 163
cycle number(s), 54–55

daacol, 89
declamatory Hausa style, 80
declamatory vocal style, 63, 95
Deep South, 3, 16, 19, 25, 29–30, 47, 82–83,
    94, 98–100, 197
Delta. *See* Mississippi Delta
"Delta" or "Deep South" blues style, 83
depression, 28, 40
devil(s), 21–24
devils' masks (Venezuela), 22, 222
Devil's Son-in-Law, The, 24
"diddley bow," 16, 100
diphonic singing, 113
divergence (processes of), 82
dog (symbolizing alter ego), 40
dominant, 105, 113, 118
dominant chord, 42, 126–27
Donald Kachamba's Kwela Band, xiii
double bells, 132–34
"dropped leaves," 12
dùndún, 131, 156

East African cattle complex, 64
Eastern Sudanic languages (II.E.), 145
ebonics, 26, 84